The Subtleties of the Ascension

The Subtleties of the Ascension

Early Mystical Sayings on Muḥammad's Heavenly Journey

Compiled by
Abū ᶜAbd al-Raḥmān Sulamī

Translated and annotated by
Frederick S. Colby

FONS VITAE

First published in 2006 by
Fons Vitae
49 Mockingbird Valley Drive
Louisville, KY 40207
Email: fonsvitaeky@aol.com
Website: www.fonsvitae.com

Library of Congress Control Number: 2006920039

ISBN 1-887752-78-1

This book was typeset by Neville Blakemore, Jr.

With gratitude to Justin Majzub for the cover image.

Printed in China by Everbest Co. Ltd., through Four Colour
Imports, Ltd.. Louisville, Kentucky

This volume is dedicated
to my wonderful parents,
William M. Colby and Mary P. Colby.

A Qurʾānic page illuminated by ʿAbd Allāh ibn Muḥammad al-Hamadānī for the Sultan Ūlljaytu, 1313 CE, Hamadan. Q 17:1–7 (Cairo, National Library of Egypt).

CONTENTS

List of Figures

Acknowlegdments

With great gratitude to Vincent Cornell and John Lamoureaux for their expert help in deciphering the script of the original text, to my parents-in-law James Blue and Lee Blue for their editorial assistance, and especially to Carl Ernst, Donald Frederick, Christiana Gruber, Kenneth Honerkamp, Scott Kugle, Omid Safi, and Laury Silvers, for their detailed comments and invaluable suggestions on earlier drafts of this work.

All mistakes and shortcomings in the translation and commentary that follows, however, are of course my own. I did my best, *wa Allāhu a*ᶜ*lam.*

With love and gratitude to my partner Jennifer Blue
for her strong and abiding support.

With special thanks to Gray Henry of Fons Vitae Press for her role in procuring the manuscript from the Faisal Foundation in Riyadh, Saudi Arabia (and to members of King Faisal's family for their kind assistance), and for her faith and encouragement in this lengthy endeavor which served as the inspiring force breathing life into this project.

With appreciation to Thesaurus Islamicus Foundation for the use of the two illuminated Qurʾānic pages (see pages vi and 28) from *Splendours of Quran Calligraphy and Illumination*, by Martin Lings, 2004.

INTRODUCTION

The work translated herein, *The Subtleties of the Ascension*, compiled by the early Sufi scholar Abū ᶜAbd al-Raḥmān al-Sulamī (d. 412 AH/ 1021 CE),[1] can be considered part of a much wider series of works on otherworldly journeys that are not limited to any particular time or cultural setting. In fact, people in seemingly every culture around the world tell stories that recount the journeys of extraordinary human beings to lands beyond everyday human experience. Sometimes such stories describe how individuals discover the secrets of the universe or the contours of the netherworld over the course of their travels. A comparative study of these otherworldly journey narratives illustrates that a common series of themes connects diverse tales of fantastic trips led by angels, giants, fairies, spirits, and in some contemporary versions, by aliens.[2] In the Abrahamic religions of Judaism, Christianity, and Islam, stories told about the journeys of prophets or heroes most commonly report how these travelers were privileged to explore the mysteries of God's creation as these mysteries were revealed to them in an ecstatic experience often presided over by a guiding angel or spirit. From the experiences attributed to Moses and later to the mysterious Merkabah/Hekhalot authors, to the experiences attributed to the Apostle Paul and later to the eloquent Italian poet Dante, to the experiences attributed to Muḥammad and later to the Andalusian Sufi mystic Ibn al-ᶜArabī, otherworldly journey narratives form a colorful strand that weaves in and out of the rich tapestries of common Abrahamic lore depicting some of the most profound spiritual realities revealed to select mortals. These narratives were and are told, interpreted, retold and reinterpreted by later generations of Jews, Christians, and Muslims seeking to explore the heights and depths of their physical and spiritual universes. Many trails have been blazed by the travelers of past centuries, which encourages those of us who come after to follow their lead in our imaginations, our minds, and our spirits.

The narrative of Muḥammad's night journey and ascension has captivated audiences since the dawn of Islamic history, and the

Muslim mystics known as the Sufis (who began to flourish in the 3rd-4th/9th-10th centuries) were among the first to recognize its rich potential for spiritual and theological enlightenment.[3] The narrative describes how the Prophet was led by the angel Gabriel in the middle of the night from a location in Mecca to a remote holy location, which came to be identified with Jerusalem,[4] and up through the seven heavens toward the divine throne.[5] Although there were disagreements about the details of the narrative even among Muḥammad's first followers, a consensus on its broad outlines emerged within the first two centuries of the Islamic era (1st-2nd/7th-8th centuries), as shown by the oral and written evidence left by early Muslim scholars. It is difficult to fully appreciate Abu ᶜAbd al-Raḥmān Sulamī's mystical compilation, *The Subtleties of the Ascension*, without some knowledge of the accounts of Muḥammad's night journey and ascension, and without some knowledge of the early scholarly discussions that a number of the sayings in the work presume. What follows thus offers a survey of some of the most important narratives and ideas that serve as the foundation upon which the mystical sayings in *The Subtleties of the Ascension* are based. The goal is to present the background necessary so that not only the specialist but also the general reader might be able to appreciate the riches uncovered in Sulamī's profound collection of Sufi sayings.[6]

The Night Journey and Ascension Narratives in the Qurᵓān

The majority of Muslim commentators turn to two main passages in the Qurᵓān for proof-texts of Muḥammad's night journey and ascension. The first of these passages is known as the "night journey verse" because of its explicit albeit brief allusion to a journey by night. It describes how one of God's servants, usually understood by Muslims to be Muḥammad himself, was taken on a mysterious journey and shown some of God's signs:

> Glorified be the one who caused his servant to journey by night from the sacred place of ritual prayer to the furthest place of ritual prayer, whose precincts we have blessed, in order to show him some of our signs. Indeed [God] is the one who hears, the one who sees.[7]

Despite the vague language in this night journey verse, the Muslim commentators who address the verse are virtually unanimous that it describes a pivotal event in the life of the Prophet, a time when he was introduced to some of his pious forebears and was shown some of God's signs in the universe. The precise content of the signs Muḥammad witnessed on his journey, however, remains a matter of speculation.

Some commentators understand a different set of verses from another chapter of the Qurʾān as providing further details about Muḥammad's otherworldly journey(s), but like the night journey verse, the details that the latter passage reveals are at least partially obscured by its ambiguous language. In this passage from the chapter (*sūra*) of the Qurʾān known as "The Star" (*al-najm*), once again a servant is shown God's signs:

> By the star when it sets,
> indeed your companion is not astray,
> nor does he speak vainly.
> It is nothing less than a revelation revealed,
> taught to him by a being of intense power,
> possessing strength. He straightened up
> while he was on the highest horizon.
> Then he drew near and descended,
> and was a distance of two bows or closer.
> He revealed to his servant what he revealed.
> The heart did not lie in what it saw.
> Will you then argue with him about what he saw?
> He saw him another time
> at the lote tree of the boundary,
> next to the garden of the refuge,
> when the lote tree was covered by what covered.
> His vision did not stray, nor was it excessive.
> He saw some of the greatest signs of his Lord.[8]

As with the night journey verse, these opening eighteen verses from "the Star" describe in cryptic language how an unnamed individual, again assumed to be Muḥammad, witnessed some sort of revelation in a series of visions. As with the night journey verse, in the first centuries after the death of Muḥammad, Muslim scholars disagreed on the exact context and meaning of the passage, but many agreed that the portion of it which describes a vision near the so-called "lote tree of the boundary" refers to the night of the heavenly ascension.[9]

In the centuries that followed the events described in these two key qurʾānic passages, the night journey verse and the opening of the chapter of the Star, Muslim scholars from a variety of backgrounds composed oral and written commentaries on these verses to explain their meaning and significance. *The Subtleties of the Ascension* makes a remarkable contribution to this corpus, providing evidence of the diverse ways in which a number of early Sufi scholars understood these verses. The Sufi anecdotes that Sulamī relates in this work do not rely solely on the pivotal qurʾānic verses. Instead, a number of the anecdotes also presume a familiarity with the oral reports attributed to the Prophet Muḥammad that were circulating in the early period.

The Night Journey and Ascension in the *Hadith* Reports

The vast majority of Sufis ground their understanding of Sufism in the two main sources of Islamic law: the Qurʾān, which records what Muslims consider to be God's final and most complete revelation to humanity, and Muḥammad's path or "*sunna*," which records the deeds and teachings of Muḥammad that his contemporaries reported and passed on to later generations. We have seen how Muslims read key passages from the Qurʾān as allusions to Muḥammad's night journey and ascension. According to Muslim scholars, Muḥammad explained to his companions and contemporaries the meaning and significance of these brief qurʾānic allusions, and these explanations formed a small fraction of the thousands of recorded "sayings of the Prophet" known as hadiths[10] that come to form the body of the Prophet's sunna. These hadiths consist of a text of a report that is preceded by a list of the individuals who transmitted the report. The "chain of transmission" (*isnād*) became one of the devices that Muslim scholars in later centuries used to determine the authenticity of hadith reports. Among the majority of Muslims, several collections of hadiths that claimed to contain only the most authentic and "sound" (*ṣaḥīḥ*) reports gained a wide circulation beginning in the third century AH / ninth century CE, and the most famous of these were the work called the *Ṣaḥīḥ* of Muḥammad b. Ismaʿīl al-Bukhārī (known simply as

Bukhārī, a scholar who died in 256/870) and the work called the *Ṣāḥīḥ* of Muslim b. Ḥajjāj al-Qurashī (known simply as Muslim, which is in this case a proper name, a scholar who died in 261/875). Even today, these two collections of hadith reports contain what most Sunnī scholars deem to be the most trustworthy of all the narratives ascribed to and told about Muḥammad, those that can be considered "sound" (*ṣaḥīḥ*) in both transmission and content.[11]

One "sound" hadith on the night journey and ascension recorded by the Muslim traditionist whose name happens to be "Muslim" illustrates the type of Islamic ascension narrative that gained a wide currency throughout the Islamic world in the centuries following Muḥammad's death. Significantly, this hadith report stretches much longer than the brief qur'ānic passages cited above. It offers a good example of the way in which such extensive hadith reports often combine basic elements of the night journey and ascension accounts from the Qur'ān, from more fragmentary hadith reports, and occasionally from extra-canonical (and at times non-Islamic) oral sources.[12] Due to its significance as a representative example of what one might call the "official" Sunnī ascension narratives, this hadith deserves to be quoted at length:

> Shaybān b. Farrūj heard from Ḥammād b. Salama who heard from Thābit Bunānī who heard from Anas b. Mālik that the Messenger of God [Muḥammad] said: "I was brought the Burāq, which is a tall white mount larger than a donkey and smaller than a mule. It places its hoof as far as the eye can see. I rode it until I came to the House of the Sanctuary [i.e. Jerusalem]. I tied it up to the ring that the prophets tie it to. I entered the mosque and prayed two cycles in it, then I exited and Gabriel came to me with a cup of wine and a cup of milk. I chose the milk, and Gabriel said, 'You chose natural disposition.'"[13]
>
> "Then he ascended with us to the [first] heaven. Gabriel sought to open the gate and someone said, 'Who is it?' He said, 'Gabriel.' 'And who is with you?' 'Muḥammad.' 'Has he been sent?' 'Yes, he has been sent.' The gate was opened, and then I found myself with Adam. He welcomed me and wished me well. Then he ascended with us to the second heaven. Gabriel sought to open the gate....[14] It

was opened for us and then I found myself with my cousin Jesus son of Mary and John son of Zakariyya. They welcomed me and wished me well. Then he ascended with me to the third heaven, and Gabriel sought to open the gate.... It was opened for us and then I found myself with Joseph, who had been given a goodly portion. He welcomed me and wished me well. Then he ascended with us to the fourth heaven, and Gabriel sought to open the gate.... It was opened, and then I found myself with Enoch. He welcomed me and wished me well. God said, '*We raised him to an exalted station.*'[15] Then he ascended with us to the fifth heaven, and Gabriel sought to open the gate.... It was opened for us, and then I found myself with Aaron, who greeted me and wished me well. Then he ascended with us to the sixth heaven, and Gabriel sought to open the gate.... It was opened for us and then I found myself with Moses, who welcomed me and wished me well. Then he ascended with us to the seventh heaven, and Gabriel sought to open the gate.... It was opened for us, and then I found myself with Abraham, leaning his back against the House of Life. Each day 70,000 angels enter [this house] and do not return to it."

"Then I was brought to the lote tree of the boundary, its leaves like the ears of elephants and its fruits like jugs. When it *was covered* by God's command with *what covered*,[16] it changed so that no creature could describe its beauty. God *revealed to* me *what he revealed*,[17] imposing upon me [the duty of performing] fifty prayers during the day and night. I descended to Moses, and he said, 'What did your Lord impose upon your community?' I said, 'Fifty prayers.' He said, 'Return to your Lord and ask him to lighten it. Your community cannot bear that. I tested the Israelites and tried them [with less and they failed].' So I returned to my Lord and said, 'O Lord, lighten [the imposition] on my community.' He removed five. I returned to Moses.... [Moses kept sending me back to get the number of prayers reduced] until finally God said, 'Muḥammad, they are five prayers each day and night. For each prayer is [worth] ten, which makes fifty prayers. One who in-

> tends to do a good deed but does not do it, one good deed is written [in the book of deeds]; if one does it, ten are written. One who intends to do an evil deed but does not do it, nothing is written; if one does it, one is written.'[18] Then I descended to Moses and informed him of it. He said, 'Return to your Lord and ask him to lighten it.' The Messenger of God said, 'I have returned to my Lord to the point that I am too shy to do so [again].'"[19]

This hadith report contains elements both from the night journey verse and from the passage from the beginning of the Star chapter, connecting the two allusions and filling in the details of the story with a rich narrative of trial and initiation.

Although the above hadith report does not include the typical opening anecdotes, for instance the recounting of where Muḥammad was praying or sleeping upon the arrival of the angels, it begins with the arrival of the fantastic mount named Burāq whom Muḥammad rides during the overland night journey from Mecca to Jerusalem. The narrative evokes Jerusalem by its epithet, "the House of the Sanctuary" (*al-bayt al-maqdis* or *al-bayt al-muqaddis*), which Muslims interpret as a reference to the site of the temple of Solomon in particular, and by extension the city of Jerusalem and its environs in general. The middle of the report consists of a repetitive account of Muḥammad's encounter with previous Abrahamic prophets in each of the heavens he visits on his ascension, concluding with his meeting with Abraham at the "House of Life" in the seventh heaven.[20] The final portion of the hadith discusses the events that took place in the vicinity of the "lote tree of the boundary" that was mentioned in the qur'ānic passage from the beginning of the chapter of the Star. Muḥammad shuttles between Moses and his Lord, eventually receiving the duty of the five ritual prayers that pious Muslims observe each day. The hadith never specifies whether Muḥammad saw his Lord at the lote tree, nor whether the two had any other interaction besides these prayer negotiations. It also concludes without discussing Muḥammad's return to Mecca, an aspect of the story that many other accounts include. Nevertheless, this hadith from the collection of the traditionist known as Muslim gives a sparse but relatively complete account of the combined night journey and ascension narrative, presenting the bare skeleton of a framework which most later scholars flesh out in their commentaries.[21]

The "sound" (*ṣaḥīḥ*) collections are a good place to start in order to learn some of the background relevant to Islamic ascension narratives, but in order to comprehend the Sufi sayings that Sulamī compiles in *The Subtleties of the Ascension* more fully, one must go beyond the "official" ascension hadiths from the "sound" collections and examine other ascension narratives that did not meet Bukhārī and Muslim's criteria for inclusion. For example, one of the earliest Muslim historical sources mentions that Muḥammad visited paradise and hellfire during his ascension, and that satisfying his desire to visit these realms was one of the purposes of the journey.[22] The biography of Muḥammad preserved in Ibn Isḥāq's *Sīrat rasūl Allāh* as transmitted by Ibn Hishām (d. 218/834) contains an account of how the angel Mālik uncovered hellfire for Muḥammad on his ascension.[23] Several of the sayings in Sulamī's *The Subtleties of the Ascension* presume that Muḥammad toured around paradise and hellfire at some point in his journey, and one discusses the significance of this tour in mystical terms.[24] Although the majority of the hadiths in the official "sound" collections of Bukhārī and Muslim downplay or omit the tour of paradise or hellfire (such as in the extended hadith report quoted above),[25] other ascension hadiths describe what Muḥammad saw on such a tour in some detail, and some of the early Sufis were well versed in these wide-ranging hadith narratives.

Another aspect of the ascension narrative that is rarely included in those hadiths that were deemed sound is the intimate conversation between Muḥammad and God, a discourse that in other accounts becomes more detailed than the formulaic haggling over the number of daily prayers that was seen in the hadith from Muslim quoted above. The collection of hadiths assembled by Abū ᶜĪsā al-Tirmidhī (d. 279/892), a collection which many Sunnīs consider as enjoying a quasi-canonical status as one of the key "six books" of hadith, offers a rare exception. The intimate colloquy between Muḥammad and his Lord appears in the following anecdote from a hadith in Tirmidhī's collection that describes Muḥammad's report of a dream:

> ...Ibn ᶜAbbās said that the Messenger of God said, "During the night my Lord came to me in the most beautiful

> form." He said, "I reckoned it a dream"—he said so in the hadith. "He said, 'Muḥammad, do you know what the heavenly host debate?' I said, 'No.' So he put his hand between my shoulderblades until I felt its coldness between my nipples"—or he said, "[between] my collarbones." "Then I knew what was in the heavens and what was in the earth. He said, 'Muḥammad, do you know what *the heavenly host debate*?' I said, 'Yes, about the penitential acts (*kaffarāt*)...and the steps (*darajāt*)....'" [26]

Although this anecdote only claims to report a dream, details from this intimate conversation and its reference to the "heavenly host debate" were collated into popular ascension narratives at an early date. Sulamī's collection of sayings preserves some evidence for the connection between the above hadith and the early ascension narratives. One of the Sufi ascension sayings quoted by Sulamī alludes to the touch of the palm of God's hand, while another discusses why Muḥammad did not know what the heavenly host debate.[27] These references illustrate why one must be familiar with narratives beyond the "official" Sunnī accounts in Bukhārī and Muslim in order to make sense of the sayings in Sulamī's work.

Ascension Narratives ascribed to Ibn ᶜAbbās

If the hadiths recorded by Muslim b. Ḥajjāj and Muḥammad Bukhārī could be said to be a type of "official" tradition on the night journey and ascension, it is important to recognize that various extra-official and/or popular traditions on the subject also circulated in the early period. One cluster of such hadiths attributed to Ibn ᶜAbbās (d.ca. 68/687), a famous early scholar and companion of the Prophet, offers a case in point.[28] The ascension narrative attributed to Ibn ᶜAbbās adds a wealth of detail to the sparse account from *Ṣaḥīḥ* Muslim quoted above, from the description of the angels encountered to the account of the seas and mountains crossed beyond the seventh heaven. Three aspects of this narrative tradition are the most significant to the present work: first, the Ibn ᶜAbbās narrative mentions explicitly that Muḥammad sees God during his ascension; second, it reports in detail the intimate conversation between Muḥammad and God at the climax of the narrative; and third, it often describes at length Muḥammad's visit to paradise and hellfire during his ascension.[29]

Notice that the "heavenly host debate" dream-vision anecdote from Tirmidhī quoted above purports to be a hadith report transmitted by the young companion of the Prophet, Ibn ᶜAbbās. A series of other ascension narratives were similarly attributed to Ibn ᶜAbbās, and one particularly extensive version that was likely in circulation by the end of the 3rd/9th century at the latest incorporates the "heavenly host debate" and other popular narrative elements that are important to the present discussion because they appear in the sayings of the early Sufis which Sulamī collects. The sayings in Sulamī's work focus largely on the events that transpire after Muḥammad travels beyond the seventh heaven, and thus when searching for the foundations of these sayings it makes sense to focus on the climax of this extensive ascension narrative attributed to Ibn ᶜAbbās. What follows is an excerpt on the encounter between Muḥammad and God taken from an early version of the Ibn ᶜAbbās ascension narrative.

> I saw a great matter, which tongues cannot discuss and imagination cannot reach. My sight was bewildered beside it to the point that I feared blindness, so I closed my eyes and put trust in God. When I closed my eyes, God returned my vision to me in my heart, and I began to gaze with my heart at what I had been gazing at with my eyes. I saw a light gleaming. I was forbidden to describe to you what I saw of his grandeur. I asked my Lord to favor me with the steadiness of vision toward him in my heart in order to complete his blessing of me. My Lord did that and favored me with it, and I gazed upon him in my heart until he made it steady....
>
> When he inclined to me from his dignity, glorified be he, he placed one of his hands between my shoulderblades, and I felt the coldness of his fingers upon my heart for some time. With that I felt his sweetness, his beautiful fragrance, cool pleasure, and generous vision. All the terror that I had encountered vanished....
>
> My Lord, glorified and praised be he, spoke to me saying, "Muḥammad, do you know what the heavenly host

> debate?" I said, "My Lord, you are most knowing in that and in all things. You are the one who knows things unseen." He said, "They debate about the steps and goodnesses"....
>
> I said, "My Lord, you *took Abraham as an intimate friend*, and you *spoke to Moses directly*. You *raised Enoch to a high place*. You gave Solomon a *kingdom not befitting to anyone after him*, and you *gave David the psalms*. What is there for me, my Lord?"[30]
>
> He said, "Muḥammad, I took you as an intimate friend just as I took Abraham as an intimate friend. I spoke to you just as I spoke to Moses directly. I gave you the Opening of the book and the "seals" of Sūrat *al-Baqara*, which were from the treasuries of my throne. I have not given them to a prophet before you. I sent you to all the people of the earth, the white, black, and red, the jinn and human. I have never sent a prophet before to them all. I made the earth, its land and its sea, ritually pure and a place of prayer for you and your community...."
>
> Then after this he informed me of matters about which he did not permit me to tell you....[31]

This excerpt from the extended ascension narrative attributed to Ibn ᶜAbbās begins with a discussion of Muḥammad's vision of God, drawing upon the qurʾānic verses from the sūra of the Star, "*the heart did not lie in what it saw*" and "*his vision did not stray, nor was it excessive*."[32] The idea of seeking steadiness (*thibāt*) of vision becomes an important subject for the Sufi sages whom Sulamī quotes.

The above passage also incorporates the detail from the "heavenly host debate" hadith about God touching Muḥammad, and it includes the text of the "heavenly host debate" discourse as part of the intimate conversation between Muḥammad and his Lord on the night of the ascension. Another refinement on this intimate conversation given above comes when Muḥammad cites verses from the Qurʾān about how previous prophets have received God's favor, and asks God about the special favor that he himself will receive. God compares Muḥammad to previous prophets, explaining how Muḥammad not only receives much of the favor received by previous prophets, but he also receives special favors never granted to any other. This section explicitly compares and contrasts Muḥammad and the other prophets in a manner that the official ascension narratives leave implicit.[33] The idea of Muḥammad's superiority to other beings becomes a central theme in the Sufi sayings that Sulamī records in *The Subtleties of the Ascension*.

Finally, the selection above both reveals and conceals details of Muḥammad's exalted experiences. While it provides more of a description of Muḥammad's encounter with the deity than does any of the official ascension hadiths, it still turns to ambiguity and silence in portions of the vision and discourse, and it ends with a reference to a secret revelation. Many of the sages whom Sulamī quotes in *The Subtleties of the Ascension* attempt to explain the ambiguity and silence of the narratives through a recourse to mystical concepts. A brief discussion of a few of these key Sufi ideas is thus in order.

Sufi Discussions of Muḥammad's Journey

Sufism, often described as the primary mystical movement within Islam, is a complex phenomenon that defies simple characterization.[34] For some, Sufism means little more than a scrupulous dedication to moral pious behavior and to the teachings of Muslim norms of conduct that come to be categorized under the umbrella term "Islamic law" (*sharīʿa*); for others, Sufism means the suspension or even rejection of the letter of Islamic law and customary norms in order to cultivate an intimate relationship with the divinity. Most early Sufis fall somewhere between these two positions, and the sharp dichotomy between Sufism and legalism commonly postulated reflects modern anti-Sufi polemic more than it does historical Sufi practices. This being said, a number of early Sufis did portray themselves as members of a spiritual elite, which sometimes brought them into conflict with Muslim legists. These Sufis looked through the letter of the law and the literal meaning of sacred texts in order to contemplate deeper spiritual truths lying beneath the surface of Muslim texts, practices, and doctrines.

For example, some Sufis understand the Muslim doctrine that affirms the essential oneness of God (*tawḥīd*) to mean that on a deeper level nothing truly exists apart from God. A few Sufis then attempt to experience this original divine unity, striving for the state of the "passing away" (*fanāʾ*) of their contingent sense of self in order that the reality of oneness might re-emerge. No dualities remain when the one divine Real (*al-ḥaqq*) becomes realized, and some Sufi texts performatively evoke that state of union by blurring the distinction between subject and object, master and servant, divine and human.[35] Muḥammad's journey through the heavens to the divine throne, therefore, becomes a metaphor for the return of the mystic to the state of union with the divine. A number of the Sufi discussions of Muḥammad's journey in Sulamī's work express this mystical insight, examining the esoteric spiritual dimensions of the narrative, dimensions that transcend the narrative's exoteric surface meaning.

Sufis apply the metaphor of the journey to the various steps and stages on the mystical path (a term that itself draws upon the imagery of travel). What is an appropriate exercise for a Sufi at the beginning of her path may not be an appropriate exercise for a Sufi further along. As a Sufi progresses on her spiritual itinerary, she rests along the way at different mystical "stations" (singular *maqām*, plural *maqāmāt*) that represent attitudes of mind or levels of mystical development and maturity. While she often rests at each station for a while before being able to progress to the next station, a Sufi may occasionally experience mystical "states" (singular *ḥāl*, plural *aḥwāl*) that are more fleeting and transitory. Many of the Sufi instructional manuals contain whole sections devoted to the description of the "stations" and "states," placing them in different hierarchical orders that reflect the author's understanding of the mystical journey.[36] A number of the sayings in Sulamī's collection translated herein understand the Prophet's night journey and ascension as a type of allegory, each stage of his journey symbolically representing a stage along the Sufi's path. By interpreting the Prophet's journey allegorically, then, a Sufi may emulate his example by progressing along the spiritual path that Muḥammad blazed during his night journey and ascension.

A few Sufis follow the Prophet's example to the degree that they actually claim to retrace Muḥammad's journey for themselves through their mystical experiences. A famous early case is the ascension narrative attributed to Abū Yazīd al-Bisṭāmī (d. ca. 261/875), which offers an example of the appropriation of Muḥammad's heavenly ascent by mystics.[37] The early Sufis quoted and discussed in Sulamī's work, however, by and large did not treat Muḥammad's journey as an experience to be retraced by the mystics. Instead, they understood the night journey and ascension to represent a source of spiritual truth revealed to an exceptional individual such as a prophet. Seen in this light, Muḥammad's actions become a teaching tool rather than a guide for imitation. The narrative of Muḥammad's journey becomes a type of manual for the instruction of moral behavior, sincere devotion, and love of the divine beloved. This didactic approach is well represented in Sulamī's *Subtleties of the Ascension*, and seems to reflect the manner in which many early Sufis approached the night journey and ascension narratives.[38]

Sulamī's Central Works and *The Subtleties of the Ascension*

Abū ᶜAbd al-Raḥmān Sulamī (d. 412/1021) spent much of his life in Nishapur, a city which in the contemporary era lies in northeastern Iran, although Sulamī traveled widely in the eastern Islamic lands collecting hadith reports.[39] In addition to receiving Sufi training from his grandfather, Sulamī was trained in the traditional fields of Qurʾān, hadith, theology, and law. His works often demonstrate his broad training and interests, combining mysticism, Ashᶜarī theology, and Shāfiᶜī Sunnī legal methodology in the project of grounding Sufism in the roots (*uṣūl*) of Muslim scholarly tradition, what has been called an "uṣūlization" of Sufism.[40] This approach can be seen in Sulamī's important biographical dictionary, *The Generations of the Sufis* (*Ṭabaqāt al-ṣūfiyya*), a work that contains just over a hundred biographies of the early Sufis divided into five generations.[41] The structure of each biography reflects Sulamī's interest in the sayings of the Prophet Muḥammad, for early in each entry Sulamī lists whatever hadith reports a Sufi was said to have transmitted. Sulamī then reports a selection of non-prophetic sayings attributed to the Sufi, illustrating how hadith methodology could be applied more broadly to Sufi sayings. Through his biographies of these early Sufi men, and through an appended work dedicated to early Sufi women,[42] Sulamī attempts to give coherence to the early Sufi movement and to demonstrate that Sufism remains fully in line with mainstream Sunnī approaches to Islam.

In addition to Sulamī's pivotal work in the field of Sufi biography and his short works on select Sufi groups and practices,[43]

Sulamī was known for his work in the field of Qur'ān commentary. He was the author of a collection of mystical glosses on qur'ānic passages entitled *The Realities of Exegesis* (*Ḥaqā'iq al-tafsīr*), a key early work that became a crucial resource for later mystical commentators.[44] As in his *Generations of the Sufis*, Sulamī's Qur'ān commentary emphasizes the sayings of the early Sufi masters, frequently citing these sayings in order to explain passages from the Qur'ān. There is a significant overlap between the glosses on the ascension-related qur'ānic verses (Q 17:1, 53:8-18) in *The Realities of Exegesis* and the first twenty-four sayings compiled in *The Subtleties of the Ascension* (approximately the first half of the work), an overlap which demonstrates the importance of the former as a tool for understanding the latter.[45]

The Subtleties of the Ascension, edited and translated here for the first time, is a collection of some fifty-six sayings by Sulamī's Sufi predecessors on the subject of Muḥammad's night journey and ascension. In his preface to *The Subtleties of the Ascension*, Sulamī states that he had been asked to assemble these Sufi sayings at the request of an unnamed party, and he claims to have done his best to bring together what the "sages of the community said about the journey (*al-masrā*) of the Prophet on the night of the ascension (*al-mi'rāj*), from the subtleties of meanings to the realities of states."[46] The first half of this quotation makes clear that the ascension of the Prophet Muḥammad is the focus of Sulamī's collection, not the ascension experiences of Sufi mystics. The second half of the quotation defines the types of mystical remarks on the Prophet's ascension that appear in his collection, from the explanation of particular subtleties or details (*daqā'iq*) on the meaning of certain words and phrases to the elucidation of the mystical states (*aḥwāl*) experienced on the journey. Sulamī thus lays out the primary focus of the collection of sayings from the start, explaining his intentions and purpose in his preface.

The majority of the sayings in *The Subtleties of the Ascension* focus upon the final stages of Muḥammad's heavenly journey. Only a single saying in the work discusses the events in Mecca prior to the night journey (saying 51, on first meeting Burāq), and no other saying unambiguously mentions Muḥammad's experiences in Mecca, what he witnesses on the way to Jerusalem, or the details of the events in Jerusalem beyond the fact that Muḥammad was said to travel there prior to ascending.[47] The various stages of the heavenly ascension itself, where Muḥammad meets one or more prophets in each of the levels of the heavens, receives little comment in the sayings. None of the sayings discuss Muḥammad's return to Mecca at the end of his night journey and ascension experience. Clearly, then, it is important to recognize that the Sufis whom Sulamī quotes are most interested in discussing the very climax of the ascension narrative, the things that Muḥammad experiences in the seventh heaven and beyond. Such an interest probably stems from the fact that these final stages of the journey represent those portions of the narrative that contain the richest material for a mystical reading of the text.

Given these parameters, one notices four major themes that appear repeatedly in *The Subtleties of the Ascension*, each of which I will describe briefly in what follows.[48] The first major theme emphasizes the night journey and ascension as proof for the unique status and favor that Muḥammad enjoyed. The sayings that discuss this theme depict the Prophet's status as being beyond the status enjoyed by any other thing in God's creation. For instance, multiple sayings compare and contrast Muḥammad's station with that of other prophets, especially that of Moses. Whereas the latter merely spoke with God through a state of separation from him, Muḥammad was able both to speak to and to witness the divinity in intimate proximity. Similarly, other sayings contrast Muḥammad's station with that of the angels, even the most exalted of angels such as Gabriel. Some draw upon the popular tradition that Gabriel would have burned up had he approached the divinity to the degree that Muḥammad is able to approach during the ascension, graphically illustrating Muḥammad's superiority to Gabriel in the eyes of God.[49] The proximity to the divinity that Muḥammad reaches on the night journey and the ascension not only illustrates his favored status, but also suggests that he achieves a mystical state of proximity to the divinity that could be interpreted as evoking the mystical state of "passing away" (*fanāʾ*).[50]

A second major theme in *The Subtleties of the Ascension* is the idea that during the ascension Muḥammad was clothed with the lights of the divine attributes. The lights are interpreted by some of the early Sufis as symbols of the mystical transformation taking place on the journey, divine attributes replacing human attributes over the course of the ascension. The theme is closely related to the first theme, in that these lights protect Muḥammad and allow him to bear what no other created being could bear. For example, the following saying combines these first two themes:

> Wāsiṭī was asked about the approach of the Prophet on the night journey. He said, "He went from his self. '*He approached*' through him, from him, to him, '*and he descended*.'[51] The veils continued to descend from Muḥammad until he arrived at what [God] pointed out with his saying: '*He was a distance of two bows or closer*.'[52] That was through the power of the lights that clothed Muḥammad in the state of his night journey. Were it not for what adorned him, the alighting of the attribute upon him and the clothing of select lights, he would have been burned by the lights of that station. Gabriel was not empowered to approach that station when he was stripped of what clothed the lover."[53]

In this saying, an early Sufi links the descent of the veils to the stripping away of the Prophet's attributes and adorning and clothing the lover in divine lights or attributes. Although the concept of the "light of Muḥammad" (*nūr Muḥammad*) was well established by Sulamī's time,[54] and some early mystics used light symbolism to refer to mystical and/or otherworldly experiences, only versions of the night journey and ascension narrative outside of the standard Sunnī hadith collections mention that Muḥammad was clothed in a garment of light.[55] Especially when understood to refer to Muḥammad's taking on divine qualities during his journey, this garment of light theme serves to exalt the figure of the Prophet to a station higher than one would expect to see in an official Sunnī hadith report from the early period.

A third theme that is prominent in a number of sayings in *The Subtleties of the Ascension* but that rarely appears in the official collections is the vision of God.[56] Unlike the visions of some Christian and Jewish mystics in which the divine is described in detail, none of the sayings in Sulamī's collection attempt to describe the vision of God in words. Rather, the sayings discuss two main issues when dealing with the vision of God: first, the way that Muḥammad's manner of gazing can be seen as a model for Sufi behavior, and second, an explanation of how Muḥammad was able to see God, especially in light of the qurʾānic idea that no mortal can do so.[57] These two issues point to what appears to have been an important discussion among the early Sufis, namely the degree to which the Prophet's experience represents a special favor from God unobtainable by any other creature and the degree to which it establishes a paradigm for Sufis to emulate in their own mystical experiences.

Some early Sufis, such as Abū Yazīd Bisṭāmī (mentioned above), allegedly claimed to have experienced a type of mystical ascension in the tradition of Muḥammad's *miʿrāj*. Significantly, the sayings that Sulamī assembles do not mention Bisṭāmī's *miʿrāj* the way that the ascension work by Sulamī's student Abū al-Qāsim ʿAbd al-Karīm al-Qushayrī (d. 465/1072) does.[58] Qushayrī's treatise is much more extensive and ambitious than Sulamī's short work, and it contains entire sections examining the idea of ascensions by figures other than Muḥammad, as well as a section that directly discusses the possibility of the human vision of God.[59] Despite the fact that none of the sayings in Sulamī's work make any explicit reference to such possibilities, one or two sayings in *The Subtleties of the Ascension* leave open the possibility that mystics can indeed follow Muḥammad and experience a type of ascension and/or vision of God.[60]

The fourth and final major theme that appears in a substantial number of sayings in *The Subtleties of the Ascension* involves explaining the reason why Muḥammad was not more forthcoming in describing his otherworldly journey. Why did he keep his experience, especially his encounter with the divinity at the culmination of the ascension, such a secret? A few sayings that Sulamī quotes portray Muḥammad and the divinity as two lovers, explaining Muḥammad's silence through the poetic trope of the lovers' secret that should not be shared with others.[61] Since the earliest period, many Sufis have expressed their relationship with God as that between a lover and a beloved, a concept that may have originated with the famous woman Sufi by the name of Rābiʿa ʿAdawiyya (d. 185/801). Some sayings in Sulamī's collection characterize Muḥammad's relationship with God in this way, and they thus seek to explain why Muḥammad kept his experiences to himself. More of the sayings, however, concentrate upon the idea that Muḥammad found mere words inadequate to describe his experience or to express the glory of the divinity. They suggest that it was not Muḥammad's unwillingness to share his experiences but rather his inability to share his experiences, due to the limitations of human language. Finally, in the sayings that express a mystical understanding of the ascension as the progressive experience of "passing away" (*fanāʾ*), the Prophet's silence could be said to result from his loss of self awareness during the ascension. Since Muḥammad's conscious sense of self (*nafs*) was not present in the highest level of the journey, these mystics contend, when he returned to his individuated sense of self he was not conscious of what had taken place and could therefore not describe it. Regardless of the various approaches to the problem of the Prophet's relative silence, each of these sayings seeks to explain why Muḥammad's descriptions of the culmination of his journey, as well as those descriptions appearing in the Qurʾān, do not offer more details about what took place.

These four themes connect and overlap in fascinating ways in the sayings that Sulamī brings together in his collection, and they represent some of the key issues that the early Sufi commentators apparently considered especially significant. Other issues that early historians, commentators, and theologians deemed important, such as the exact date and time of the night journey and ascension, or the exact identity of the companion(s) with whom Muḥammad was sleeping on the night of his journey, do not appear at all in Sulamī's collection. As Sulamī explained in his preface, he attempted to relate "what the sages of the community said about the journey of the Prophet on the night of the ascension, from the subtleties of meanings to the realities of states."[62] Since the term "meanings" (*maʿānī*) in this opening sentence refers to deep spiritual or mystical meanings, one can understand why historical, political, or theological questions do not receive much attention in these early Sufi sayings. Rather, the sayings that Sulamī collects explain how Muḥammad's journey serves a didactic function and how it describes one of Muḥammad's preeminent mystical experiences.

The inclusion of narrative elements in Sulamī's collection that do not appear in the standard accounts of the night journey and ascension, from the clothing of light to the vision of and conversation with the divinity, however, merits some consideration. One might justifiably wonder why there are so many references to images and symbols outside of the "official" scope of the "sound" hadith collections. To what degree were Sulamī and his Sufi predecessors circulating and commenting upon "unofficial" hadith reports, such as the ascension narratives attributed to Ibn ᶜAbbās, that the scholars of the generation after Sulamī might have considered problematic? It is not possible here to attempt to resolve this issue definitively.[63] Nevertheless, the evidence from *The Subtleties of the Ascension* suggests that up through the 5th/11th century a wide diversity of ascension narratives were not only in circulation, but also were accepted by pivotal early Sufi scholars as preserving insights into mystical truths about Muḥammad's night journey and ascension.

The Authenticity of the Text

The discussions above on what can be learned from *The Subtleties of the Ascension* about the history of ascension narratives and about the types of issues Sulamī and his predecessors deemed important have all been predicated upon the hypothesis that *The Subtleties of the Ascension* represents an authentic work by Sulamī. Rather than taking this hypothesis for granted, however, critical scholars see the importance of testing it in light of the available evidence. For instance, no reference to *The Subtleties of the Ascension* appears in the major bibliographies of Sulamī's works.[64] This difficulty is not insurmountable, however, since Sulamī's biographer mentions that Sulamī had written almost seven hundred works in his life, and the present treatise is so short as to be easily overlooked.[65]

It is possible that *The Subtleties of the Ascension* was composed by a later scholar in Sulamī's name, drawing material from Sulamī's Qurʾān commentary and/or Qushayrī's later ascension work. The substantial overlap between portions of these larger works and *The Subtleties of the Ascension* makes such a possibility intriguing.[66] One could make an argument that *The Subtleties of the Ascension* was composed after the ascension portions of Sulamī's Qurʾān commentary, *The Realities of Exegesis*, since only the sayings from the first half of *The Subtleties of the Ascension* (the first 24 sayings) draw upon ascension-related sayings from *The Realities of Exegesis*. One could imagine Sulamī or a later compiler drawing upon the latter work, going on to supplement it with an additional thirty sayings that do not appear in the latter. If a compiler after both Sulamī and Qushayrī had access to both Sulamī's *Realities of Exegesis* and Qushayrī's *Book of the Ascension*, she or he could have begun compiling sayings from the former and expanded it with a number of additional sayings from the latter.

In contrast, one could argue that *The Subtleties of the Ascension* represents a work compiled and written prior to Qushayrī's *Book of the Ascension*, for the latter text often supplements the sayings preserved by Sulamī with further explication and editorial commentary. One example here will suffice, Qushayrī's transmission of Sulamī's saying 6:

> Wāsiṭī was asked, "How was his [i.e. the Prophet's] (peace be upon him)[67] state on the night of the ascension?" He said, "He clothed him in the clothes of his attribute, he permitted him the witnessing, and he addressed him face to face."[68] And the meaning of this is that he clothed him in the clothes that suited his attribute (*libāsan yaṣlaḥu lina*ᶜ*tihi*), that is, [suited] to the truthful witness of his description." [I believe that] it means: "He strengthened him and steadied him for what he specified exclusively for him and his family."[69]

In this passage, Qushayrī faithfully transmits Wāsiṭī's answer exactly as it appears in Sulamī's *Subtleties of the Ascension*, and he then goes on to offer a further explication of its meaning as he understands it. In the process, Qushayrī modifies the sentiment of the original saying, explaining away its possibly objectionable aspects, and making its meaning correspond to his own theological perspective. Qushayrī's text then continues to the beginning of the next saying, which corresponds to the very next saying in Sulamī's text as well (saying 7). This type of exegetical interjection is consistent with the thesis that Qushayrī took the sayings from his teacher's work and adapted them to his own later text on the same subject.

Such an argument proves little about the authenticity of Sulamī's text, however, for there remains no guarantee that even Qushayrī's text is genuine or reliable. The sole extant manuscript of Qushayrī's *Book of the Ascension* is relatively late, copied in

880/1475-6 according to its colophon. Moreover, even if one were to assume that Qushayrī's text is genuine, a later fabricator could have composed *The Subtleties of the Ascension* using both Sulamī's *Realities of Exegesis* and Qushayrī's *Book of the Ascension* as sources. Without discovering further bits of evidence, internal or external, there is simply no way to prove the authenticity of *The Subtleties of the Ascension* in any definitive manner. Having worked with hundreds of manuscripts of Arabic ascension narratives from different centuries, however, I maintain that the balance of evidence that we have at this point weighs in favor of accepting the authenticity of *The Subtleties of the Ascension*.

Proceeding on the working hypothesis that Sulamī wrote *The Subtleties of the Ascension*, the text presents equivocal evidence about the date at which Sulamī might have composed the work. The evidence does not come in the form of references to historical events or places, but rather consists of the use of an honorific formula typically given after the names of revered figures who are no longer living. The name of Sulamī's spiritual teacher Abū al-Qāsim al-Naṣrābādhī (d. 367/977-8) is cited twice in *The Subtleties of the Ascension*, yet in neither case does the honorific formula "God have mercy upon him" (*raḥamahu Allāh*) appear after his name, suggesting that Naṣrābādhī may still have been living when Sulamī compiled the text.[70] One could then date the composition of the work to a period between 360/970, when Sulamī began his literary career,[71] and 367/977-8, when Naṣrābādhī died. However, this honorific formula does in fact appear in one citation after the name of one of Sulamī's important sources, Abū Bakr Muḥammad b. ᶜAbd Allāh Ibn Shādhān al-Rāzī (d. 376/987).[72] This detail therefore suggests that the text was composed after Ibn Shādhān's death, that is, after 376/987. Given that a later copyist may have inserted this formula in one case and neglected to copy it in another, such honorific phrases cannot be used as reliable evidence for ascribing a definitive date to Sulamī's compilation of *The Subtleties of the Ascension*.[73] More suggestive is the fact that the sayings that are present in both *The Realities of Exegesis* and *The Subtleties of the Ascension* all appear in the first half of the latter work. Were Sulamī to have composed *The Subtleties of the Ascension* early in his life and later drawn upon it in his Qurᵓān commentary, *The Realities of Exegesis*, one would expect that he would have drawn sayings from throughout *The Subtleties of the Ascension*, not just from its beginning. The fact that the overlap occurs only in the first half of the text, therefore, leads one to believe that *The Subtleties of the Ascension* was compiled after *The Realities of Exegesis* was written, which scholars date to the period between 360/970 and 370/980.[74]

While I am not aware of other internal evidence in *The Subtleties of the Ascension* that could allow one to date the text definitively, and while there is no colophon at the end of the text that reports the date it was completed or copied, nevertheless the unique "Sulamiyyāt" manuscript in which *The Subtleties of the Ascension* is preserved offers evidence to suggest that the text was copied at an early date, perhaps as early as the same century in which Sulamī died.[75] For instance, the colophon to the text immediately following *The Subtleties of the Ascension* in the manuscript, a work called *Memorial of Female Sufi Devotees* (*Dhikr al-niswa al-muta^cabbidāt al-ṣūfiyyāt*) states in the same hand that the latter text was copied in the year 474/1081, or approximately sixty years after Sulamī's death.[76] If the manuscript is indeed as old as this colophon indicates, then there is a significant possibility that the treatises it contains are indeed the authentic works of Sulamī. As such, *The Subtleties of the Ascension* offers a valuable glimpse into the discussions and debates among the early Sufi masters about this central journey in the Prophet's life and into the depths and dimensions of its mystical significance.

Notes on Translation

Translating a text involves a number of decisions on the part of the translator, and it has become almost a truism that translation involves interpretation. Few accept the idea that a translation can produce an equivalent text in another language, and contemporary translation theorists speak more of approximation than equivalence.[77] One issue a translator must struggle with is how closely he or she sticks to the nuances of the original text in an effort to be accurate, and how freely he or she changes the expressions of the original text to accommodate the rhythm and flow of the new language and new cultural context. In translating *Laṭā^cif al-mi^crāj* into *The Subtleties of the Ascension*, I have attempted to strike a balance between attention to accuracy and attention to the exigencies of contemporary American English. If I tend to give more weight to accuracy, even when the resulting phrases are somewhat awkward in English, I erred in this direction not out of scorn for lucid American English but out of a desire to convey the ambiguity and subtlety of the original prose. Such rich semantic openness deserves to be preserved in translation, especially in mystical passages in which subject-object interplay becomes a device for undermining the multiplicity inherent in human language.[78] I would much rather produce an English translation that faithfully but somewhat awkwardly reproduces the nuances of the original than to impose a delimited meaning onto the text in the name of artificial clarity, destroying the original's semantic openness in the process.

For this reason, with few exceptions, I have not capitalized adjectives, pronouns and nouns that might be understood to refer to the deity. Arabic has no capital letters, and therefore any time they appear in a translation from Arabic they reflects the decision of a translator more than the requirements of the original text. Usually such decisions are relatively harmless, but in mystical passages where a third person masculine singular pronoun might on one level refer to the deity and on another level to someone or something else, capitalizing may do real violence to the multivalent meaning of the text. For this reason, with the exception of the divine names "God," "the Lord" and "the Real" (a name Sufis often use for the divinity), I generally resist imposing capital letters at the beginning of words that either explicitly or potentially refer to the divinity. I see it not as a matter of respect or faith, but rather as a matter of preserving the richness and openness of the original text.

At times I do feel that the brevity of the original text merits explanation or expansion to make its meaning more comprehensible in English. Whenever I have added words or phrases not present in the Arabic text, for whatever reason, I enclose those words or phrases in square brackets [ ] . I use rounded parentheses ( ) for words or phrases present in the original text, such as honorific formulae, that may otherwise unduly disrupt the flow of the English prose. In addition, I replace the honorific phrase that comes after Muḥammad's name, "God's blessings and peace be upon him" (Ar: *ṣallā allāhu ʿalayhi wa-sallam*) with a special symbol that represents this phrase in Arabic calligraphy.[79]

It is important to bear in mind that the numbering of the sayings and the titles at the head of each section are not a feature of the original text. Rather, I have added these devices to the English translation, and the Arabic text in the case of the numbers, in order to facilitate subsequent references to and cross-references between the various sayings in *The Subtleties of the Ascension*. While an argument could be made that one or two of the sayings that I have treated together should actually be divided into separate sayings, I follow the lead of the original Arabic manuscript and its use of a symbol to indicate when one saying ends and a new one begins.[80]

A word must be said about the use of *italicized* text within the translation and commentary of *The Subtleties of the Ascension* that follows. When text in italics appears within quotation marks in the body of the translation, the words in *italics* are direct quotations from the Qurʾān. Since allusions to qurʾānic words or phrases that might be clear to a Muslim or Arabic-speaking audience may well be obscure for other audiences, I have also used *italics* in Sulamī's text to indicate when such indirect allusions occur. Following the text, the paragraphs of text in italics represent my own annotations and commentary on each saying. In addition, I use italics (or the lack thereof, when the rest of the passage is italicized) to indicate words transliterated from Arabic into Latinate characters. It is my hope that by using italics, additional headings, and other editorial insertions, the text will become more accessible to an English-speaking audience.

Technical Issues of Transliteration, Names, and Dates

I transliterate Arabic terms into English characters by the Library of Congress system as described in the *International Journal of Middle East Studies*. A few Islamic words that have become so common in Islamic texts as to be familiar, such as *ḥadīth*, will not be transliterated with their formal diacritic marks but will rather be represented in their common form (i.e. hadith). I have attempted to follow the lead of Michael Sells and others in introducing names, new words, and new concepts through the "familiarization" principle.[81] That is, the first time that a name or a term is introduced in the text it will appear in formal form, including diacritic marks (e.g. Abū ᶜAbd al-Raḥmān al-Sulamī); subsequent references will appear in a more informal and familiar form, without the definite article and without some or all of the diacritics (e.g. Sulamī). The part of the name representing "son of so and so," indicated by the Arabic term "Ibn," will be written out in full when it is the common way to refer to an individual (e.g. Ibn ᶜAbbās), but abbreviated in the conventional fashion as "b." when it is not (e.g. Muslim b. Ḥajjāj). The text of the translation will preserve the Arabic form of the names of famous individuals (e.g. Mūsā), while the commentary will refer to them in the form more familiar to English readers (e.g. Moses). When a death date of an individual is known, it will be given it in parentheses after the formal mention of the individual, first with the Islamic *hijrī* dating system (*anno Hegirae* or A.H.) based on the years after the traditional date of the *hijra* from Mecca to Medina, immediately followed by the Western *mīlādī* dating system (*anno Domini* or A.D., presented in less Christianocentric form as the "Common Era" or C.E.) based on the years after the traditional date of the birth of Jesus. For example, Sulamī's death date in the year 412 A.H., which is equivalent to the year 1021 C.E., will be given after Sulamī's name in the following form: (d. 412/1021).

The Illustrations that Accompany this Text

Nearly all the images that are interspersed throughout the text are from a famous *Miᶜrājnāma* manuscript held in the Bibliothèque Nationale in Paris and published in facsimile edition by Marie-Rose Seguy.[82] This incredible manuscript, purportedly produced in Herat circa 1430-36 CE, bears on its surface no direct connection to Sulamī's work. Sample paintings have been included here, however, in order to highlight the thematic parallels between some of the early mystical sayings in Sulamī's *Subtleties of the Ascension* and this later ascension text whose narrative can also be traced to early non-canonical sources.[83] Just as the figural representations of the Prophet in the *Miᶜrājnāma* push the boundaries of some contemporary Muslim notions of artistic propriety, so a number of the sayings in *The Subtleties of the Ascension* push the boundaries of some contemporary Muslim conventions of authentic and acceptable discourse attributed to the Prophet. The intention is not to offend anyone's sensibilities, but rather to discuss the historical record honestly, and to open up a creative space for mystical insight and imaginative speculation as one contemplates the subtle mysteries of Muḥammad's ascension as elucidated by the early Sufi masters.[84]

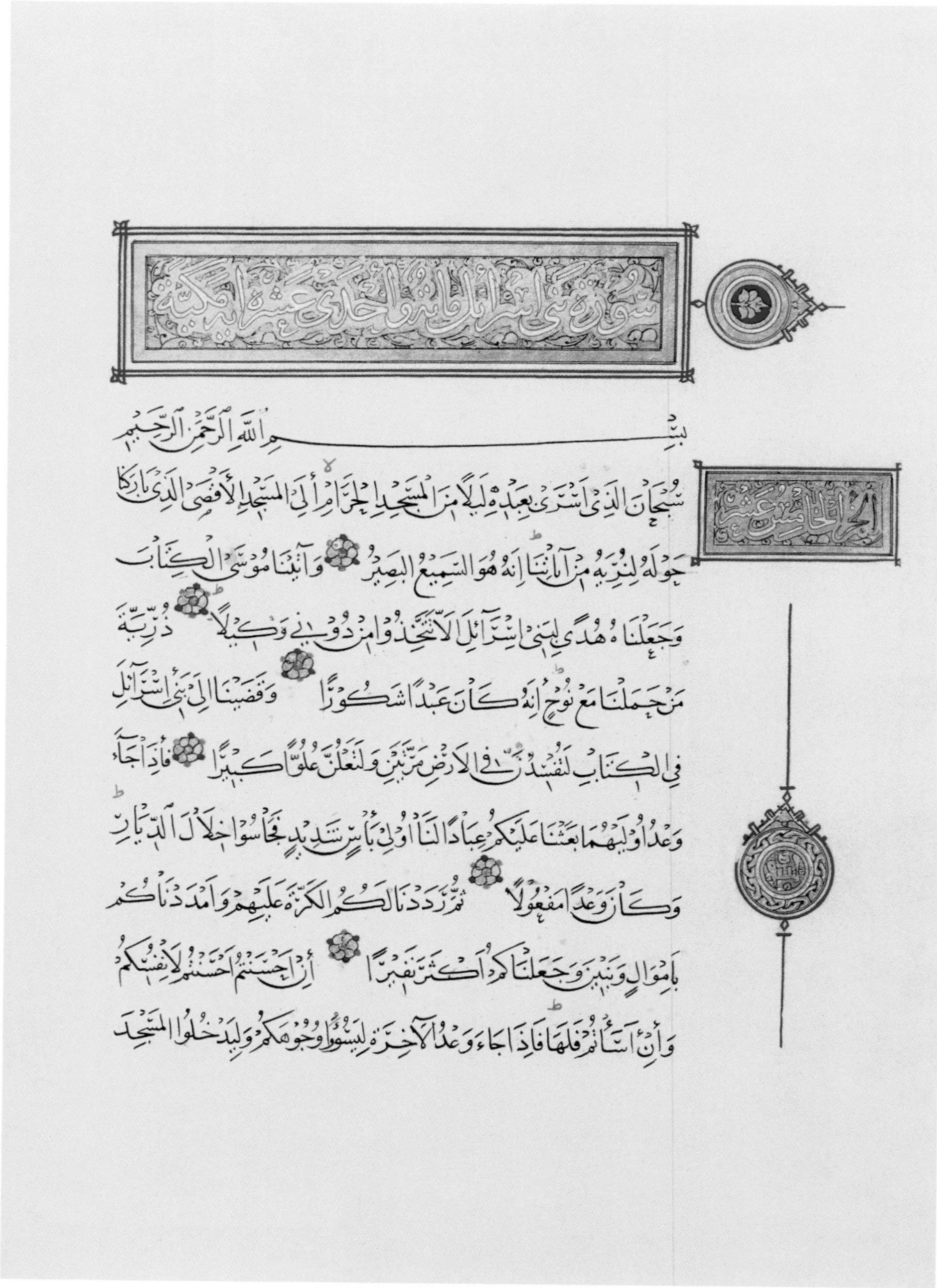

Figure 1. The beginning of the Sura of the Children of Israel/The Night Journey, Q 17:1. A Qur'ānic page written by Aḥmad ibn ash-Shaykh as-Suhrawardī, the grandson of the founder of the Suhrawardī Sufi order, 1318 CE, Iraq. (Istanbul, Turkish & Islamic Museum).

The Subtleties of the Ascension

by

Abū ᶜAbd al-Raḥmān Sulamī

In the name of God, the Compassionate, the Caring;
My Lord is my sufficiency, and with him is success....

The Issue of
The Elucidation of the Subtleties
of the Ascension

Praise be to God, Lord of the worlds, the first and the last,and may God's abundant blessings and peace be upon Muḥammad and his family....

[PREFACE]

You asked (may God help you to success) what the sages of the community said about the journey of the Prophet on the night of the ascension, from the subtleties of meanings to the realities of states. I assembled selections on that for you, to the best of my capacity and ability, after beseeching God for goodness in it and a blessing on it. It is a good and a blessing for the believer.[1]

Sulamī's brief prefatory remarks suggest that he composed the work at the request of an unknown student, companion, or patron. This type of introduction is fairly common in premodern Muslim texts, and one need not assume that an actual correspondent requested that Sulamī compose this work. The request may, in fact, be nothing more than a literary device. Whether genuine or not, it is worth examining the parameters for the work that the request establishes. Instead of asking Sulamī simply to recount the story of the Prophet's night journey and ascension as found in the Qur'ān and hadith reports, the request asks that Sulamī gather sayings that point to the deeper truths and hidden meanings in the story. It also requests him to recount how the story might illuminate Sufi spiritual practice, asking for an explanation of the "realities of the states" (ḥaqā'iq al-aḥwāl) *or the mystical experiences that the Prophet's journey illustrates. The sayings that follow presume an intimate knowledge of the qur'ānic allusions and hadith reports of the*

Prophet's journey discussed in the introduction above, moving beyond this level of discourse into a deeper level of mystical discussion.

Sulamī collects the sayings that were attributed to the "sages of the community" (ḥukamā᾽ al-umma), *primarily the Sufi masters that preceded him. Although Sulamī does not transmit any hadith report in its entirety in this work, we will see that many of the following sayings are introduced by a chain of Sufi transmitters in a fashion similar to the transmitter chains* (isnāds) *that introduce hadith reports. In both cases, the chains of transmitters serve as authenticating devices. Sulamī claims to have done his best in assembling this collection of sayings, and that through God's help his project met with success. How successful the sayings are in communicating to contemporary readers mystical truths about Muḥammad's ascension depends upon a number of factors, but I have done my best in the translations and annotations that follow to attempt to make the sayings accessible to the general reader. The hope is that each may catch at least a glimpse of the light that shines from these brilliant elucidations, both to learn more about Sulamī and the early Sufi movement, as well as to learn more about Muḥammad's ascension and the subtle realities that some have seen in it.*

1 - GOD AS THE SOLE CAUSE OF THE JOURNEY

God, be he glorified and exalted, said, "*Glorified be the one who caused his servant to journey by night. . . .*" [Regarding this phrase from the night journey verse,] Wāsiṭī[2] (may God be compassionate to him) said, "He distanced himself from anyone [else] having a movement or thought in sending out his Prophet ﷺ,[3] who would thus be a partner in the night journey and the sending out."

With this saying, Sulamī immediately takes up a detailed discussion of the night journey verse, "Glorified be the one who caused his servant to journey by night from the sacred mosque to the furthest mosque whose precincts we have blessed in order to show him some of our signs, indeed [God] is the one who hears, the one who sees" (Q 17:1). *Wāsiṭī, the authority whom Sulamī draws upon in this saying, analyzes the use of the very first word in the verse, subhāna ("glorified be"), discussing the significance of this word in the context of the night journey. This approach is what one might expect in a work of Qur'ān gloss or commentary, and indeed in his Qur'ān commentary or* tafsīr, *Sulamī begins his exegesis of the night journey verse by citing this very same saying by Wāsiṭī.*[4]

Along with the famous early Sufi named Ḥusayn b. Manṣūr Ḥallāj, Muḥammad b. Mūsā Wāsiṭī (also known as Ibn Farghānī) is one of the most frequently cited authorities in the present work. Wāsiṭī was an important companion of Junayd and Nūrī, pivotal figures from the formative period of Sufism. Short biographical notes on these figures and others whom Sulamī mentions in the text appear in the appendix to this translation.

The theme of this concise yet profound saying is God's incomparability. According to Wāsiṭī, by using the word subhāna, *God distanced himself* (nazzaha nafsahu) *from any human conception. It suggests that God cannot be compared with other beings. This idea of distancing or setting apart here, conveyed by the Arabic term* tanzīh, *was central to the articulation of Islam's rejection of both anthropomorphism (the idea that God has a human form) and polytheism (the idea that there is more than one God). Not only the early mystics but also other Muslim scholars applied this theological concept to the beginning of the night journey verse. For instance, a contemporary of Wāsiṭī, the famous exegete Muḥammad b. Jarīr Ṭabarī (d. 310/923), explains the purpose of the phrase "glorified be..." as "distancing* (inzāh) *God from [all] others."*[5] *Wāsiṭī's saying develops the argument further to reach its logical conclusion. God begins the verse with an expression of "distancing" because God wants to emphasize that no other being has the power or ability to send Muḥammad on the night journey. Although Gabriel may help to carry out God's orders, God ultimately has no partners or equals, and God alone merits praise for bringing about Muḥammad's journey.*[6]

2 - THE NATURE OF THE JOURNEY

> Ibn ᶜAṭāᵓ said, "He purified the place of nearness and the stopping place of approach from being influenced by a created thing through a state. He was caused to journey by night in his self, he journeyed by night in his spirit, and he was dispatched in his secret-heart. The secret-heart did not know what engaged the spirit, the spirit did not know what the secret-heart witnessed, and the self had no report from either of them or from what engaged them. Each stopped at its limit, witnessing the Real, apprehending something of it without intermediary or abidance of humanity. Rather, a real became realized in his servant, making him realized. He stood him where there was no station and addressed him. *He revealed to* him *what he revealed.*[7] Lofty and exalted is our Lord.

This saying discusses how a contingent and created being could approach the eternal and uncreated divinity. According to Ibn ᶜAṭāᵓ in this saying, nothing created or human reaches the divinity. Ibn ᶜAṭāᵓ seems to bridge the gap between the early theological positions on the debate about whether the Prophet's journey took place in body or in spirit. Evidence for this debate already appears in the account from Ibn Isḥāq's biography of Muḥammad. Here, Ibn ᶜAṭāᵓ claims that three different aspects of Muḥammad's being participated simultaneously on the night journey, each arriving at a different limit. The self (nafs) of the Prophet, sometimes identified with the portion of the soul connected with the physical body, was the aspect of Muḥammad that was sent on the night journey. It is the faculty that was first acted upon, connected to the qurᵓānic verb asrā. *The second aspect or spirit* (rūḥ) *of the Prophet actively "journeyed by night"* (sarā), *a different form of the same root as the verb* asrā, *reaching a farther limit. Finally, the innermost secret-heart* (sirr) *was "dispatched"* (sayyara), *making use of a different verbal root to refer to the final stage of the journey, perhaps standing for the final stages of the heavenly ascension. The saying makes it clear that the spirit and the secret-heart both reached a station beyond what the self was able to reach. Although all three aspects witnessed the Real to some degree, none of the three aspects could comprehend what the others experienced.*

Ibn ʿAṭāʾ introduces the idea that each of the faculties witnessed the divine Real in its own manner, and each transcended its connections with the human body in order to reach that point. The Sufi concept of "passing away" (fanāʾ) *comes to the fore in the saying as the Prophet-subject dissolves into the mystical experience of divine self-revelation, and ambiguous verbs and pronouns near the latter half of the saying evoke the apophatic mystery of non-duality. The Real* (al-ḥaqq), *one of the divine names, merges with the servant insofar as "a real* (ḥaqq, indefinite) *became realized* (taḥaqqaqa) *in the servant, making him/it realized* (ḥaqqaqahu)." *The combination of the complex use of the root* ḥ-q-q *and the polysemic ambiguity in this passage makes it extremely difficult to translate, but particularly rich in potential mystical meaning.*[8]

The phrase "he stood him (aqāmahu) *where there was no station* (maqām)*" points to the fact that this experience transcended human rational categories of thought and speech. Such a phrase resonates with the language from the Book of the Stan*dings, *a mystical treatise on intimate dialogues with the divinity by a near contemporary of Ibn ʿAṭāʾ named Muḥammad b. ʿAbd al-Jabbār Niffarī (d. 354/965).*[9] *In the above saying, the enigmatic location of "no station" also yields a divine colloquy ("he addressed him"), the content of which remains a mystery. Ibn ʿAṭāʾ connects the key qurʾānic verse from the sūra of the Star,* "He revealed to his servant what he revealed" (Q 53:10), *with this colloquy. The verse seems to conceal more than it reveals about the nature of the experience, and a number of other sayings offer mystical commentary on this verse and its qurʾānic context.*

3 - BEARING THE VISION IN THE HEART

I heard Manṣūr b. ᶜAbd Allāh say that he heard Abū al-Qāsim Bazzāz say that Ibn ᶜAṭāᵓ said regarding God's saying "*The heart did not lie in what it saw,*"[10] "The heart did not believe differently than what the eye saw."

[Bazzāz] said that Ibn ᶜAṭāᵓ continued, "Not everyone who sees has a heart enabled [to comprehend it],[11] since sight may overcome and unsettle the secret-heart from bearing what reaches it. But the Messenger ﷺ was able to bear it in his heart, intellect, sensation, and gaze. This indicates the sincerity of his inner heart when he bore it in what was witnessed."

The previous saying ends with a gloss of a qurᵓānic verse, "He revealed to his servant what he revealed" (*Q 53:10*)*; the present composite saying, which actually appears separately but in close proximity in Sulamī's Qurᵓān commentary, continues in exegetical mode by analyzing the next verse,* "The heart did not lie in what it saw" (*Q 53:11*). *The object of the vision was a matter of debate among early scholars, some understanding it as vision of God and others as a vision of Gabriel's true created form. Some theologians who defended the former position, troubled by the idea that Muḥammad could have seen God in a physical form, cited this qurᵓānic verse as a proof that the vision took place in Muḥammad's heart rather than with his eyes. Others, on the contrary, insisted that Muḥammad saw the vision with the eyes of his head.*[12] *Here Ibn al-ᶜAṭāᵓ does not comment on the object of the vision, but he supports the idea that the original vision was seen by Muḥammad with the eyes of his head.*

Instead of focusing upon this debate, however, Ibn ᶜAṭāᵓ takes a different approach. The saying portrays the central point of the verse as the fact that Muḥammad's heart was able to bear the extraordinary thing that his eyes were made to witness. That is, while the vision took place through the physical faculty of the eyes, the heart believed (iᶜtaqada) *and correctly understood what the eyes perceived. The hearts of lesser creatures, by contrast, might have disbelieved the vision and formulated a false opinion about what was seen.*

The second half of the saying, which may well have originated as a separate but related anecdote, develops the idea that only certain individuals possess hearts that can bear what their eyes witness in such circumstances. Muḥammad, the saying asserts, was one such individual whose faculties faithfully supported him throughout the experience. The saying leaves open the possibility that other gifted individuals, such as the Sufi saints, could similarly bear fantastic visions such as those Muḥammad witnessed. Ibn ʿAṭāʾ concludes by drawing a connection between the ability to bear the vision and the sincerity of one's inner heart (ṭawiyya), *an organ which enfolds the innermost secret-heart* (sirr).

4 - A CHOICE OF WORDS

> I heard Abū al-Qāsim Naṣrābādhī say, "The Real (be he exalted) cast down all objections and uncertainties about the ascension with his saying, '*He caused* [his servant] *to journey by night*.'[13] He did not say, 'He journeyed by night,' since [then] there would be no wonder in the power and lordship [displayed], nor astonishment over them."

Here Naṣrābādhī explains the importance of the verb "to cause to journey by night" (asrā) *in the night journey verse, addressing the issue of why the verb could not instead have been in the simple active form "to journey by night"* (sarā). *He asserts that the latter usage might have implied that Muḥammad undertook the journey of his own accord, without receiving any divine command or assistance. Were the latter to have been the case, then the night journey and ascension would have focused exclusively upon Muḥammad and his power, rather than recognizing the one who caused his servant to journey by night. The qurʾānic choice of words, according to Naṣrābādhī, deliberately evokes wonder and astonishment at the power* (qudra) *and lordship* (rubūbiyya) *displayed in causing Muḥammad to journey (presumably the Real's power and lordship, but the text does not state the agent explicitly in the final phrase). According to this saying, the use of the verb* asrā *rebuts "all objections and uncertainties" of those who doubt that Muḥammad could have accomplished such a journey. The ones with objections and uncertainties are presumably the Meccan polytheists who refuse to believe the truth of Muḥammad's account. The verse answers their objections by hinting at the divine agency involved in the journey.*

It is significant that this saying equates the two terms night journey (isrāʾ) *and ascension* (miʿrāj), *for it states that objections about the ascension were cast down by the revelation of the night journey verse. Such a usage shows that a sharp distinction between these two terms in a technical sense, i.e., reserving the night journey for the terrestrial trip from Mecca to Jerusalem and the ascension for the celestial trip in the heavenly realms (as one finds, for example, in Ibn Isḥāq), was a convention no longer recognized by the Sufis whom Sulamī quotes. Indeed a large number of the hadith reports on the night journey in the early official collections describe much less about the terrestrial journey and much more about the journey through the heavens. The sayings that Sulamī compiles also contain such an emphasis, perhaps, as hypothesized in the introduction above, because of the greater potential for mystical interpretation in the latter portion of the narrative.*

Figure 2: The Prophet in the garden of paradise.

5 - THE PROPRIETY OF WITNESSING

One of them was asked, "On the night of the ascension, why was the Prophet ﷺ shown paradise, hellfire, the prophets and the angels before the approach to the Real?"

The response was, "So that he would learn propriety by [seeing] them in the place of empowerment. He veiled the realm of being with what he used to veil it: a throne, a seat and their pillars. Were it not for that, nothing would have been steady for him, and something of imagination would have approached his view. When he alone had a single witnessing apart from [other] witnessings, all save him shrank from every sensation to one sensation."

"Existing beings were offered to the Prophet in order that he could speak to the prophets and angels ﷺ. When he knew that the thing desired of him was not that, he closed his eyes to them and all that they contained. He undertook the obligation of the propriety of witnessing until 'he *approached and descended*' and '*he revealed to his servant what he revealed*.'"[14]

The Prophet's encounter with earlier prophets such as Abraham, Moses, and Jesus, and his encounter with angels such as Gabriel and Michael, the various gatekeepers, and the angels worshipping God in Jerusalem, at the lote tree, or near the divine throne form standard elements of the Islamic ascension narratives. The question that prompts this anonymous saying, however, presumes that all these encounters are secondary to Muḥammad's encounter with the divinity at the culmination of his journey. If encountering the Real can be said to be the purpose of the night journey and ascension, one wonders why Muḥammad was shown so many other created realms and living beings before being ushered into this ultimate encounter. The anonymous response that Sulamī reports here alleges that the journey was a gradual process of training the Prophet to observe the rules of propriety or adab. *The meaning of the term* adab *comes to signify a broad semantic range, encompassing courtly etiquette, good manners, proper conduct, culture in general, and literature in particular. The type of* adab *that this saying discusses is the proper manner of looking at both the creation and the creator.*[15]

The anonymous respondent maintains that the Prophet was made to view created things first in order that he could have a steady frame of reference from which to approach the witnessing of the creator. Seeing the various aspects of the created universe grants the Prophet first-hand knowledge of this world and the next, assuring that it is not his faculty of imagination (tawahhum) *by which he perceives the highest stages of his journey. Even the most exalted of created things such as the divine throne and seat* (kursī) *are nothing but veils that obstruct one's view of the Real.*[16]

Over the course of the above saying, one can identify the steps through which the Prophet learns proper conduct and abandons the vision of created things. This process begins with the Prophet turning from created multiplicity to focus on divine unity: "When he alone had a single witnessing apart from [*other*] *witnessings, all save him shrank from every sensation to one sensation." Notice how this sentence itself performatively evokes the movement from many to one. Objects of sensation, which are little more than veils, diminish before the strength of the Prophet's purpose. At this point he realizes that the created beings and realms that he was shown were little more than a test, for they encompass things other than what was desired* (al-murād) *of him. Turning away from them reflects a knowledge of the propriety of witnessing, and this action leads to an encounter with the divinity as understood in the two qurʾānic verses quoted at the end of the saying.*

Such a mystical interpretation of the stages of the ascension as a test to the one ascending resonates with the account of the dream ascension attributed to the early Sufi master Abū Yazīd Bisṭāmī (d. ca. 261/875). In both cases the person ascending is offered honors and realms, gifts which should properly be refused in the single-minded purpose of reaching the divinity. In his dream, Abū Yazīd continually repeats the phrase, "O my dear one, my goal is other than what you are showing me."[17] *The saying above provides a simple formulation of this idea, a theme that the dream vision attributed to Abū Yazīd develops to hyperbolic lengths.*

Finally one notices that this saying presumes that the visit to paradise and hellfire precedes rather than follows Muḥammad's divine audience. As mentioned previously, the official ascension hadiths discuss these visits less frequently than other less official ascension narratives, and when references do appear in the official accounts they often place the visits after the divine audience.[18] *The extended ascension narratives in Ṭabarī's* Tafsīr *on the night journey verse provide noteworthy exceptions, as do the popular ascension narratives attributed to Ibn ᶜAbbās. It is possible that the person who asked the question that led to the saying above could have had one of these alternate versions of the ascension narrative in mind.*

6 - GOD'S GIFT TO THE PROPHET

Wāsiṭī was asked, "What was the gift of the Prophet ﷺ from his Lord on the night of the ascension?" He said, "He clothed him in the clothes of his attribute, he permitted him the witnessing, and he addressed him face to face."

Official narratives on the night journey and ascension of the Prophet rarely discuss the idea that Muḥammad received a gift (hadīya) *from his Lord that night, unless the daily ritual prayers were considered that gift. In addition, one hardly ever encounters the idea that Muḥammad returned from his journey with any physical object of otherworldly origin. Recensions of the popular ascension narrative attributed to Ibn ᶜAbbās, in contrast, do enumerate the various honors and dispensations that God grants Muḥammad near the end of their intimate conversation. Some versions of this narrative describe specific qurʾānic verses that God presents to the Prophet as "gifts." No early ascension narrative still extant contains all three of the "gifts" that Wāsiṭī lists in this saying. Each of these gifts deserves brief comment.*

As mentioned in the introduction above, the idea that God clothed (albasa) *the Prophet on the night of the ascension appears in a number of the sayings in* The Subtleties of the Ascension. *In some instances the sayings allege that on the journey Muḥammad becomes clothed in the divine attributes, in others that he becomes clothed by resplendent lights. Here God is said to have clothed Muḥammad in the dress* (libās) *of his attribute* (naᶜt), *the "his" presumably but not unambiguously referring to the divinity. One only has to consider the debate that surrounded the hadith that "God created Adam in his form" ("his" meaning God's or Adam's form?) to realize that such debates were not restricted to Sufi sayings. If one understands the saying to mean that the Prophet was clothed in God's attribute, then it may well designate a mystical state. A related expression appears in saying 13.*

The "witnessing" (mushāhada) *or vision of God represents another controversial issue discussed by Muslim theologians with respect to the Prophet's journey. Both the night journey verse and the opening passage of the sūra of the Star allude to visions involving some type of signs* (ayāt), *but the content of those visions remained a point of contention. This and other sayings in Sulamī's work refer to Muḥammad's "witnessing" as a dispensation, and by "witnessing" the sayings apparently refer to a vision of the divinity that Muḥammad received as a special gift on the night of the ascension.*

The idea that God spoke to Muḥammad face to face (mukāfaḥatan) *on the night of the ascension recalls the qurʾānic designation of Moses as one to whom God spoke directly* (taklīman; *Q 4:164*). *The word used in the Qurʾān is not the same as the word used here, but I would nevertheless argue that the above saying presents Muḥammad's status as being at least equivalent to if not superior to that of Moses. The official ascension narratives do depict Muḥammad conversing with God—or at least a mysterious voice from above speaking on behalf of the divinity—in the Prophet's intercessory role, pleading for the reduction of the number of the daily prayers to five. As mentioned in the Introduction, the narrative attributed to Ibn ʿAbbās contains a more extensive account of the intimate conversation between Muḥammad and God. It remains possible, therefore, that the above saying offers a mystical commentary upon a popular version of the ascension narrative similar to that attributed to Ibn ʿAbbās, one that perhaps is no longer extant. This being as it may, this saying should be compared to other sayings in* The Subtleties of the Ascension *which discuss the rank of Muḥammad's station relative to that of Moses and the other prophets (e.g. saying 13 where the experiences of Moses and Muḥammad are treated with a certain equivalency; cf. sayings 15, 20, 22, and 23*).

7 - BEARING THE VISION OF GOD

> Yūsuf b. al-Ḥusayn was asked, "By what means was the Prophet ﷺ[19] capable of witnessing on the ascension?" He said, "He did not cease to induce him out of the continual reverence of the Real toward him, thus he empowered him for that [witnessing] out of the witnessing of the reverent-one."

The previous two sayings suggest that the Prophet was able to witness (or view) the divinity on the night of the ascension, and this saying addresses the issue of how he was able to do so. Here the questioner asks how Muḥammad was able to bear the vision of God, a vision that some Muslim theologians deny is possible in this world. The Qurʾān offers a precedent that supports the impossibility of such a vision in its description of the events on Mount Sinai, when God told Moses, "You will never see me," *and the latter collapsed thunderstruck when God appeared on the mountain (Q 7:143). If such was Moses' fate when witnessing the divinity, it becomes a legitimate issue how Muḥammad was able to witness the divinity without suffering such dire consequences.*

In this saying, Yūsuf b. al-Ḥusayn alleges that God, one of whose names is "the reverent one" (al-bārr), *induces Muḥammad to bear the vision through his reverence. The use of the divine names the Real* (al-ḥaqq) *and the reverent* (al-bārr) *make it clear that God was one of the actors in this process. The divine clearly initiates the interaction: The "reverence of the Real"* (birr al-ḥaqq) *and the "witnessing of the reverent"* (mushāhidat al-bārr) *are precursors to Muḥammad's own reverence and witnessing, and they in turn empower him to be able to bear what he saw.*

8 - THE WISDOM OF THE ASCENSION

I heard Muḥammad b. ʿAbd Allāh [Ibn Shādhān] who said that Muḥammad b. Mūsā [Ibn] Farghānī [Wāsiṭī] was asked, "What was the wisdom of the ascension?" He said, "God (be he exalted) wanted to lift up the state of the beloved ﷺ from the station of servanthood to the station of eternity, and from the station of eternity to the station of lordship."

"He showed the Prophet ﷺ in the station of servanthood in order to show the proprieties of servanthood to the community. Then he moved him to the station of eternity in order to teach through it the propriety of who he is in that station. Finally he moved him to the station of lordliness, namely the ascension, to which he was caused to journey by night. At that, the stations and traces were eliminated from him. He was moved to the station which was created out of approach and nearness."

The question in this saying addresses the "wisdom" (ḥikma) *of the ascension, and Wāsiṭī's response deals largely with a discussion of the purpose behind the ascension, and specifically the rationale behind the different stages of the journey. According to Wāsiṭī, God brought his beloved on this journey in order to illustrate different mystical levels or stations* (maḥallāt *and* maqāmāt, *here used interchangeably*). *Instead of seeing the night journey as a physical journey from one place to another, Wāsiṭī implies that it was rather a journey between different states of being, a movement linking servant and Lord.*

Many Muslims see the gap between the all-powerful and eternal Lord and his dependent and contingent creatures to be ontologically unbridgeable. From this perspective, the appropriate human response to God's revelations is humble submission and abundant praise. Both Sufis and non-Sufis describe how the most exalted station that a human being can reach, therefore, is that of a faithful servant or slave (ʿabd) *of God. As the introduction dis-*

cusses, however, some Sufis believe that the ontological gap between servant and Lord can be bridged through mystical experiences in which the one eternal God becomes realized to the degree that the contingent nature of his creatures pass away. The above saying by Wāsiṭī suggests that the narrative of Muḥammad's ascension is but a type of allegory for the process by which the servant is able to pass away as the Real becomes manifest.[20]

That the movement described in the saying above reflects a return to the original pre-created essence becomes clear through the use of the concept of azaliyya, *an Arabic term which designates eternity in terms of primordial unity. God wanted to show who "he" is in such a station, the pronoun "he" able to refer both to the lover and the beloved. Such ambiguity potentially renders polarized dichotomies meaningless by performatively evoking an original unity. The equation between the ascension and the station of lordliness* (rabbāniyya) *at the end of the saying is remarkable, depicting the ascension itself as the process of stripping away contingent qualities which ultimately ends in passing away* (fanāʾ). *The Sufi concepts of propriety* (adab) *and learning propriety* (taʾaddaba) *link the above saying to saying 5. Both focus upon the purpose behind the stages of the journey, and both maintain that moral instruction was at least one such purpose. They differ, however, in the degree to which they identify the Prophet as the one receiving instruction and the degree to which they support or subvert the distinction between creator and creation.*

9 - TOUCHING THE HEAD TO THE GROUND AT THE LOTE TREE OF THE BOUNDARY

> Someone was asked, "Why did the Prophet ﷺ not touch his head to the ground at the lote tree of the boundary?" That person said, "Because [implicit] in touching one's head to the ground is the sight of the self, the appearance of servanthood, and the magnification of the Real. But he was in the station of passing away from his descriptions, dressed in the manner of dress of the reality upon witnessing the Real. So how could one ascribe to him turning towards something or applying himself to touching his head to the ground?"

This saying asks about Muḥammad's actions when he arrives at the famous "lote tree of the boundary" (sidrat al-muntahā) *mentioned in the* sūra *of the Star* (*Q 53:14*). *This fantastic tree is usually said to be found in the seventh heaven, and its name is sometimes explained in reference to the idea that it stands at the very outer limit of creation, beyond which the vast majority of created beings are not allowed to pass. Traditional depictions of the lote tree in both official and non-official ascension accounts graphically describe its enormous size. For example, they maintain that its leaves are as big as elephant ears, its fruits are the size of water jugs, and its shadow extends for hundreds of leagues. Drawing upon the imagery of paradise, accounts of the lote tree often name and describe the blessed rivers that flow from its base. In a number of the accounts of Muḥammad's ascension, the heavenly lote tree of the boundary serves as the site where the Prophet experiences some sort of audience with the diety, receiving among other things the duty of the daily ritual prayers.*

Before we consider this anonymous response to the question of why the Prophet refrained from the act of touching his head to the ground (sujūd) *at the lote tree of the boundary, we must examine the assumption upon which the question is predicated, namely the idea that one would have expected the Prophet to do so. There are two principal reasons that the Prophet may have been expected to touch his head to the ground at the lote tree: 1) he would have done so at this holy site as part of the traditional movements performed during cycles of ritual prayer, praying there just as he prayed at other stages of the journey, such as in Jerusalem; 2) he would have touched his head down in prostration when he witnessed a manifestation of the divinity at the lote tree, having been expected to act this way in adoration and/or submission. The first explanation draws upon versions of the ascension narrative in which the Prophet leads other prophets and angels in prayer in various stages of the heavenly journey. The second explanation draws upon the narratives that interpret the qurʾānic verses* "He saw him another time / at the lote tree of the boundary" *as referring to a vision of God at the lote tree. The questioner and respondent may well have presumed that such a theophany took place at the lote tree, for the phrase the "witnessing of the Real" in the response to the question apparently refers to a vision of the divinity. In any case, the fact that the same issue arises again in saying 13 shows that this subject represents a significant topic of discussion among the early Sufis.*

In the saying above, the anonymous Sufi respondent points out that the act of touching one's head to the ground (sujūd) *is a self-conscious physical act, invoking the vision of the self* (nafs). *The act likewise performatively demonstrates the submissive relationship of the servant* (ʿabd) *to the divine Lord* (rabb). *According to this anonymous Sufi respondent, however, at the lote tree of the boundary the one ascending was in the process of transcending this dualistic master-servant relationship, approaching the station of passing away* (fanāʾ) *from his contingent attributes. In witnessing the Real* (al-ḥaqq), *he becomes clothed in divine attributes, as represented by the phrase "dressed in the manner of dress of the reality"* (lābisan libsat al-ḥaqīqa). *In such a mystical state, the anonymous Sufi master contends, it was no longer appropriate or even possible to demonstrate humble submissiveness through touching one's head to the ground. In such a mystical state, the master-servant relationship no longer exists.*

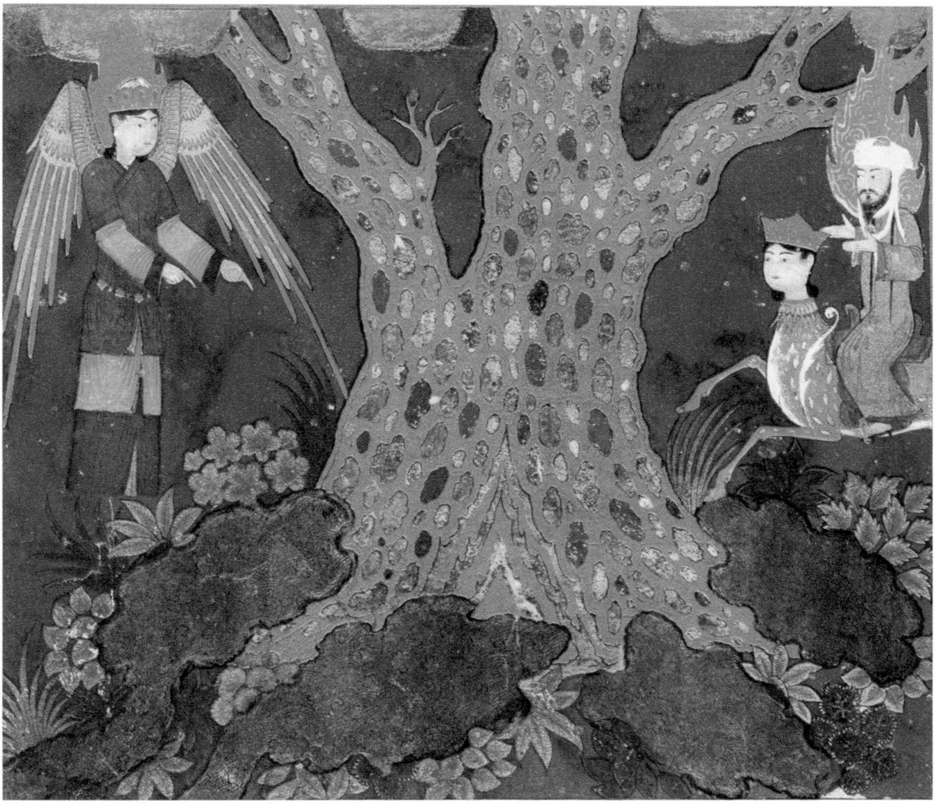

Figure 3: The lote tree of the boundary.

10 - SEEING WITH GOD'S EYES

> Ḥusayn b. Manṣūr [Ḥallāj] was asked why Muḥammad ﷺ did not observe existing beings during the ascension. He said: Because he observed things with the eye of God (be he exalted). One who observes them like that does not see anything other than God.

Ḥallāj was one of the most controversial of the early Sufis discussed in Sulamī's work. He was supposedly killed by the authorities in Baghdad for his extreme beliefs, although recent studies suggest that there may well have been more political reasons behind his execution.[21] *In any case, he has been best remembered for the ecstatic utterance attributed to him in which he was said to have exclaimed, "I am the Real." The phrase scandalized some of Ḥallāj's contemporaries, who accused him of claiming divine status. Ḥallāj's supporters defended him by explaining that the phrase was a divine utterance spoken when Ḥallāj was no longer present, i.e., in a state of* fanā᾿. *The above saying on Muḥammad's ascension can be interpreted as alleging that a similar state came over Muḥammad during his journey, a state in which divine faculties replaced human faculties. According to Ḥallāj's saying, the perspective of divine vision is not to observe* (lāḥiẓa) *created beings in their contingent particularity, but rather to observe them as part of the totality of divine unity.*

This saying should be compared with saying 5, which similarly discusses the idea of not dwelling upon created existing beings (al-akwān). *In both instances, these beings represent a kind of distraction that diminishes in importance once human existence is left behind. Whereas in saying 5 the issue of avoiding existing beings takes the form of a test of the sincerity of the one ascending, in this saying the test has already been passed. Ḥallāj's saying above, therefore, discusses the issue in the context of a description of the divine vision, one that perceives only divinity.*

11 - HUMANNESS TRANSFORMED

> Ḥusayn [b. Manṣūr Ḥallāj] said, "Humanness does not lack the strength to witness its shape from [the perspective of] the contingent. When lordliness shows, the rules of humanness pass away. Do you not see that when Muḥammad ﷺ was surrounded by the divine manner of dress, Gabriel عليه السلام, despite the magnitude of his station, lacked the strength to look at him or accompany him? He said, 'Were I to approach [the length of] a fingertip, I would burn up.'"

Once again Ḥallāj comments on the mystical transformation that he understands to take place during the ascension, human qualities "passing away" (fanāʾ) *into divine attributes. The essence of humanity or humanness* (bashariyya) *is capable of witnessing its own form in the contingent, created realm of accidents* (al-ḥadath), *but in the presence of the state of divinity* (rabbāniyya), *the rules* (aḥkām) *pertaining to the human form no longer apply. Divinity envelops humanity as a dress envelops a body, a clothing metaphor that also appears in sayings 6, 9, 11, 13 and 35. In such a state of transformation, all contingent things are threatened with annihilation or dissolution into the divine oneness.*

To illustrate the point, Ḥallāj draws upon a popular hadith report in which Gabriel explains to Muḥammad why he could not accompany him all the way to the divine throne. This anecdote, not a part of the official ḥadīth collections but present in some Sufi works and in certain versions of the ascension narrative attributed to Ibn ʿAbbās, was popular for its assertion of Muḥammad's superiority to all other created beings. In the above saying, according to Ḥallāj, Gabriel was unable even to look at Muḥammad after the latter's transformation. Through his use of the verb ʿajaza (*"to lack the strength / be unable"*), *Ḥallāj directly contrasts the angel Gabriel's visual inability to the human prophet's visual ability, emphasizing the human potential for even greater vision than that achieved by angels. Ḥallāj suggests that Muḥammad is able to proceed to a higher level because his humanity has been surrounded or overcome by divinity, and Gabriel is unable to proceed because he remains a contingent being. Just as the light of the throne in Jewish Merkabah mysticism was thought to burn up all but the most exalted of beings who attempted to come near, so here the divine radiance is said to be so intense as to consume Gabriel had he approached even the slightest distance towards it beyond his allotted station.*

Some Sufis might understand the consuming nature of the divine radiance and fire as a positive rather than negative characteristic, seeing in it a symbol for the passing away of contingent qualities as they merge with the eternal one. From such a perspective, Gabriel's refusal to approach and "burn up" could also represent his inability or unwillingness to pass away into divine unity.

12 - THE INEXPLICABLE APPROACH

Jaᶜfar al-Ṣādiq (may God be pleased with him) said: The Real caused his lover Muḥammad ﷺ to approach his self through his saying "*he approached and descended*"[22] without qualifying how, because he sent him out from the limits of the how. He sheltered him at a stopping place that had no description. The approach to the Real has no limit and no end.

He said: He caused him to *approach* the intimate knowledge and belief that he deposited in his heart, *and he descended.* He calmed his heart for that which he was caused to approach, and he removed from his heart doubt and suspicion.[23]

Jaᶜfar al-Ṣādiq, considered the sixth Imām in most Shīᶜī circles and arguably one of the most famous scholars of the early period, was claimed by the Sufis as an early mystic. Although there is reason to doubt that the sayings attributed to Jaᶜfar al-Ṣādiq in Sulamī's Qurʾān commentary actually originated with Jaᶜfar, the Sufi sayings ascribed to him by Sulamī appear to be relatively consistent.[24] *The above saying, which is actually two different sayings presented together,*[25] *will be treated here as the source treats them, as two related halves of a single saying. A theme that links the two halves is the idea of the ascension as an interior journey, a movement deeper and deeper in toward the true self in the innermost heart.*

The first half of the saying discusses the theological idea that God cannot be said to be enclosed by any limit or finite place. Muslim theologians debated how one could approach God if God could not be said to reside in any specific location. The "solution" offered above, that the approach took place even though we are unable to understand how, resembles the famous position of the theologian Abū al-Ḥasan Ashᶜarī (d. ca. 330/947) that the anthropomorphic references to God in the Qurʾān are to be accepted without asking how (bi-lā kayf). *The idea of a location without description* (waṣf) *satisfies this theological requirement while simultaneously appealing to the mystical insight that human language and logic remain inadequate to describe the divine abode. The qurʾānic verse* "then he approached and descended" (Q 53:8) *is cited to suggest that the journey was an interior one in which the divine Real caused Muḥammad to approach his self* (nafsuhu). *The ambiguous possessive pronoun "his" in the phrase "his self" could refer both to the Real and to Muḥammad, and thus the journey inward could be seen as a mystical journey in which duality is transcended.*

The second half of the saying further underscores the idea of an interior journey in its description of the approach toward the intimate knowledge or insight and religious belief or faith that were deposited in the heart. The reference at the end of the saying remains equivocal, perhaps alluding to several different ideas at once. One interpretation might listen to this portion of the saying and hear echoes of the initiatic scene in many night journey and ascension narratives, including hadiths in both Bukhārī and Muslim, in which Muḥammad's heart is split open and cleansed by one or more angels prior to the night journey. In some versions, the angels place "faith and wisdom" in his heart after they are finished cleaning it.[26] *Usually this scene represents a prelude to the outward movement of the night journey, but in the second half of the saying above it would have to represent the ultimate destination that Muḥammad moves towards on his inward journey, a fact that makes such a reading more difficult to maintain. In favor of such a reading, however, is the idea that the qurʾānic phrase* "he approached and descended" (*Q 53:8*) *which seems to describe an interior and spiritual rather than exterior and physical journey.*

Moving inward, Muḥammad becomes tranquil and calm as God removes doubt and suspicion from his heart, phrases that conjure up other potential associations. Muḥammad's being upset and later being made tranquil recalls a scene in the ascension narrative attributed to Ibn ʿAbbās in which a heavenly being, sometimes Gabriel and other times God himself, speaks to or touches Muḥammad in a way that removes all his fear.[27] *The mention of "doubt"* (shakk) *also potentially resonates with the qurʾānic phrase,* "if you are in doubt about what we send down to you..." (*Q 10:94*), *a passage that early Imāmī Shīʿī commentaries at the turn of the*

4th/10th century nearly unanimously associated with the night journey and ascension, understanding Muḥammad's "doubt" to have come when ᶜAlī's high status was revealed to the Prophet that night.[28] *While there is nothing explicitly Shīᶜī about the above saying that would demand such a reading, given that this saying is attributed to (pseudo-) Jaᶜfar al-Ṣādiq, I would argue that one should not rule out the possibility that an originally Shīᶜī-oriented hadith report was subsequently purged of its overtly Shīᶜī content, leaving behind a vague reference to Muḥammad's doubt.*

13 - WHEN OBEISANCE IS APPROPRIATE

Someone was asked: Why did Muḥammad ﷺ not touch his head to the ground at the lote tree of the boundary, yet he will do so at the resurrection during [his] intercession for creation? He said: No doubt the compensation for that act of touching his head to the ground is the intercession for that which has neither weight nor value. The need makes obligatory the entreaty. Do you not see how Mūsā ﷺ did not touch his head to the ground during the address [on Mount Sinai]? When the witnessing of the stopping place drew near, he was obliged to observe the proprieties of servanthood.

Yet because the Real clothed them [both] in his attributes, it would have been impossible for them to touch their heads to the ground before him, since in that station he stripped them of all trace of servanthood. That is why Muḥammad ﷺ did not touch his head to the ground at the lote tree of the boundary, nor did Mūsā ﷺ do so during the address [on Sinai].

The question of the Prophet's touching his head to the ground at the lote tree of the boundary, discussed above in saying 9, here resurfaces in a different form. On the day of judgment, some hadith reports and popular ascension narratives state that Muḥammad will be able to intercede on behalf of individuals who would otherwise be bound for punishment in the hellfire. The question above presumes a belief in this power of intercession (shafāᶜa), *and also in the idea that Muḥammad will bow down before God while attempting this intercession. Muḥammad certainly accomplishes a certain type of intercession in almost every version of the heavenly ascension narrative, for through Moses' suggestion Muḥammad requests and eventually succeeds in getting the duty of fifty prayers reduced to five. Some versions of the narrative contain even more elaborate intercession scenes that are placed near the end of the divine colloquy. The fact that the Prophet intercedes during the ascension, therefore, leads to the question posed above. What makes this intercession and/or theophany at the lote tree different from the eschatological intercession and/or theophany, such that the former does not require the acts of obeisance required in the latter?*

The respondent answers the question in two parts, corresponding to the two different situations. First, with regard to the reason Muḥammad will touch his head to the ground on resurrection day, he will do so out of the gravity of the situation. The image of the scales of judgment is invoked, and the ones for whom Muḥammad intercedes will not have the weight of the scales of deeds inclining on their behalf. He will thus touch his head to the ground before God because these people are in dire need of his utmost assistance. Second, with regard to Muḥammad's lack of touching his head to the ground during the intercession at the lote tree, the respondent compares this situation to that of Moses (Arabic: Mūsā) and his discussion with God on Mount Sinai. The surface level of comparison between these situations illustrates that since Moses was not said to have touched his head to the ground while speaking with God on Mount Sinai, accordingly Muḥammad should not have been expected to do so when speaking with God in the heavens. On a deeper mystical level of interpretation, the respondent adds that both Moses and Muḥammad were clothed in divine qualities and stripped of created qualities during their respective experiences. With the disappearance of all created traces, the very act of obeisance, which is predicated upon the distinction between master and servant, no longer applies. When Moses was prevented from viewing the divinity, however, the dualistic relationship was reinstated, and Moses was forced to observe the proper behavior (adab) *required of a servant.*

The comparison between Muḥammad's experience on his heavenly ascension and Moses' experience on his ascent of Mount Sinai bears further examination, especially in light of the Jewish traditions that interpret Moses' ascent of the mountain as a heavenly journey. What is remarkable about the above saying is that it equates the two experiences on a mystical level (cf. saying 6). Other sayings in this work (e.g. sayings 15, 20, 22, 23) will contrast the two experiences, portraying the differences between them as a clear sign of Muḥammad's superiority not only to Moses but also to the rest of the prophets.

14 - THE INEFFABLE LIMIT

Junayd (may God be compassionate to him) said, "On the night of the ascension, the Prophet ﷺ reached a limit for which there is neither expression nor description. [It is ineffable] because of his union with the one and the singular in that assembly, the uncertainty of what happened in it, the silence of the Prophet, and the abandoning of reports about it."

Official accounts of the night journey and ascension such as those that appear in the standard Jamāʿī-Sunnī collections of prophetic sayings do not give details about what happened to the Prophet at the very highest stage of his journey. One reason for the lack of discussion of this narrative climax, this saying attributed to Junayd asserts, has to do with the ineffability of the limit (ḥadd) *reached. Junayd explores some of the reasons that this ultimate experience was difficult to describe, ranging from the idea that the Prophet was reticent to talk about it, which meant that people did not have any reports to transmit, to the idea that the mystery of union* (ittiḥād) *defies human understanding, which meant that the experience was necessarily ineffable.*

If the highest stage of the journey contained a description of the most intimate discourse between Muḥammad and his Lord, then why would his companions not transmit this information for later generations of Muslims? Viewed in the light of union, the "silence of the Prophet" and "the abandoning of reports about it / him" may allude to the mystical concept that at that ultimate limit the Prophet was no longer really there anymore. The Prophet had passed away, leaving nothing but the divine one and singular (al-wāḥid al-aḥad). *At that limit, according to Junayd, "there is neither expression nor description" that human beings can comprehend.*

15 - THE SPEECH OF MOSES AND MUḤAMMAD

Junayd was asked about the saying of God (be he powerful and lofty), "*You were not next to Mount Sinai when we called.*"[29] He said, "He called to Mūsā ﵇ because he was behind the veil, and he whispered to Muḥammad ﷺ because he had torn through the veils. The one who is behind the veil is called to, and the one who crosses the veil is whispered to. As for the one who passes away from these stations, he shelters him and honors him above the realms of being. Do you not see how when Muḥammad ﷺ was asked about the heavenly host debate,[30] when the lights of his descriptions alighted upon him and he stripped him of his description, he spoke about all places and reported about them?"

As a number of sayings in this work illustrate, the comparison between Moses' experience on Mount Sinai and Muḥammad's experience during his ascension provoked the interest of some of the early Sufis. The above saying focuses upon the comparison between the two in terms of speech and knowledge. It should be examined along with saying 20, which focuses upon the comparison between the two in terms of vision. In both cases, as one would expect in most Islamic texts (in contrast, however, to saying 13), Muḥammad is said to have achieved a higher station than that reached by Moses.

The occasion for the above saying is a verse of the Qurʾān that refers to the events of the exodus from Egypt and to Moses' dialogue with God on Mount Sinai, explaining that God recalls these events in the Qurʾān in order to inform those of us who were not present. Instead of commenting on the content of Moses' dialogue, however, Junayd isolates a phrase ascribed to the divinity in the verse, "We called" (nādaynā). *The verb implies a certain distance between the two parties in the dialogue, and Junayd contrasts this implied distance between God and Moses with the implied nearness between God and Muḥammad on the latter's ascension. That Muḥammad had reached an extreme degree of nearness is clear, according to Junayd, from the fact that Muḥammad whispered* (nājā) *with God. Junayd concludes that a veil continued to separate Moses and God, but no veil separated Muḥammad from the divine presence. Therefore, Muḥammad enjoys a higher status than Moses, the former having obtained a station that the latter could not obtain. Junayd asserts, however, that both of these aforementioned stations fall short of the ultimate experience of passing away* (fanāʾ).

In order to illustrate this ultimate station, Junayd turns to a scene from some ascension narratives in which Muḥammad speaks with God in the vicinity of the divine throne. Near the beginning of most versions of this intimate conversation (munajāt), *God asks Muḥammad whether or not he knows the subjects that the heavenly host debate, drawing upon a passage from the Qurʾān (Q 38: 69) in which Muḥammad is instructed to say that he does not know what they debate.*[31] *God then informs Muḥammad about it, sometimes transmitting the knowledge to him by the touch of his hand. With this touch, according to the version of the hadith-report in Tirmidhī's hadith collection, Muḥammad "knew what was in the heavens and what was in the earth."*[32] *This passage helps to explain Junayd's claim that "he spoke about all places and reported about them." Unlike Tirmidhī, however, Junayd shies away from the idea that God touched Muḥammad with his hand, perhaps because of the anthropomorphism that this idea requires. Junayd instead transforms the physical image of the descent of God's hand upon Muḥammad's shoulderblades into the mystical image of the descent of the divine lights upon the one ascending, lights that replace the description* (ṣifa) *of human qualities with divine qualities. The resulting mystical experience, in which one possesses a knowledge of all places, comprises an ultimate station beyond all stations.*

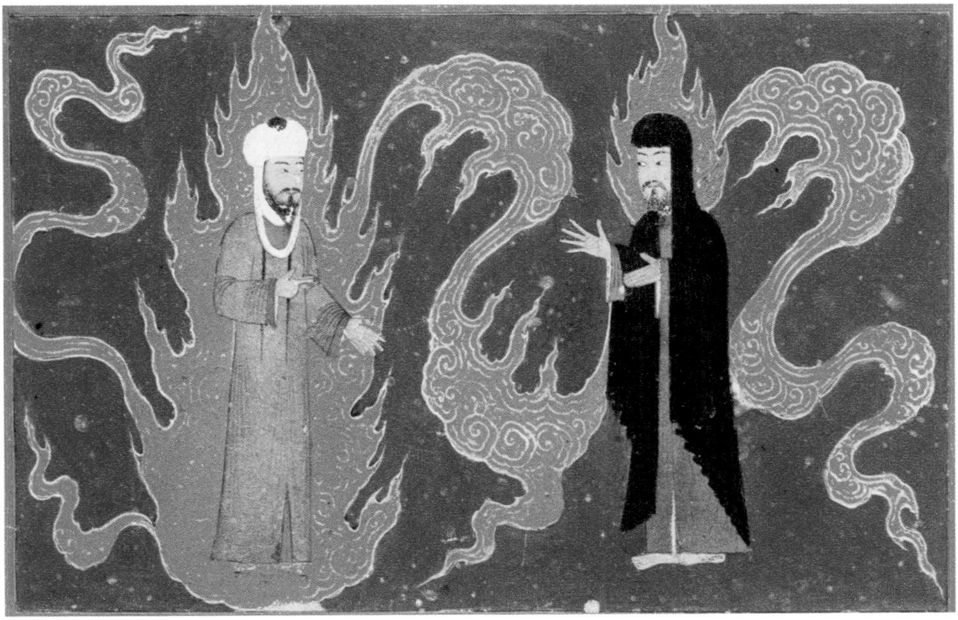

Figure 4: Moses and Muḥammad talking.

16 - INCREASE IN SECRET KNOWLEDGE

Abū Saᶜīd Kharrāz said, "The Prophet ﷺ was commanded to invoke through the saying '*My Lord, increase me in knowledge.*'[33] He used to be given knowledge through intermediaries and mediators. When this invocation was made to flow on his tongue, it was answered for him. That did not happen out of a deliberate intention for it on his part, nor from any request, but rather to demonstrate his favor."

"So he was caused to ascend to the most close and most elevated station, where the knowledge of the whole of creation was severed from him. At the station of the approach he began to address and was addressed, without intermediary, face to face. He was strengthened in that station by steadiness, and he was given bounty by the increase in knowledge which no one in creation had been taught. That station is something most like what I hold to be the '*praised station*,'[34] because it is a secret between him and his beloved that no one else uncovered."

While the previous saying discusses a portion of the intimate conversation between Muḥammad and his Lord on the night of the ascension, this saying asserts that the details of this conversation remained a secret known only to the conversing lovers. Interestingly, Kharrāz depicts the ascension as a journey granted by God in order to reveal secret knowledge to Muḥammad. Kharrāz thus creatively links the ascension narrative to the petitionary invocation (duᶜā) *from the Qurʾān,* "My Lord, increase me in knowledge" (*Q 20:114*) *He insists that Muḥammad did not selfishly repeat this invocation in order to receive such a revelation, rather God decided to respond in this way in order to proclaim Muḥammad's special favor among created beings.*

The idea that Kharrāz mentions in the second half of the saying, namely that Muḥammad was cut off from the rest of creation during his ascension, is not explicitly articulated in the standard ascension narratives. It does appear, however, in the popular version of the ascension narrative ascribed to Ibn ʿAbbās. In one of the earliest extant recensions of this version, Muḥammad remarks that as he approaches nearer and nearer to the divine throne, "I thought all those who were in the heavens and the earth had died, because I did not hear any of the angels' voices, nor did I see any of his creatures...."[35] *I would contend that this passage serves as the basis for Kharrāz's statement that "knowledge of the whole of creation was severed from him."*

Although he does not record the detailed account of the intimate conversation that follows in the Ibn ʿAbbās ascension narrative, perhaps out of the belief that the conversation was actually a secret between lovers, Kharrāz draws upon the separation idea from the Ibn ʿAbbās narrative in order to underscore the fact that the conversation took place apart from the rest of creation. No other creature was privy to the secrets that were revealed there. Unlike the qurʾānic revelations that Muḥammad received via the mediation of Gabriel, this intimate discourse was face-to-face and unmediated. He was granted steadiness (thibāt) *in this station, a term commonly applied to the firm certainty of Muḥammad's gaze during his vision of God. At that point he received the "increase in knowledge" that had been the subject of the original invocation.*

Kharrāz concludes his saying by equating this secret conversation between lovers with the "praised station" (al-maqām al-maḥmūd) *mentioned in the Qurʾān in connection with supererogatory prayers. Several official hadiths understand this "praised station" as a reference to Muḥammad's power of intercession on the day of judgment,*[36] *while some later scholars link it to Muḥammad's power of intercession on the night of the ascension.*[37] *In contrast to both positions, Kharrāz identifies the* "praised station" *as an isolated and intimate nearness to God. He makes use of the poetic trope of the lovers' secret in order to explain the reason why the revelatory conversation remained a mystery to all outsiders, including the highest of angels. Such a concept reinforces the idea that Kharrāz introduces earlier in the saying, namely that the purpose of the ascension was to reveal an unmediated revelation to Muḥammad that no other creature witnessed or received.*

17 - ON THE APPROACH

Wāsiṭī was asked about the approach of the Prophet ﷺ on the night journey. He said, "He went from his self. '*He approached*' through him, from him, to him, '*and he descended.*'[38] The veils continued to descend from Muḥammad ﷺ until he arrived at what [God] pointed out with his saying: '*He was a distance of two bows or closer.*'[39]

That took place through the power of the lights that clothed Muḥammad ﷺ in the state of his journey. Were it not for what adorned him, the alighting of the description upon him and the clothing of select lights, he would have been burned by the lights of that station. Gabriel عليه السلام was not empowered to approach that station when he was stripped of what clothed the lover ﷺ."

The first half of this saying consists of Wāsiṭī's exegesis of two verses from the sūra of the Star, brief remarks that contain rich insights. The night journey represents a departure from the Prophet's physical self (nafs)*, suggesting a spiritual journey as discussed in some of the previous sayings. The concise phrase which states that he approached "through him, from him, to him"* (bihi minhu ʿilayhi) *can be interpreted in multiple ways. One should compare its usage here to the pairs of similar phrases attributed to Abraham, Moses, and Muḥammad in saying 22. In the above saying, the repetitive use of the third-person singular pronoun "he" together with three different prepositions heightens the ambiguity of the passage.*

One way to understand the series of three prepositional phrases is that in all three instances the pronoun refers to the divinity, that is, it illustrates the idea that God was present in every stage of the journey: its starting point, its means, and its ultimate goal. Another way to interpret the passage is to read the pronouns as all referring to Muḥammad, he journeyed "through himself from himself to himself," discovering his "true self" in the final destination. In addition, one could interpret the ambiguous pronouns through a combination of these possibilities, for example, that "he (Muḥammad) approached through Him (God) from him (Muḥammad) to Him (God)." The Arabic phrase allows for all of these possibilities and more. The danger of using capital letters to indicate a pronoun referring to the divinity is that such a usage forces a single reading to take the place of the openness of the original. Preserving this openness becomes especially important in light of the mystical insight that as one approaches fanāʾ *the subject and object intermingle and/or potentially become confused. Finally, the idea of movement from a place where God is not to a place where God is raises difficulties discussed by some Muslim theologians, who object to the idea that God can be said to be limited to any particular location. In that sense, the pronouns could once again be understood as all referring to the divine, for from a mystical perspective all movement (and indeed all being) happens by the grace of and subsumed in the divinity.*

Wāsiṭī interprets the verb "descended" in a unique way here, understanding it not to refer to Muḥammad, Gabriel, or God, but rather to the descent of the veils that Muḥammad crossed on his ascension. After crossing these veils, Muḥammad finally reached the highest station, a station that Wāsiṭī equates with the qurʾānic verse that follows: "He was a distance of two bows or closer" (*Q* 53:9). *Although Wāsiṭī never explains who or what Muḥammad approached this close distance, the context makes clear that the station of "two bows" indicates proximity to the divine presence. The verse presents an allusion to that state of proximity, therefore, rather than a concrete description of it.*

The second half of the saying deals with the theme of the protective clothes that allowed Muḥammad to reach the state indicated by the phrase "two bows or closer."[40] *Whereas previous sayings (e.g. numbers 6 and 9) refer to the fact that Muḥammad was clothed in divine attributes, here the attributes metaphorically assume the form of "select lights"* (al-anwār al-makhṣūṣa). *Had these lights not clothed Muḥammad through the alighting of the divine description* (ṣifa), *the lights of the highest station would have burned him up. In other words, he was transformed by the light, perhaps transformed into light, in order to protect him from the awesome power of the divine light. The fact that Gabriel was unable to approach without this clothing*[41] *illustrates the favor that*

Muḥammad was granted, and the transformation required as a prerequisite to the divine encounter.

18 - APPROACHING THE DIVINE VISION

Ja^cfar al-Ṣādiq (may God be pleased with him) said, "One who imagined that he '*approached*' with his self thus produced a distance, [and] only '*descended.*'[42] Indeed as much as he drew near to him with his self, he distanced him from types of intimate knowledge, since there is neither approach nor distance. As much as '*he approached*' with his self toward the Real, '*he descended*' a distance. In the reality he was '*turned back . . . driven off and tired,*'[43] since there really is no way to examine the reality."

"As for the reports about the station of regard and favor, the Real made him take one of his vessels, thus making him bear witness to him. In reality, his essence was a witness to his essence. In reports from Muḥammad ﷺ, however, he did not describe him through him from the noble station and the exalted stopping place."

As mentioned previously, early Muslim scholars struggled with the issue of how one could move toward or away from God in space, as if God were bounded by or located in a particular place. This saying interprets the qur'ānic verse "he approached and he descended" (*Q 53:8*) *in light of this issue. Insofar as Muḥammad attempted to move toward the divinity with his self* (nafs), *he was forced further away from the realization that God cannot be bound by space. Each "approach," then, becomes a "descent" or a distancing from the Real. Yet the Sufi speaker, here identified with Ja^cfar al-Ṣādiq, states that with the divine Real "there is neither approach (i.e., drawing near) nor distance." He makes an allusion to another qur'ānic passage* (*Q 67:4*) *which denies that a person could gaze at all of God's creation without becoming bewildered and exhausted, quoting the passage presumably in order to explain by analogy the futility of moving toward God in a physical sense.*

If one understands the verse "he approached and he descended" *as recounting Muḥammad's rejection from the divine presence, how then is one to understand the various reports (here:* akhbār) *about Muḥammad's experience at the highest station? The second paragraph of the saying, absent from Qushayrī's recension of the text and substantially different in Sulamī's Qur'ān commentary, suggests that God gave Muḥammad the choice of the various "vessels"* (aniya), *through which he "made him bear witness to him."*[44] *This allusion to vessels immediately calls to mind the trope in the hadith reports where Muḥammad is asked to choose between two to four cups or vessels, one of which invariably contains milk and stands for correct guidance, and is the cup that Muḥammad drinks from in every version.*[45] *Through this initiatory trial, according to this version of the saying, an ambiguous witnessing takes place: he bears witness to him/it. Lest one understand this idea in simplistic and dualistic terms, however, the saying goes on to offer the mystical insight that "in reality, his essence* (dhāt) *was a witness to his essence* (dhāt)*." At the unified level of non-duality that is the realm of reality* (al-ḥaqīqa), *subject and object merge, and the ambiguous third person masculine pronouns evoke this mystical state.*[46] *Such a state cannot be described by human language. Therefore, in his reports of the experience, Muḥammad had to describe God from the perspective of a certain station, a delimited, if exalted, point of view. He was not able to describe God through the divine perspective, nor to articulate in words the reality of his essence.*

19 - SPECIAL CLOTHING AND GREETINGS

I heard Ḥusayn b. [Yakhtar] say that he heard Jaᶜfar b. Muḥammad [Khuldī] say that he heard Junayd say, "The night of the ascension, Muḥammad ﷺ was clothed in the manner of dress attributed exclusive to him, separate from all creatures. Gabriel ﷺ lacked the strength for it, so he said, 'Were I to approach the length of a fingertip, I would burn up.'

That manner of dress was that he flooded him with his lights, emptied him of all his descriptions, and adorned and beautified him with the lights of his descriptions. He was thus able to bear the assault of speaking with, witnessing, consulting, and apprehending the Real in salutations. The Real welcomed him with all the salutations, not just one. Then he made him to understand that he should receive the Real in a like fashion, so he said, 'Rather salutations, blessings, and goodnesses are for God, for you are worthy of that.'"

The idea that Muḥammad was given special clothes to wear on the night of the ascension appears only in select versions of the ascension narrative, and here that idea merges with the mystical metaphor of his becoming clothed in the divine lights. In wearing such a garment, human qualities are replaced by divine qualities through a process of removing previous descriptions (ṣifāt) *and adorning the being with new ones. This divine vestment protects the one ascending from being overwhelmed and destroyed by contact with the Real. Speaking and seeing the Real comes as an assault upon anyone who does not wear such a garment, and Gabriel admits that he could neither wear these special clothes nor approach the Real the slightest distance (see also sayings 11 and 17). In contrast to Gabriel, Muḥammad, or the presence that remains from the traces of Muḥammad after the process of "emptying," is able to bear the encounter with the Real that begins with an exchange of salutations.*

The final portion of the saying turns to the subject of these salutations (taḥiyyāt), *a feature found at the beginning of the conversation between Muḥammad and God in the ascension narrative attributed to Ibn ᶜAbbās. This exchange follows the same basic formulae that appears near the beginning of a cycle of Muslim ritual prayers, "salutations, blessings, and goodnesses are for God"* (*al-taḥiyy*āt wa 'l-mubārakāt wa 'l-ṭayyibāt li-lāh). *God addresses Muḥammad with all these greetings, a sign of Muḥammad's high station and honor. Junayd also states that God taught these phrases to Muḥammad on the night of the ascension, informing him of the appropriate formulae to use when addressing the divinity. The reciprocity of the exchange, the fact that the one ascending addresses the Real in the same manner he himself was addressed, suggests that the two have become virtual equals through the replacement of human with divine qualities.*

20 - MOSES AND MUḤAMMAD

> One of them said, "The difference between his speaking to Muḥammad ﷺ in the seventh heaven and his speaking to Mūsā عليه السلام upon Mount Sinai is that Mūsā عليه السلام only saw thunderbolts because of his preoccupation. He did not obtain the power that would bear the indications of the essence. However, Muḥammad ﷺ was strengthened by the vision of the heavens and the earths and the placing of the palm [of the hand]. After these, he was capable of [bearing] each thing received by his secret-heart from the command of his Lord."

As in sayings 13, 15, 22 and 23, here we find a comparison between Moses' experience of theophany on Mount Sinai and Muḥammad's experience of theophany in the heavens. This anonymous saying is more explicit in Muḥammad's superiority to Moses. Moses failed to see more than thunderbolts, a notion that likely draws upon the qurʾānic narrative from Q 7:143, a verse that reports how Moses became as if thunderstruck when God appeared upon the mountain. In contrast, Muḥammad was able to bear every sight and sound he witnessed. Just as Gabriel falls short of Muḥammad's level of favor and perfection, so Moses and the other prophets fall short as well. This theme appears throughout ascension literature, and suggests that ascension narratives played a crucial role in constructing Muḥammad as a prophetic figure,[47] *and perhaps a role in promoting Muḥammad's image in the context of conversion efforts and/or interreligious polemics.*

Of particular interest in this saying is the way it explains how Muḥammad is able to bear what Moses is not. Unlike other sayings in The Subtleties of the Ascension, *it offers no indication that Muḥammad received special clothes or experienced a transformation. Rather, it proclaims that Muḥammad became "strengthened" by two physical encounters: first, his vision of the heavens and the earths* (sic, *plural in the Arabic); second, his experience of "the placing of the palm* [*of the hand*]*"* (waḍaʿ al-kaff). *Previous sayings in this collection discuss Muḥammad's vision of the heavens and earths before his arrival at the divine throne, and the early Sufis appear to be especially interested in explaining the reason that God made the night journey and ascension to precede the divine audience. Only this particular saying, however, refers to the mysterious "placing of the palm," an apparent reference to an anthropomorphic passage in some ascension narratives where God places his hand upon Muḥammad's shoulderblades in order to calm him and/or transmit knowledge to him.*[48]

This "placing of the palm" motif, which apparently circulated in the earliest period, was deemed objectionable by later theologians who excised the motif from the narrative. The text of the narrative transmitted by Sulamī's student Qushayrī provides an example of how the palm detail comes to be removed from the Ibn ᶜAbbās ascension narrative.[49] *The presence of the above saying in Sulamī's collection proves that while scholars such as Qushayrī may have disapproved of such details, these details were not altogether unknown or rejected among the earliest generations of Sufis from whom Sulamī quotes. The fact that Sulamī transmits this saying from an anonymous source suggests that this controversial anthropomorphic element does not constitute sufficient grounds in Sulamī's estimation to disqualify this anonymous saying from his collection. The fact that the saying is anonymous, however, may also say something about its controversial status.*

21 - THE DISTINGUISHING SIGN

Fāris [Baghdādī] said, "The descriptions of Gabriel, with their abiding in the Real, lacked the strength of those of Muḥammad ﷺ while he passed away in the Real. He reported about it in his saying: '*He saw some of the greatest signs of his Lord.*'[50] He only referred to '*the greatest*' because it represents a hyperbole of greatness, and there is no extreme beyond [such] hyperbole. It only became a sign because he was manifested through the perfect completion of loftiness.

When the attribute of loftiness gave him his due, he was made undistressed. He hindered Gabriel ﷺ from ascending to him, because he did not extend to him that in which he bore him. But he strengthened Muḥammad ﷺ by that which bore him of what was his due. Both of the stations are for him and with him; one of them is covering, and the other is unveiling."

Here Fāris Baghdādī explains the distinction between the stations of Gabriel and Muḥammad near the climax of the ascension, and the reason why Gabriel was prevented from following Muḥammad to the highest station. The saying portrays Gabriel as representing the state of "abiding in the Real" (baqāʾ bi-'l-ḥaqq) *and Muḥammad as representing the state of "passing away in the Real"* (fanāʾ bi-'l-ḥaqq), *each of which is appropriate to its own mystical station. He further elucidates the distinction between the two through a commentary on the final verse from the visionary passage at the opening of the sūra of the Star, 53:18. That verse, like the verse of the night journey (Q 17:1), mentions that Muḥammad was shown "signs" during his experience. Fāris interprets one of the "greatest signs" as being the divine manifestation to Muḥammad. God acts through his divine quality of loftiness* (jalāl), *conveying Muḥammad to the highest station while being careful not to distress him. Gabriel, who often comforts Muḥammad when he becomes distressed, is ultimately forced to stay behind. Gabriel is not sent the device for the final ascent, "that in which he bore [Muḥammad]," which is described in some ascension narratives as a type of green cushion* (rafraf),[51] *but here left unidentified and thus perhaps offered as a metaphor for Muḥammad's mystical transformation.*

It is interesting to notice that while Fāris initially asserts that Muḥammad's state is superior to Gabriel's, for Gabriel's attributes make him essentially unable to follow Muḥammad, he concludes the saying with the assertion that Gabriel's and Muḥammad's positions represent two important mystical stations (maqāmayn). *What distinguishes the two stations is their degree of contact with the divine manifestation. Fāris employs the metaphor of the veil or cover to represent the degree of disclosure in each case. Despite the fact that God remains covered for Gabriel during Muḥammad's ascension, Gabriel abides with the Real in the state of* baqāʾ, *a state that Sufis often describe as the stage following the mystical experience of* fanāʾ. *Ultimately, both stations are intimately connected with the Real, both being "for him and with him."*

Figure 5: Gabriel in his true form.

22 - TRIALS OF THE PROPHETS

> I heard Muḥammad b. Muḥammad b. Ghālib say that Ḥusayn b. Manṣūr [Ḥallāj] said, "The Intimate Friend [Ibrāhīm] ؑ said, 'From you to me,' so he tried him with the fire. The Speaker[52] [Mūsā] said, 'From me to you,' so he tried him with the sea. Muḥammad ﷺ said, 'From you to you,' so he tried him with the journey."

The Qurʾān reports that "God took Abraham as an intimate friend (khalīl)" *(Q 4:125), and the nickname "Intimate Friend" becomes synonymous with Abraham* (Ibrāhīm). *The Qurʾān contains a number of examples of Abraham petitioning favors from God, for instance asking to be granted righteous progeny, but the phrase "from you to me" is not applied to Abraham anywhere in the Qurʾān, so the source of this reference remains something of a mystery. Given the variations upon the phrase applied in this saying to both Moses and Muḥammad, one suspects that Ḥallāj employs it symbolically in all three cases. That is, Ḥallāj understands the phrase "from you to me"* (*minka* ᶜilayya) *to say something symbolic about Abraham's prophecy rather than something actually recorded as spoken in Abraham's name. Unlike this mysterious phrase, the Qurʾān does record Abraham's "trial by fire," reminiscent of the story of Shadrach, Meshach, and Abednego in the Hebrew Bible (Daniel 3:8f.), recounting how idolaters attempted to burn Abraham in a fire but God turned the fire cold and saved him. This is probably the trial by fire mentioned in the saying above. The connection between the phrase "from you to me" and this particular trial, however, remains unclear.*

The reference to Moses in this saying is equally cryptic. Moses' trial by sea, of course, is most likely a reference to the miracle of the crossing of the Red Sea by the Israelites as they fled from Pharaoh's armies (Q 2:50, 7:138, 10:90, 26:63). However, Ḥallāj never explains the connection between the phrase "from me to you" (minnī ᶜilayka) *and the sea trial ascribed to Moses. Both Abraham's trial by fire and Moses' trial by water took place as the prophets' neighbors threatened them with death, and in both cases God comes to their aid to help them to survive the trial. Perhaps Ḥallāj would say that the fact that both Abraham and Moses saw themselves as having an independent will or ego, symbolized by the phrases "from you to me" and "from me to you," led to these trials. The trials allowed God to show the prophets how they would have died if not for him, how they are nothing apart from him.*

It is difficult to understand how Muḥammad's journey (here: al-masrā) *could be a trial in a sense analogous to the deadly trials faced by Abraham and Moses. Muslims traditionally date Muḥammad's journey to the period just before the emigration to Medina when the Muslim community was undergoing hardship and Muḥammad's life was even threatened, but this context would not explain why the night journey itself was portrayed as a type of trial. Muḥammad did pass various tests on his journey, such as the test of which drink to select out of the cups offered to him. One could imagine that it was a trial for Muḥammad to endure some of the visions he was shown, such as the terrors of hellfire, or the splendors of the vision of God. Nevertheless, the above saying implies that the actual journey was itself a test for Muḥammad.*

The night journey certainly was a trial for Muḥammad's community upon his return, a test of their faith in believing his story, and this is perhaps the closest that one can find to a connection between the night journey and a trial. Indeed, several versions of the narrative turn to a later verse in the Night Journey sūra in order to explain this post-journey trial: "We only made the vision that we showed you as a strife (fitna) among people..." (Q 17:60). Members of the Quraysh tribe challenge the veracity of Muḥammad's story, and according to the earliest versions of the narrative, a certain number of Muslims turned away from Islam after hearing Muḥammad's tale. Muḥammad's friend and companion Abū Bakr, by contrast, earns the title of "the one who testifies to the truth" (al-Ṣiddīq) *by believing what Muḥammad says. From the perspective of this anecdote, the miracle of the night journey and ascension itself becomes a potential crisis for Muḥammad upon his return, a trial that he and his entire community must face and strive to overcome.*[53]

Beyond this interpretation of the journey as trial, Ḥallāj may intend a more mystical sense of the concept of trial. Perhaps as in the visionary ascent ascribed to Abū Yazīd Bisṭāmī, each stage of the journey was a trial for the one ascending, tempting one to stop and take pleasure in each abode. Alternately, it could be that the very idea of a journey to the divine abode, as if God resides in a particular place set apart from his creation, represents an illusion and thus a trial for Muḥammad. When he overcomes the trial of seeing himself as an individuated entity, effacing and transcending himself through passing away, only God remains.

Regardless of how it is interpreted, Ḥallāj relates Muḥammad's "trial by journey" to the phrase "from you to you" (minka ᶜilayka), *a phrase that bears comparison with the triple prepositional phrase of saying 17: "Through him, from him, to him." Here the phrase "from you to you" may symbolize Muḥammad's recognition of the primary importance of God's will. When one recalls that Ḥallāj is frequently associated with multiple ecstatic utterances that blur the distinction between the mystic and the divinity in the state of passing away, one recognizes that in such a state, God is both the subject and object of one's actions. Part of Muḥammad's "trial"*[54] *on the journey, then, was the way that he was called to let go of his own individuated will and ego.*

23 - DIVINE AND PROPHETIC ATTRIBUTES

> I heard Naṣrābādhī saying that he heard Ibn ᶜĀᵓisha saying that he heard Abū Saᶜīd Qurashī say, "God (be he exalted) manifested himself to our Prophet, Muḥammad ﷺ, through the attributes of bounty and beauty. He spoke to him with cordiality '*at the lote tree of the boundary*.'[55] He welcomed him with reverence and kindness, so he increased his kindness, reverence, compassion, and intercession with people. However, he unveiled to Mūsā ﵇ through the attributes of dread and loftiness. From there, Mūsā was increased in roughness and intensity."

This saying builds upon previous sayings that attempt to distinguish the theophany witnessed by Moses and that witnessed by Muḥammad. It explores further the idea alluded to briefly in saying 21, namely that certain divine descriptions or attributes (ṣifāt) *preside over the divine unveiling* (kashf) *and manifestation* (tajallī). *According to Abū Saᶜīd Qurashī, two different characteristics were employed in each of the two prophet's experiences, each affecting the future personality of the prophets. God treated Muḥammad with kindness, and as a consequence Muḥammad became more kind to people with whom he interacted; God treated Moses with terrifying majesty, and as a consequence Moses become more harsh when dealing with those with whom he interacted. While not filled with deep mystical insight, this concept and others like it could be said to pave the way for mystical theories built upon the various roles played by different divine attributes.*[56]

24 - A SECRET BETWEEN LOVERS

Jaᶜfar al-Ṣādiq was asked about the saying [of God] (powerful and magnified), "*Then he approached and descended.*"[57] He said, "When the lover drew near to the lover at the extremity of nearness, extreme dread got hold of him. The Real kindly favored him with extreme kindness, because only extreme kindness can bear extreme dread."

"That is [the meaning of God's] saying, '*He revealed to his servant what he revealed.*'[58] In other words, what was was, what happened happened. The lover said to the lover what a lover says to a lover, he kindly favored him with the kind favor of a lover to a lover, and he divulged to him what a lover divulges to a lover. The two concealed and did not disclose their secret to any but themselves. For that reason he said, '*He revealed to his servant what he revealed,*' and no one knew what he revealed except the one who revealed [it] and the one to whom it was revealed."[59]

"There is an indication of extreme reverence by what [God] said, '*The heart did not lie in what it saw,*'[60] [that is,] rather the heart sincerely testified to what it saw. No one knew what it saw except the one who showed [it] and the one who saw.[61] The lover drew near to the lover, becoming a confidant and intimate to him, until he became bewildered. God (powerful and magnified) said, '*We raise by degrees whom we will.*'"[62]

Initially this saying draws upon the theme discussed in the previous saying, namely the manner in which the Real received the ascending Prophet. The passage abounds with hyperbolic expressions indicating the extreme limit (ghāya) *of emotion, which reflects the intensity of this ultimate experience. The quality of dread* (hayba) *that the previous saying connected with God's theophany to Moses here becomes an emotion that manifests itself in Muḥammad as he reached the limit of proximity to the divine. God treats Muḥammad with kindness* (luṭf) *as in the previous saying, but in this context, the purpose of this approach was to overcome the extreme dread that Muḥammad felt.*[63] *The opening paragraph of this saying illustrates the intensity of the feelings confronting Muḥammad at the highest stage, and the care and sensitivity with which God comforted his beloved.*

The second paragraph lyrically describes the interaction between the two parties as a meeting between two lovers. One finds such imagery throughout Sufi poetry, but only a few sayings in The Subtleties of the Ascension *explicitly draw upon this poetic convention.*[64] *The trope of the secret meeting between lovers serves two purposes here. First, it underscores the loving intimacy shared between the two parties in this mystical encounter. Second, it explains the ambiguity of the qurʾānic verse and the absence of descriptions of this highest encounter in the hadith reports. Just as lovers keep their secrets between themselves, so neither God nor Muḥammad discloses the details of their intimate meeting.*

Moreover, the final paragraph applies a similar insight to the vision of the heart witnessed by the ascending Prophet, claiming that while his heart faithfully reported the vision to him, neither he nor the one who brought about the vision revealed to another the content of the vision. Instead, the vision was a private matter between lovers, who exchanged whispers and confidences with one another. At this climactic point in the text, The Subtleties of the Ascension *preserves a phrase that does not appear in other versions of this saying, stating that the lovers became intimate "until he became bewildered"* (ḥattā ṣāra wālihan). *The term used for a bewildered person here,* wālih, *can also refer to someone who is afraid or bereaved. The mystical state of bewilderment or perplexity* (ḥayra) *could logically follow from such an intense experience of intimacy, and it may allude to the loss of the sense of self that characterizes the state of passing away* (fanāʾ). *In any case, the saying closes with a reference to the qurʾānic verse that appears in two contexts to explain how God favors some individuals over others. This citation justifies the unique favor that Muḥammad enjoyed as God's beloved and confidant, and it subtly refers back to the discussion of Muḥammad's superiority to the other prophets.*

25 - THE GREATEST VISION

One of them said, "The Real severed the secret-heart of Muḥammad ﷺ from all changes. He gazed at his Lord with the *eye of certainty*, and he became realized in the lights of the Real until the *eye of certainty* returned to him the *real-truth of certainty*. He summed up the face-to-face address with his saying, '*He revealed to his servant what he revealed.*'"[65]

"When he caused him to approach, '*he descended*.'[66] He showed him his he-ness and eliminated from him his I-ness. He cast down his traces, and he adorned him with his lights. Thus he was able to witness that witnessing. He never saw a created light above his light. It occupied him. For that reason nothing awed him and nothing pleased him after what he witnessed, which God (be he exalted) recounted in his saying '*Indeed he saw some of the greatest signs of his Lord.*'[67] And '*his vision did not stray nor was it excessive*'[68] out of the exaltedness of his light and the purity of his trace."

The connection between the vision of the divinity and Muḥammad's mystical experience serves as the theme of this anonymous saying. The opening sentence signals the idea that Muḥammad's created and contingent nature was left behind when he witnessed and thus partook in the essence of the uncreated and eternal divinity. The vision moves him to the final stage in what elsewhere in this work (e.g. saying 32) is described as a three-stage progression: the knowledge of certainty (ᶜilm al-yaqīn, *from Q 102:5*), *the eye of certainty* (ᶜayn al-yaqīn, *from Q 102:7*), *and the real-truth of certainty* (ḥaqq al-yaqīn, *from Q 56:95 and Q 69:51*). *In the final stage,* ḥaqq al-yaqīn, *the distinction between the divine Real* (al-ḥaqq) *and his lover is blurred as the latter becomes realized* (taḥaqqaqa) *in the lights of the Real. This anonymous saying equates this powerful visionary experience with crucial verses from the sūra of the Star.*

Initially, the saying cites the mysterious verse "He revealed to his servant what he revealed" *(Q 53:10), which highlights the vague language with which the exchange is described while underscoring the dichotomy between master and servant. However, turning next to an earlier verse in the same passage,* "he approached and descended" *(Q 53:8), the anonymous exegete describes the stripping away of Muḥammad's individual identity as divine qualities replace human qualities. While no actual union is spoken of here, the process of divine "infusion" or more precisely "investiture" is portrayed as a necessary step that makes possible the visionary experience that follows.*

The image of the divine lights appears throughout this saying, both as a garment worn by the visionary and as the content of the vision. To a certain degree, the lights become both the subject and the object of the visionary experience. All created lights pale in comparison with these divine lights, the anonymous master states, and thus after this experience Muḥammad was never impressed by worldly things (compare saying 56).

26 - ABIDING IN THE PRESENCE

Abū Muḥammad Jurayrī (may God be compassionate to him) said, "When the chosen one ﷺ gazed at the Real through the Real, he saw the Real through the Real. He abided with the Real through the Real, neither in time nor in space, for he remained with one for whom there is neither time nor space. He was stripped of his descriptions by the descriptions of the Real.[69] In that state he did not have a self, knowledge, tongue, or elucidation until the Real restored him to his description. His exterior was stripped of the lights that had been let down upon it. The benefit to him is the restoration of the figure to its description in order for his undertaking the duties of his message, while the secret-heart remained in the [divine] presence. For that reason, he concealed what happened in that assembly. He said: '*He revealed to his servant what he revealed.*'"[70]

Like the previous saying, this saying attributed to Jurayrī describes the visionary experience at the climax of Muḥammad's heavenly ascension. On one level it states that Muḥammad saw God through the grace of God, a vision of the Real through the Real. On another level, one notices that the name "Muḥammad" never appears in the saying, rather it substitutes for it his common nickname, "the chosen one" (al-muṣṭafā). *Such a substitution may not always be all that significant, but the effect in this instance is that Muḥammad as an agent becomes quickly effaced by the repetitive mention of "the Real" along with the ambiguous pronoun "he." Thus, when "he saw the Real through the Real," the active subject seeing and the passive thing being seen are no longer as distinct as it may appear upon first glance.*

As in other sayings, here the vision itself accompanies and seemingly rests upon the transformation of the visionary. Having passed away (fanāʾ) *from his created self, the visionary abides* (baqāʾ) *in the Real outside of space and time. The image of the divine lights that descend upon the visionary during this experi-*

ence are described here only in terms of their being removed afterward. Ultimately, the Real restores the exterior body of Muḥammad to its original physical form (the term here is "figure," shabaḥ), *in order that he might be able to transmit God's message. Nevertheless, despite the outer restoration, the innermost secret-heart remains in the state of abiding in God. Jurayrī concludes by suggesting that the mystery of this mystical experience, and the desire to conceal the fact that the secret-heart remained in the divine presence, together explain the ambiguous language with which Muḥammad and God ("he") describe the intimate encounter.*

27 - THE BENEFIT OF RITUAL PRAYER

> Ḥusayn b. Manṣūr [Ḥallāj] was asked about the realities of ritual prayer. He said, "God (be he exalted) and his Prophet ﷺ addressed ritual prayer at the most exalted assembly. He said, 'Lord, what is in it for me [on behalf] of the one who performs the ritual prayer?' He replied, 'Following my command and avoiding what I forbid.' He said, 'And what is in it for me?' He replied, 'My praise of you in following the command and my thanks to you in avoiding the forbidden.' He said, 'If you praise, you praise your good character, and if you thank, you thank your beneficence. The servant has no station with you in anything.'"

The scene where Muslims receive the duty to perform five daily ritual prayers (ṣalāt) *appears in a position of prominence near the end of most accounts of Muḥammad's heavenly ascension. In many hadith reports, the emphasis of this scene rests upon the bargaining session which Muḥammad initiates on the prompting of Moses, in which God gradually lightens the original imposition of fifty daily prayers to a final total of five daily prayers. The haggling over the number of prayers does not play much of a role in the saying of Ḥallāj quoted above, although one may see a brief allusion to it in the introductory sentence: "God and his Prophet addressed ritual prayer...."* (literally: God spoke/preached to his Prophet about ritual prayer....) *Instead of developing this common theme, the above saying comments on the subtle realities behind the performance of ritual prayer through its report of the verbal exchange that followed. It presents a conversation between Muḥammad and his Lord, each identified with the third person pronoun as "he," in which they discuss who benefits from the performance of* ritual *prayer and in what way.*

According to the surface level of Ḥallāj's saying, the servant benefits from the servant's performance of ritual prayer insofar as it represents his or her obedience to God's commands and prohibitions, and God benefits from the servant's praise which is expressed through this act of obedience. This type of binary division of benefit is nothing out of the ordinary, for one finds such sentiments in the official exegesis of the first sūra of the Qurʾān, the "Opening" (al-fātiḥa)*: half of the sūra is said to be for the benefit of the servant, and half for the benefit of the Lord.*[71] *In this understanding of ritual prayer, neither God nor God's servant actually requires the performance of the prayers in and of themselves, rather the prayers serve to affirm the master-servant relationship: God commands and forbids, the servant obeys. The saying ends by apparently reinforcing this sharp dichotomy between master and servant, emphasizing God's goodness and his transcendence of worldly matters.*

The abundant use of the third person pronoun in Ḥallāj's saying, however, could suggest another level of meaning that complicates this surface-level reading. I would argue that Ḥallāj's use of the pronoun throughout the saying engenders a certain degree of confusion about the speaker in each case, forcing the reader to look for clues as to who is speaking. Clues can be found to guide a person to the meaning that she would expect. For instance, the phrase that begins "Lord" appears to signal a speech expressed by the Prophet as the representative of the servant before his Lord. In the second question and answer exchange, it is God's turn to address the question to the Prophet about what God stands to gain through observing the servants' ritual prayer. So far there is nothing that unusual, despite the fact that one might find it curious that the all-knowing God would ask Muḥammad what God's portion might be, implying a certain degree of reciprocity between his question and Muḥammad's initial question. Still, the identity of each of the speakers can be generally established in both of the first two exchanges. That raises the issue, however, of precisely who is speaking and addressing whom in the culminating sentences of Ḥallāj's saying.

The issue of the identity of the speaker in the closing statement is more complicated than it first appears. As seen above, the text can be translated as follows:"He said, 'If you praise, you praise your good character, and if you thank, you thank your beneficence. The servant has no station with you in anything.'"[72] *Here the party speaking is understood to be the divinity, who tells Muḥammad that his praise reflects back onto him. That interpretation has the benefit of internal consistency within Sulamī's work, for it evokes the hadith cited in four different sayings that states how praise falls short of the Real: "I cannot enumerate the praise of you as you have praised yourself."*[73] *However, the last sentence calls such an interpretation into question, for one wonders why God would then tell Muḥammad that "the servant has no station with [Muḥammad] in anything." Perhaps the translation above should be maintained, but the party speaking should be understood to be Muḥammad, who more logically tells the divinity that "the servant has no station with [God] in anything." But this interpretation raises the question of why God would praise his own good character and why God would thank his own beneficence, particularly in the context of a discussion of ritual prayer. The hadith cited above may suggest a solution through the idea that God praises himself in the Qur'ān in a manner that lies beyond the ability of human beings to produce themselves. In this interpretation, then, Muḥammad affirms for the divinity that the servant does not share in his station. The final phrases of the saying are ambiguous, especially in their present written form.*[74] *Given that Ḥallāj was said to have composed these words, one might theorize that the ambiguity may have been deliberate.*

Ḥallāj's use of ambiguous pronouns causes a certain amount of confusion, and it is possible that he intended to subvert the Arabic language to a certain degree, playing upon its ambiguity to achieve a type of apophatic effect that seeks to transcend the dualism and reification that much of human speech presumes. If this thesis can be maintained, clearly the apophasis here is less pronounced than in other sayings in The Subtleties of the Ascension. *Nevertheless, I have attempted to show that the final phrases of the saying above may either function to reinscribe the master/servant distinction, or they may function to develop the more subtle point that as long as one remains on one side or the other of this dualistic divide, one experiences nothing of the sublime station where the Real alone abides.*

Qushayrī's ascension text does not include the above saying on ritual prayer, but the section of his book entitled the "Subtleties of the Ascension" concludes with a hadith report about ritual prayer that he claimed to have transmitted via his teacher, our compiler Sulamī himself: "I heard Shaykh Abū ʿAbd al-Raḥmān Sulamī say that he heard Naṣrābādhī say: One of the special attributes of ritual prayer was that God commanded it to his Prophet without intermediary [on the ascension]. An act of devotion that is commanded without intermediary has a higher virtue than any other."[75] *Since both saying 27 and this latter saying cited by Qushayrī deal with a similar subject, and both follow what is defined in* The Subtleties of the Ascension *as saying 26, these details suggest that despite the difference in organization, the two texts often run closely parallel to one another. Qushayrī's direct citation of a report attributed to Sulamī could be seen to support the idea that* The Subtleties of the Ascension *represents an authentic work of Sulamī. That is, in Qushayrī's text, the student (Qushayrī) adapts and appropriates the work of his teacher (Sulamī) as part of his own, and he preserves the title of his teacher's text in one of his own section headings. In addition to appropriating Sulamī's work as his own, Qushayrī furthermore transmits an additional report from his teacher, quoted above, and collates it together with the rest of the ascension-related sayings.*[76]

28 - LETTER MYSTICISM WITH L AND B

> One of them said, "When on the ascension the Prophet ﷺ said, 'I am with you (*bika*),' the answer on the part of the Real was, 'If you are with me, I am for you (*laka*),' since the [letters] L and B alternate with each other. One whose attribute is L, his description is B."

The narrative context from which this mystical saying is drawn remains largely a mystery, although it clearly presumes a dialogue between the Prophet and the divinity on the night of the ascension. The saying's mystical insight revolves around the similarity between the Arabic prepositional phrases "bika" (with you) *and* "laka" (for you, yours) *in this reported exchange. Since the short vowels 'a' and 'i' are not normally written in Arabic, only the letters 'b'* (*Arabic:* ba) *and 'l'* (*Arabic:* lam) *distinguish* "bika" *and* "laka" *in the original text. The anonymous commentator maintains that the two phrases naturally follow one upon the other, the letters 'b' and 'l' being inherently connected in a manner not obvious to the uninitiated. Despite the fact that a complete understanding of this saying requires a familiarity with a system of letter mysticism* (ʿilm al-ḥurūf) *that may be difficult to decipher today, the apparent message that Muḥammad and his Lord expressed their close connectedness during their intimate conversation on the night of the ascension seems clear enough. The final sentence of the saying implies that the two positions in reality apply to a single entity, linking the attribute* (naʿt) *and description* (ṣifa) *of such a one.*

29 - DRAWING NEAR TO THE DIVINE VISION

One of them said, "When the Real purified Muḥammad ﷺ in his pre-eternity from the interminglings of the secret-hearts and the witnessings of others, he purified him from desire, compensation, and invocation. He faced the station of the invocation of God, so he said, 'Greetings to God.' He faced the station of request for compensation through longing for the compensator. In epochs and ages, he faced [each] station by passing away from them and abiding with their creator."

"When he was in the latter station, he drew near and was caused to *approach*. Some of the lights of the descriptions *descended*[77] upon him and attracted him to the carpet of empowerment. He thus witnessed the Real. He drew near until through nearness he was caused to pass away from the station of nearness."

"That was the time that he was permitted to ascend. The self associated with the spirit through that which remained of it, reserved for the self of the spirits. The self observed what then remained of the heart, and the secret-heart was his in observance. That is [God's] saying: '*The heart did not lie in what it saw*.'[78] The heart did not lie to the self in what it witnessed."

The idea of the Prophet's primordial purification and vision of the divine is here associated with his experience of purification on the night of the ascension that culminated in the theophany. Muḥammad transcends mystical stages by passing away from them and abiding with the divine source. In the above saying, this process of transformation is represented physically with the descent of the divine lights trope that we have discussed previously.[79] *When he arrives into the divine presence, Muḥammad comes to the heavenly carpet (bisāṭ) and witnesses the Real.*[80]

But the process of transformation does not stop with this vision, for he is brought so near that he passes away from the station of nearness, the self (nafs) *practically merging with the spirit* (rūḥ).[81] *Both aspects participate in the vision of the divine, a domain normally reserved for the spirit and the secret-heart. The anonymous exegete ends by citing the verse from the sūra of the Star on the vision of the heart, claiming that on an esoteric level the verse proves that the inner heart faithfully transmitted what it witnessed to the self or* nafs. *It is tempting to read into this final exegetical comment the theological position that Muḥammad was taken on the night journey and ascension both in body (here represented by the* nafs) *and spirit (here represented by the* sirr). *While this mystical exegesis does allow for such a position, clearly in the present context, in which Muḥammad has passed away into divine proximity, this type of mundane theological debate is largely moot.*

30 - MUḤAMMAD'S RANK

I heard ʿAbd Allāh b. Muḥammad Dimashqī say, "I asked one of our teachers from Syria, 'Does the rank of any other prophet عليه السلام approach that of Muḥammad ﷺ in terms of favor?' He responded, 'Neither near angel nor sent prophet approaches the rank of Muḥammad ﷺ. How could their rank approach his, while he is in the presence and witness [of God]?'"

"Upon the witnessing, he did not lose his spirit and secret-heart until he was approached, spoken to, and whispered to. Marks and traces were cast down from him, and he stood with the Real in the closest station in which one can stand. The expression for this on the night of the ascension is: '*He was two bows or closer*'[82] and '*The heart did not lie in what it saw.*'"[83]

As we have seen in previous sayings, here the initial question deals with the issue of the relative status of Muḥammad in comparison with the other prophets, specifically how his rank (martaba) *compares to theirs. The anonymous "Syrian teacher" alleges that Muḥammad's experience of the divine presence and his visual witness of the divinity, presumably during his heavenly ascent, as the context here suggests, establishes Muḥammad's superiority to all other prophets and indeed to even the most favored of angels. The teacher expands upon this idea by describing the degree to which Muḥammad was able to bear the vision of God. Whereas most creatures would immediately perish when faced with such a vision, Muḥammad's soul endures the experience until the point in which the divinity approaches and speaks. Only at this point are all traces of Muḥammad obliterated in the state leading to "passing away"* (fanāʾ)*, allowing for extreme proximity and togetherness. One should note that despite the allusion to* fanāʾ*, however, this saying stops short of postulating an ultimate union. At the highest stage two parties remain, "he" (the traces left of Muḥammad, here unnamed) and the Real. The Syrian teacher quotes two qurʾānic verses from the sūra of the Star at the end of the saying, interpreting them as referring to this intimate experience.*

Figure 6: Muḥammad talking with other prophets.

31 - THE PURPOSE OF THE ASCENSION

One of them was asked, "What was the benefit of the ascension while the Prophet ﷺ was not hidden from the presence, rather he [already had] witnessed hidden things through the realities of faith?" He responded, "Muḥammad ﷺ was the beloved, and of all creation he was the most intense in longing for his Lord because of the sincerity of his love. The Real knew of his longing for him and the paucity of his patience for witnessing him. Thus he hastened that [vision] to him, before [granting it to] all of the prophets and messengers عليهم السلام. That only increased his longing for him. Do you not see how he chose when given a choice? He said, 'Rather, the most exalted companion.'"[84]

An anonymous Sufi is here asked how the ascension was of any benefit or advantage (fāʾida), *since according to the petitioner Muḥammad regularly had access to the unseen realm even before the ascension through the "realities of faith"* (ḥaqāʾiq al-īmān). *The Sufi responds that God brought the Prophet on the ascension as a reward for his devotion. He contends that while initially it appears that the purpose of the ascension was to help satisfy Muḥammad's intense longing* (shawq, *compare saying 33 below*), *the journey actually achieved the opposite effect of making his longing even more intense. The reader is left to conclude that one benefit of the ascension is that it simultaneously satisfied and magnified Muḥammad's yearning for God's presence.*

The Sufi who was originally questioned then responds to his petitioner with a question of his own: "Do you not see how he chose when given a choice?" The choice mentioned here is probably Muḥammad's choice to die rather than to go on living, a reference to a hadith describing Muḥammad's final illness. Ibn Hishām's recension of Ibn Isḥāq's biography of the Prophet records the narrative as follows:

> *Ibn Shihāb al-Zuhrī told me from ʿUbayd b. ʿAbdullah b. ʿUtba from ʿĀʾisha that she used to hear the apostle say, "God never takes a prophet to Himself without giving him*

> *the choice." When he was at the point of death the last word I heard the apostle saying was, "Nay, rather the Exalted Companion of paradise." I said (to myself), "Then by God he is not choosing us!" And I knew that that was what he used to tell us, namely that a prophet does not die without being given the choice.*[85]

This hadith explains why the disjointed phrase "Rather, the most exalted companion" is given in this saying, despite it appearing out of context, for it reports Muḥammad's alleged response to an unheard question from the realm of the unseen. Muḥammad's experience on the night of the ascension, therefore, is connected here and in saying 47 to Muḥammad's choice at the end of his life to return to the divine realm rather than to stay in the world. This connection illustrates how the night journey and ascension served to reconcile the Prophet with his later illness and death, and moreover it served to increase his longing for his future reunion with the divine beloved.

32 - HIERARCHY OF RANKS

I heard Abū ʿAlī Aḥmad b. ʿAlī Shāmī say that in Samarqand he heard Fāris Baghdādī say, "The Real stood creatures at [different] ranks from him. For the people of intimate knowledge there was the *knowledge of certainty*, for the prophets عليهم السلام there was the *eye of certainty*, and for Muḥammad ﷺ there was the *real-truth of certainty*."

"The people of intimate knowledge inscribed the *knowledge of certainty*, since they were certain of what they knew. The prophets عليهم السلام arrived at the *eye of certainty*, since they witnessed from it the reality of certainty. Muḥammad ﷺ passed away from his descriptions, and he was realized in the realities of the Real. Thus he was granted the sustenance of the *real-truth of certainty*. That is a station beyond which there is no station."

Fāris Baghdādī here applies the tripartite division of degrees of certainty (yaqīn)*, which were alluded to briefly in saying 25, to the discussion of the ranking of creatures in a manner reminiscent of saying 30. While the latter context restricts the discussion to a comparison between Muḥammad and the other prophets and angels, here the tripartite division allows Fāris Baghdādī to insert the Sufis (the "people of intimate knowledge,"* ahl al-maʿrifa) *into the equation. He claims that these intimate knowers have a limited access to certainty* (yaqīn) *through their command of science or knowledge* (ʿilm, *drawing upon the phrase* ʿilm al-yaqīn *from Q 102:5*). *Prophets have greater access to certainty through their ability to visualize its reality* (ḥaqīqa) *through the "eye of certainty"* (ʿayn al-yaqīn, *from Q 102:7*). *Muḥammad, of course, has access to the highest stage, the "real-truth of certainty"* (ḥaqq al-yaqīn, *from Q 56:95 and Q 69:51*)*, which is only reached by passing away* (fanāʾ). *He becomes "realized in the realities of the Real," a phrase that strings together three words that are all based upon the same key Arabic root,* ḥ-q-q: "yuḥaqqiqu bi-ḥaqāʾiq al-ḥaqq." *This third degree of certainty represents the ultimate station beyond which* *there can be no other, since at this point all traces of created being have vanished into the unity of the Real.*

The word choice in this saying merits close attention. For instance, one can detect more than a little irony in the fact that the Sufi masters of intimate knowledge (ma^{c}rifa) *are on the one hand elevated by being placed on the same spectrum as the prophets, while on the other they are debased for being so certain about what they discover through worldly knowledge* (^{c}ilm). *Moreover, the idea that the prophets "arrived"* (waṣalū) *at the "eye of certainty" suggests a sense of movement which culminates in Muḥammad's "passing away" into mystical union. Indeed this sense of movement toward the divinity through stages of certainty becomes the only real connection between the above saying and the narrative of Muḥammad's night journey and ascension. The final station reached through passing away remains the most exalted of all (compare saying 44), and Muḥammad's external night journey symbolizes his mystical transformation, a process by which this ultimate station becomes more and more realized.*

33 - THE UNSWERVING AIM

Nūrī (may God be compassionate to him) said, "The Real viewed the hearts [of creatures] and did not see any heart that longed for him more than the heart of Muḥammad ﷺ. So he was bountiful toward him with the ascension, hastening the vision and the conversation."

"When he was welcomed to that magnificent assembly, realms of being were diminished in his eyes to the point that he did not turn towards anything. He neither deemed anything pleasing nor magnified anything next to the aim for which he aimed."

As in saying 31 above, Nūrī's saying identifies Muḥammad's intense longing (shawq) *as the decisive factor in God's decision to reward him by hastening his ascension. God compares Muḥammad to the other creatures in creation and deems him the most worthy, an idea that relates to the other sayings in which Muḥammad is extolled through his superior qualities that become apparent by comparing him with other beings. In addition, God's look into Muḥammad's heart in the saying above complements Muḥammad's vision of the divinity, the latter often understood as being a vision of the heart.*

The second half of Nūrī's saying quoted above describes how the realms of being (akwān) *grew insignificant in comparison with the divine vision and his sincere "aim"* (qaṣd) *to reach the divine presence. The final phrase evokes the qurʾānic verse* "his sight did not waver nor was it excessive"[86] *without quoting the verse directly. Compare this passage to sayings 42 and 55, where the reference to this verse is explicit.*

As in these two other sayings and elsewhere in Sulamī's text (e.g. saying 48), here one is reminded of the visionary ascension attributed to Abū Yazīd Bisṭāmī. [87] *For instance, just as Nūrī describes Muḥammad as being devoted to his aim, so Abū Yazīd's dream ascension repeatedly illustrates how Abū Yazīd overcomes temptations through the sincerity of his aim or quest* (qaṣd) *to God.*

The idea described above that "realms of being were diminished in his eyes" becomes graphically and hyperbolically depicted in Abū Yazīd's journey, where immense kingdoms and towering angels become as if tiny gnats in Abū Yazīd's eyes. Nūrī's saying above develops a similar but more modest idea, namely that through Muḥammad's sincere longing and determination, he neither paid attention to nor offered praise for anything that stood apart from his unswerving aim.

34 - CHEERFULNESS AT RESURRECTION

> One of them was asked, "Why will the Prophet ﷺ be made expansively cheerful at the resurrection, when the [other] prophets عليهم السلام will be silent and contractively distressed?" He said, "Because his stopping place on the ascension, his conversation with the Real, and his address to him [together] eliminated his distress. Thus the stopping place will not make him faint-hearted, because of the portion of the magnificent station that he witnessed before that. The prophets عليهم السلام, [on the other hand,] will be taken by surprise, so they will be made silent and contractively distressed."

Once again the Prophet Muḥammad's superiority to other prophets comes to the fore as the main theme of this anonymous saying. On the day of resurrection (al-qiyāma), *Muḥammad's prior experience of the divine presence during the ascension and the assurances that he received while at that station will mean that he will be made cheerful* (inbasaṭa) *rather than distressed* (inqabaḍa) *that day. The other prophets, who never had the advantage of such an experience, will be overwhelmed and terrified. Thus they will be unable to intercede on behalf of their communities in the way that Muḥammad will intercede on behalf of Muslims. Muḥammad's intercession on the day of resurrection is a theme that is the subject of a number of hadiths,*[88] *and the concept appears again in sayings 41 and 44, which both similarly link the possibility of intercession with the paired concepts of expansive cheerfulness and contractive distress.*

The verbs translated above as "to be made expansively cheerful" (inbasaṭa) *and "to be made contractively distressed"* (inqabaḍa) *come to serve as technical terms for the contrasting Sufi states of "expansion"* (inbisāṭ) *and "contraction"* (inqibāḍ). *While such technical usage must be kept in mind as a deeper level of mystical meaning underlying both the question and answer, in this context and in the other sayings that evoke this pair of terms (sayings 41 and 44), there is no reason that they only be understood in the technical sense in which they come to be employed. For this reason, I have decided to add the sense of expansion and contraction adverbially, rendering Muḥammad's state of being "expansively cheerful" as juxtaposed to the state of the others as "contractively distressed." In this way I hope to supplement the emotional connotations of the two terms with the more nuanced mystical connotations that also become part of their semantic range in Sufi discourse.*

35 - RECEIVING SELECT ROBES OF HONOR

I heard Muḥammad b. ᶜAbd Allāh [Ibn Shādhān] say that he heard ᶜAlī b. Hind Fārisī say that Abū Saᶜīd Kharrāz said, "Muḥammad ﷺ reached beyond the trial boundary, thus he reached the approach boundary.[89] God (be he exalted) said, '*He was a distance of two bows or closer.*'[90] That was when there was no station for feet, so he saw his feet in a state. Then he was stripped of everything with which the commoners clothe themselves, and he was clothed with the most select of robes of honor. After that he praised him with his saying, '*You are indeed of magnificent character.*'"[91]

This saying attributed to Abu Saᶜīd Kharrāz is based upon a version of the narrative of Muḥammad's ascension that is no longer widely known. A precise understanding and contextualization of its various references becomes difficult without access to the original underlying narrative. Details such as the "trial boundary" (al-miḥnat al-muntahā, sic)*, the idea of Muḥammad's feet being supported despite the lack of place to stand, and the trope of the robes of honor* (khilaᶜ) *that Muḥammad receives in place of his common clothes, all would require further investigation into their textual provenance. For instance, various "trials" commonly take place in the night journey and ascension accounts. The most important of the trials is the choice of cups scene, which in some accounts takes place in Jerusalem, in others near the "lote tree of the boundary," and some in yet a different place entirely (e.g. just prior to entering paradise).*[92] *The terminology of the above saying suggests that the "trial boundary" might well be the cup test that Muḥammad faces at the heavenly lote tree of the boundary, yet other interpretations of the phrase are possible. Indeed, one has only to think of the many trials that Abū Yazīd faces as he ascends through various stages to realize that the precise nature of the trial alluded to in the above saying cannot be so easily determined without access to the version of the narrative that it presupposes.*

Despite the fact that its base narrative is not well known, and therefore the exact meaning of its references will remain elusive, the saying's general meaning can be surmised from context. Muḥammad overcame some trial near the culmination of his ascension, and that accomplishment allowed him to approach to within two bows' lengths from the divinity. Moving beyond the created realm into a realm in which there was no material foundation upon which to stand, the divine power held him suspended and supported him. At this highest station, Muḥammad's earthly garments were exchanged for select heavenly garments as a sign of his honor and favor. God then praised Muḥammad for his moral character, drawing upon a phrase from an early sūra that Muslims consider to represent one of the earliest of the Meccan revelations.

The expression "there was no station for feet, so he saw his feet in a state" merits further commentary since the words "station" (maqām) and "state" (ḥāl) are often crucial technical terms in Sufi discourse. While the stations are often understood as more permanent stages of mystical progress, the states are generally fleeting and transient. In light of the idea expressed in sayings 32 and 44 that Muḥammad was made to stand in a station beyond which was no station, the allusion here to him standing at "no station" takes on a deeper mystical significance. Whether Muḥammad's feet were "in a state" (floating?) or whether by seeing his feet miraculously suspended caused Muḥammad to be placed "in a state" cannot be determined from the text. In either case, the state immediately precedes the physical imagery of stripping and investiture that could be interpreted as symbolizing the mystical states of fanāʾ and baqāʾ.

The mention of the most select robes of honor (singular: khilʿa; plural: khilaʿ) near the end of this saying is particularly intriguing when examined in the context of other mentions of robes in the text and other uses for robes by later Sufis. Recall that a number of sayings in The Subtleties of the Ascension describe how Muḥammad was stripped of his outer qualities and descriptions on the ascension, being wrapped instead in a garment of divine lights that transform and/or protect him.[93] In the saying above there is no description of the robes beyond the fact that they are said to have select qualities or virtues (khaṣāʾiṣ). As mentioned in the Introduction, none of the official ascension narratives contain a reference to the

Prophet receiving a robe on the night of the ascension, but a few other popular and Shīᶜī narratives do. The idea of a sovereign bestowing robes of honor upon choice subjects was widespread in the Middle Periods of Islamic history, and later Sufis will adapt this practice to serve as a symbol of the ceremony of initiation into a Sufi order, the master giving the disciple a robe that is frequently called a khirqa.[94] *In this saying there is no trace of such a Sufi initiatic meaning being given to the Prophet's investiture at the highest station, a silence which suggests that in Abū Saᶜīd Kharrāz's time this Sufi ritual had not yet become established.*

36 - ILLUMINATING THE HEAVENS

> One of them said, "God (be he exalted) desired to illuminate the heavens with the lights of Muḥammad ﷺ, just as he illuminated the earths with his blessings, so he took him on a journey to the ascension-ladder."[95]

This short saying depicts the purpose of the night journey and ascension as the spreading of Muḥammad's light and blessings throughout the heavens. As mentioned previously, the concept of the "light of Muḥammad" (nūr Muḥammad) *and the related concept of an essence of spiritual authority or blessing* (baraka) *that could be transmitted physically were ideas sometimes associated with Shīʿism. Both ideas come to be important for some of the early Sufis.*[96] *Here the two concepts are combined, Muḥammad's light(s) being explicitly linked to his blessings. Muḥammad had already illuminated the lower world like the sun when it rises (a connotation conveyed by the use of the verb* ashraqa), *and thus he was brought on the ascension so that he could also shine his light upon the heavens. Implied but not expressed in this concise saying is the notion that Muḥammad was sent as a prophet not only to humanity, but also to the angels. Certainly the idea that the heavens could benefit from Muḥammad's light (and by extension, his blessings) suggests that Muḥammad's station is superior to that of the angels, an idea addressed in other sayings that Sulamī transmits in this compilation.*

Two things about the end of this short saying are worth noticing: first, the divine appears as an active agent, and second, the ascension-ladder appears as a physical object. Unlike in saying 4, which insists that the Qurʾān uses the fourth verbal form asrā *instead of the simple first form* sarā *to emphasize the divine power which sends Muḥammad on his journey, here the first form* sarā, *"to journey by night," is used with the divine as its presumed active subject. That is, in order that Muḥammad's light could be spread throughout the heavens, "he took him on a journey"* (sarā bihi), *or in other words, "he (God) journeyed by night with him (Muḥammad)." While one could imagine other ways to read this phrase, the combination of the divine as an active participant on the night journey and the* mi^c^rāj *used to refer to a physical ladder or stairway in the above saying raises the possibility that its underlying narrative employed more concrete and anthropomorphic elements than the vast majority of ascension narratives that have survived to date.*[97]

37 - PROOF IN JERUSALEM

Abū al-ᶜAbbās Dīnawarī was asked, "Why was the Prophet ﷺ caused to journey by night first to the house of the sanctuary [Jerusalem] before he was caused to ascend to heaven?" He said, "God (be he exalted) knew that the unbelievers of the Quraysh would accuse him of lying about what he reported to them about heaven. So he wanted him to report to them about [a place on] the earth that they had reached and viewed. They knew that the Prophet ﷺ had never entered the house of the sanctuary. When he reported to them about the house of sanctuary, after they had declared him sincere in [his] reports of the world, they were not able to accuse him of lying about reports of heaven."

As mentioned in the introduction, most Muslims by the 10th century had come to view the night journey from Mecca to Jerusalem (the house of sanctuary, bayt al-maqdis) *as the precursor to the heavenly ascension from Jerusalem through the seven heavens and back. Just as the people who addressed questions to the Sufis asked to know the purpose behind the ascension, here someone asks the reason why the night journey to Jerusalem was made to precede the ascension. Could not the Prophet have ascended directly from Mecca to the heavens, as some early versions of the ascension narrative contend? The answer recorded here, ascribed to Aḥmad Dīnawarī, maintains that God caused the Prophet to travel to Jerusalem first so that he could later prove the truth of his miraculous journey to his skeptical contemporaries.*

Dīnawarī asserts that because the unbelievers accepted Muḥammad's account of Jerusalem, they therefore could not reject his account of the heavens. Although the logic of this assertion is questionable, it makes sense that Muḥammad needed to appeal to something that the Quraysh themselves could verify in order to have any hope to win over his critics. In fact it is remarkable to note that the "proofs" given at the end of every narrative of the night journey and ascension almost without exception refer solely to places or people that Muḥammad encountered during his journey to or stay in Jerusalem. Elements of the heavenly ascension are never offered as proofs, presumably because they could not be verified by others. The answer given above, which helps to explain such an emphasis, becomes one of the methods adopted by later Sunnī scholars for explaining the purpose of the terrestrial night journey prior to the heavenly ascension.[98]

Figure 7: Muḥammad praying with other prophets in Jerusalem.

38 - THE SANCTIFICATION OF JERUSALEM

I heard Manṣūr b. ʿAbd Allāh say that he heard Qāsim b. al-Qāsim Sayyārī say that he asked Wāsiṭī, "Why was the Prophet ﷺ caused to journey by night to the house of the sanctuary [Jerusalem] before the ascension?" He said, "The Real (be he exalted) desired that [such] a favored ground would not be devoid of his assembly and the tread of his feet upon it, so he completed the sanctification of the house of the sanctuary with Muḥammad's ﷺ ritual prayer in it. When he thus completed its sanctification, the Prophet ﷺ reported that one should only set out in the direction of three mosques: the sacred mosque [i.e. the Kaʿba in Mecca], because it was the place of his birth, his childhood, and the site of his prophecy; the mosque of Medina, because it was the mosque of his emigration and site of his tomb; and the furthest mosque, because it was the land of his night journey and the site of his miracle. God (be he exalted) said: '*Glorified be the one who caused his servant to journey by night from the sacred mosque to the furthest mosque.*'"[99]

The city of Jerusalem is revered by Muslims for a number of reasons, not only because the night journey and ascension are frequently linked to the city, but also because it was the first direction of prayer or qibla *for the early community. Although the qurʾānic reference to the "furthest mosque" is open to interpretation, the hadith collections record two major opinions concerning its identity: either it stood for the city of Jerusalem and the site of Solomon's temple, the so-called "house of the sanctuary," or it stood for a location in the heavens. The former interpretation eventually came to be the one supported by the consensus of Muslim scholars, but the issue remained a matter of debate among Muslims in the centuries after Muḥammad's death.*[100]

The question posed in the saying above presumes that Jerusalem was the destination for the night journey and the starting point for the heavenly ascension. This presumption can be inferred by the fact that the questioner does not ask whether the Prophet was taken to Jerusalem but rather why he was taken to Jerusalem, and why this visit preceded the ascension. Clearly, then, the narrative being discussed here is one of the composite versions that begins with the night journey to Jerusalem and continues from there into the ascension through the heavens.

The answer to the question attributed to Wāsiṭī here alleges that the Prophet was first taken to Jerusalem in order to sanctify it by his presence there. That is, he is not brought to Jerusalem because it represents the closest point on earth to heaven, the "navel of the earth" as maintained by some popular accounts that probably originated in Jewish oral narratives. Rather, just as Muslims believe that the line of prophecy was not complete before Muḥammad came as the "seal of the prophets," so too Jerusalem was not fully sanctified until Muḥammad walked in it and prayed in it.

The saying concludes with a discussion of the hadith that states that a Muslim should only journey in pilgrimage to three mosques, those of Mecca, Medina, and Jerusalem.[101] *The hadith plays a major role in the later Muslim discussions of the "favors of Jerusalem" (faḍāʾil al-quds), and its citation here extends the argument that Muḥammad was brought to Jerusalem in order to demonstrate and fulfill its position as a sacred space for Muslims. It is interesting to note that in the discussion of the "three mosque" hadith in the saying above, it states that Jerusalem was the "site of his miracle"* (mawḍiᶜ muᶜjizatihi), *presumably a reference to the "miracle" of his heavenly journey. The word "miracle" here may even represent a corruption of the Arabic word for "ascension," and the original phrase may have read "site of his ascension"* (mawḍiᶜ miᶜrājihi). *In any case, the use of the phrase "furthest mosque" for Jerusalem in this concluding discussion and the citation of the night journey verse at its end make it clear that Wāsiṭī had no doubt that the destination of the night journey was Jerusalem. The reason Muḥammad was taken to that destination had less to do with what Muḥammad gained in Jerusalem than with what Jerusalem gained through Muḥammad's visit. The above saying thus recalls the idea from saying 36 that Muḥammad was brought to the heavens in order to bless them with his presence. Similarly, here Muḥammad is said to bless Jerusalem with his presence and prayers.*

39 - THE PROPHET'S SPEECHLESSNESS

> Someone said, "When Muḥammad ﷺ reached the boundary in [his] approach to the Real,[102] he had to follow the way of amazement and dying down. Therefore he did not report anything that he viewed, nor did he boast about it. Upon his return, he said, 'Were you to know what I know....'[103] In that assembly, at the appearance of the dawn he spoke words of praise: 'I seek refuge in you from you. I cannot enumerate the praise of you as you have praised yourself.'"[104]

On the night of the ascension, Muḥammad advanced farther and farther into the otherworldly realm until he finally reached the limit or boundary (al-muntahā). *If Muḥammad in fact encountered his Lord at this liminal station, one wonders why the subsequent hadith reports of Muḥammad's journey seldom describe any details of this sublime experience. This saying offers at least three explanations for the Prophet's silence on this subject. First, it suggests that Muḥammad's mystical experience at that exalted station brought him amazement and distraction* (dhuhūl), *causing him to fade out like the embers of a dying fire* (khumūd). *The anonymous Sufi speaking here does not explicitly attribute the state of "passing away" to Muḥammad, but the metaphor of the dying fire may well evoke the concept of* fanāʾ. *On one level, then, Muḥammad is unable to speak of his encounter with the divinity because the individuated created being "Muḥammad" had faded into ashes.*

The second explanation for Muḥammad's silence given in the saying above hinges upon the idea that the horrors Muḥammad witnessed during his tour of hellfire were too shocking to be repeated. The allusion to the hadith "Were you to know what I know, you would laugh little and cry much" clearly expresses such a sentiment. Instead of boasting to his community about what he witnessed on his journey, Muḥammad counsels his followers to repent.

Finally, a third explanation for Muḥammad's silence derives from the ineffability of the highest encounter. The Prophet literally cannot find words to describe adequately what he experienced. To further underscore this idea, the anonymous Sufi here cites a well-attested hadith report in which Muḥammad addresses God and proclaims his own inadequacy in praising God compared to the way that God has praised God's self (in the Qurʾān). The central message of the hadith appears to be that human words fall short of any satisfactory description of divinity, and God's own words in the Qurʾān are far superior to any utterances that humans may formulate.

40 - THE LIMITATIONS OF PRAISE

> Ḥusayn b. Manṣūr [Ḥallāj] was asked why the chosen one ﷺ was uncertain about praise on the ascension. He replied, "When he knew that praise, even if pure and plentiful, falls short of reaching the Real, that it returns nobility to the praiser not to the one praised, and that it shows the ability of its speaker and no other, his tongue once again faltered. Thus he said, 'I cannot enumerate the praise of you. . . .'"[105]

The hadith report introduced in the previous saying, "I cannot enumerate the praise of you as you have praised yourself," is here once again applied to the question of why the Prophet used such sparse and cryptic language to describe the climax of his journey on the night of the ascension. The opinion attributed to Ḥallāj here is based upon two ideas about praise: first, the idea that any human praise utterly falls short of the divine reality, and second, the idea that all praise serves to elevate the status and/or demonstrate the eloquence of the one praising rather than the status of the one praised. When the Prophet realized these truths, his tongue falters when describing his experience, because his praise for the divinity would not do him justice (compare sayings 46 and 54). Thus, Muḥammad was uncertain (abhama) *in his praise for the divinity, according to Ḥallāj, out of the recognition of his inability to praise the Lord adequately using human speech.*

Significantly, Ḥallāj's explanation above does not account for the concise language that the Qurʾān uses to refer to Muḥammad's ascension experience, for believing Muslims understand the Qurʾān as God's speech rather than Muḥammad's speech. God's own speech is clearly up to the task of praising God, whereas human speech falls short of that task. Other sayings in Sulamī's collection do address the Qurʾān's relative silence on the Prophet's ascension experience, such as Jaʿfar al-Ṣādiq's thesis in saying 24 that the experience remained a secret between lovers, something not to be talked about openly. The question then becomes not the ability to describe the experience but rather the propriety of doing so. In the above saying, by contrast, the emphasis rests more on the question of the human ability to express adequate praise in the description of a sublime encounter. The mystical point that Ḥallāj makes here is that an experience of the Real defies conventional human expression.

41 - THE PROPHET'S EXPANDING CHEERFULNESS

> Someone was asked: On the night of the ascension, why was the pure one ﷺ made expansively cheerful through the witnessing and speech upon the carpet of nearness?" [He said, "That is because when the Prophet was specified on the night of the ascension for witnessing and speaking on the carpet of nearness,] bewilderment was eliminated from him at the times of witnessing, and constrictive distress was eliminated during of the conversation. He thus was made expansively cheerful in the intercession and requesting."

Two important technical terms for contrasting mystical states, cheerfulness or expansion (inbisāṭ), *and distress or contraction* (inqibāḍ), *are juxtaposed in this anonymous saying.*[106] *Someone asks an unnamed Sufi the reason that the Prophet was in a state of expansive cheerfulness at the time of his encounter with God on the night of the ascension. Would not one expect Muḥammad, in contrast, to be terrified and distressed during such an encounter? The anonymous Sufi sage answers that the states of bewilderment* (ḥayra) *and constrictive distress* (inqibāḍ) *were removed from the Prophet at this exalted station, rendering him expansively cheerful, and thus able to play a role as intercessor for his community during his ascension.*

The idea that Muḥammad was made at ease during the divine encounter and therefore able to intercede reflects a mystical appropriation of a scene that appears concretely in some versions of the ascension narratives. In many versions attributed to Ibn ᶜAbbās, for instance, both Gabriel and the divinity calm Muḥammad and remove his terror, sometimes through words, other times through the physical contact of a touch or an embrace. The use of the passive voice in the above saying allows the anonymous respondent to avoid the issue of exactly how the distress and bewilderment were eliminated. The respondent instead focuses attention upon the results of their elimination, the Prophet's state of expansive cheerfulness during his divine audience.

Muḥammad's expansive cheerfulness enables him to petition and to intercede on behalf of his followers. As sayings 34 and 44 state, those prophets who do not achieve this state of expanding cheerfulness but instead remain in contracting distress will be powerless to intercede in this way on the day of resurrection. In contrast to these sayings which discuss Muḥammad's intercession on the day of resurrection, the above saying focuses upon the Prophet's ability to intercede much earlier, on the night of the ascension. As for what exactly Muḥammad requested on the night of the ascension on behalf of his community, whether it was forgiveness for their misdeeds or a reduction of their ritual obligations (number of daily prayers, number of months of fasting, etc.), the above saying does not specify.[107]

The anonymous saying given in the Sulamī manuscript is incomplete as it stands, for it is missing one or more lines that contain the words indicating the end of the query and the beginning of the response. The way to amend the text in a minimal fashion would be to insert only the words "He said" at the appropriate point, and that is the path I followed in my Arabic edition of Sulamī's text. By comparing the Sulamī text to the text of the same saying preserved in Qushayrī's manuscript, however, I have attempted to restore the missing line(s), offering the reconstructed portion in brackets in the English translation above in order to indicate the words not present in the Arabic text of Sulamī's unique manuscript.

42 - UNSWERVING VISION

> Ruwaym said, "When Muḥammad ﷺ was bountifully favored with the most magnificent honor during the night journey, his aspiration was exalted beyond turning towards the signs or bounties, paradise or hellfire. '*His sight did not waver*,'[108] that is, his glance did not wander to anything of the existing beings. One who witnesses the sea makes little of river beds and rivers."

Unlike most of the sayings in The Subtleties of the Ascension*, this saying is a statement about the night journey rather than an answer to an explicit question. The implicit question, here and in saying 55, is why the Prophet did not describe the otherworldly locales in more detail, and how he was able to keep his vision focused throughout his experience. At issue regarding the latter question is the meaning of the verse* "His sight did not waver" (*Q 53:17*). *This verse was of interest to Sufi exegetes, some of whom saw in it a model for the proper Sufi attitude toward mystical visions. According to the above interpretation that is attributed to Ruwaym, Muḥammad proves the sincerity of his aspiration* (himma) *toward the divine by not being distracted by created things, no matter how glorious or horrifying they may seem. The saying concludes with the sentiment that next to the majesty of his ultimate experience in the divine presence, the experience of created realms and beings along the way pales in comparison, appearing less worthy of notice or comment. Within the faculty of sight, created things shrink before the presence of the divinity, just as created traces are in the process of passing away* (fanāʾ) *as the divinity becomes more fully realized.*

As seen in sayings 33, 48, and 55, the dream vision of Abū Yazīd Bisṭāmī evokes general themes similar to those expressed above.[109] *The use of the Arabic term* himma (*aspiration*) *in this saying and its emphasis on intense dedication to the divine goal resonates with the poetic manner in which the same term appears in the Abū Yazīd ascension narrative. Next to Abū Yazīd's powerful* himma, *all the offerings that the angels produce in order to tempt*

Abū Yazīd from his quest shrink away, just as created things shrink away from Muḥammad in the saying above, becoming like tiny streams that diminish in significance next to the majesty of the ocean.[110]

43 - REAL PRAISE

> Wāsiṭī was asked why the Prophet ﷺ was uncertain about praise. He replied, "Praise is for those sufficient [to it]. For one who has not reached the reality of praise, praise is incapable of [real] praise."

The Prophet did not report much detail about his praise on the night of the ascension, a topic that has been discussed previously with regard to other sayings. Saying 40, ascribed to Ḥallāj, is closely related to the saying above, ascribed to Ḥallāj's contemporary Wāsiṭī. Wāsiṭī's version likewise expands upon the idea introduced in the hadith in which the Prophet pleads his inability to enumerate adequate praise (thanāʾ) *of the divinity.*[111] *Here the hadith is not mentioned explicitly, but its key Arabic term* thanāʾ *serves as the touchstone for Wāsiṭī's response. Whereas the earlier saying discusses how every act of praise turns out to reflect upon the one expressing the praise rather than the one receiving the praise, the above saying underscores the idea that praise of the divinity is essentially impossible unless the praiser has achieved the state which is called "the reality of praise"* (ḥaqīqat al-thanāʾ). *That is, the successful praiser must have some degree of insight into reality* (al-ḥaqīqa), *a term connected to and semantically related to the Real* (al-ḥaqq). *The praise of one whose insight is not sufficient* (kafī) *for such a level of praising becomes ineffective and meaningless.*

44 - MUḤAMMAD THE INTERCESSOR

I heard Manṣūr b. ^{c}Abd Allāh say that Abū Bakr b. Ṭāhir [Abharī] was asked, "Why was the Prophet ﷺ caused to ascend without the rest of the prophets عليهم السلام?" He responded, "For several reasons. First, because he is master of intercession on the day of resurrection. He was made to mediate by night before that [last day], so that the bashfulness of surprise would befall him [in advance], as it will befall other prophets [on resurrection day]."

"And [second], because he is master of the praised station. Prior to that, the Real (be he powerful and lofty) desired that the station of contracting distress would leave him in order that he may be empowered in the praised station. So he welcomed him before the heavenly host to witness and to speak. Then he lifted him up to a place for which there is no place after his place, and no station beyond his station, in order that he could be a witness to the totality. He will entreat in the highest assembly for intercession and for empowerment in the praised station."

In nearly every account of Muḥammad's heavenly ascent, Muḥammad completes the journey unaccompanied by any other prophet or human companion. In fact, the narratives that describe Muḥammad's journey beyond the lote tree sometimes describe how the Prophet leaves even Gabriel behind in the final stages. This saying discusses the reason why Muḥammad was caused to ascend without the other prophets accompanying him. Since all of the prophets had gathered together in Jerusalem and had prayed together, one might have expected them all to ascend together into the divine presence. The answer attributed to Abū Bakr Abharī above states that Muḥammad was caused to ascend alone because of his unique role and position on the day of resurrection (compare to sayings 34 and 41).

As in saying 34, the above saying draws upon the popular Muslim belief that Muḥammad will serve as an intercessor (shafī^{c})

on the day of resurrection. At times Muḥammad's role as intercessor appears to be limited to intercession for the Muslim community, and at other times it is expanded to include all of humanity. The above saying does not specify for whom Muḥammad will intercede, merely that his experience on the night of the ascension was intended to prepare Muḥammad for this future role. The rest of the prophets will be shocked and tongue-tied when facing the divinity on the day of resurrection, but because Muḥammad will have experienced the shock of the vision of God prior to the day of resurrection, he will be able to retain his composure and to carry out his duty as intercessor that day.

Furthermore, as in saying 34 and 41, the above saying alludes to the station of distress or constriction (maqām al-inqibāḍ) *that Muḥammad experienced, suggesting here that the Prophet's solitary ascension was meant to help him leave behind this station in favor of the praised station* (al-maqām al-maḥmūd). *As with intercession, the purpose of bringing the Prophet to this praised station before the day of judgment was to give him a foretaste of his future position so that he might be able to accept it and adapt to it more easily on that day. This connection between the concept of intercession and the concept of the praised station is not surprising, for the two concepts become virtually synonymous in some commentaries, the praised station being precisely the position in which Muḥammad has the ability to intercede. Here, however, the praised station signifies something further: the exalted position in which Muḥammad is able to witness the divine totality* (al-kull). *Such a position might be associated with the mystical state of seeing the world through the eyes of the divinity,*[112] *but it falls short of invoking the state of* fanāʾ *that other Sufis ascribed to the highest stages of the heavenly ascension.*

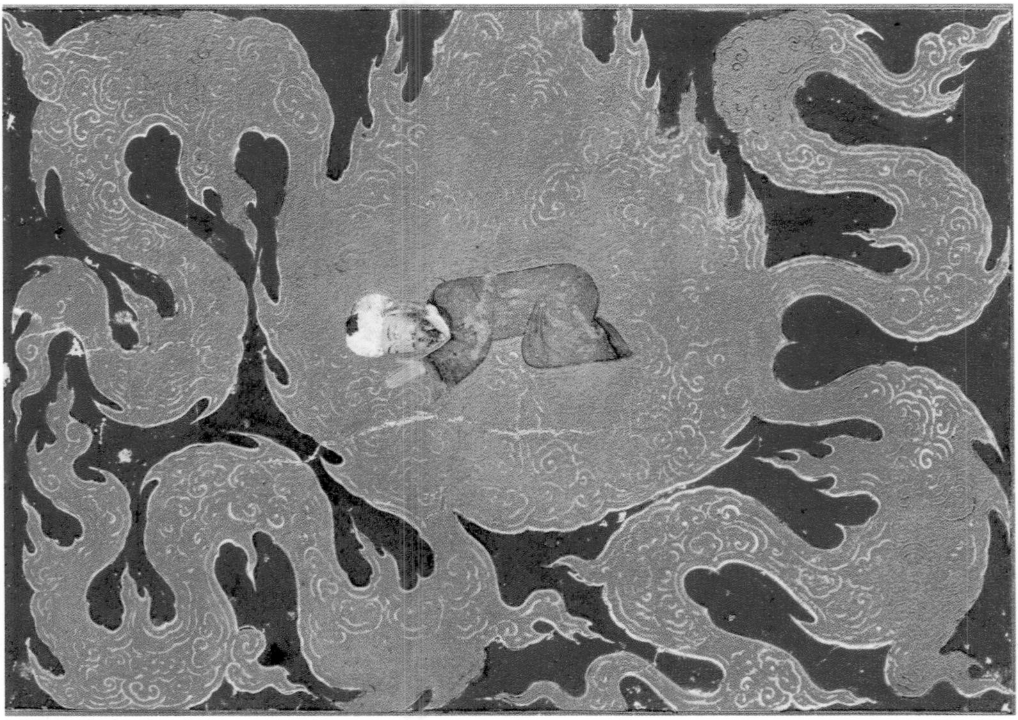

Figure 8: Bowing down in the heavens.

45 - PREPARATION FOR THE ENCOUNTER

I heard Manṣūr b. ᶜAbd Allāh say that Shiblī was asked, "On the ascension, how did the Prophet ﷺ withstand encountering the [divine] address?" He replied, "He was prepared for a matter, so he was empowered to [withstand] it."

The question of how Muḥammad was able to bear meeting and conversing with the divinity was a natural one, especially given the story of Moses' encounter with the deity on Sinai (compare saying 20, as well as sayings 13 and 15). In the qurʾānic account of Moses' experience, the deity tells Moses that he will not be able to bear looking upon the deity. Even simply looking at the mountain when the deity revealed himself to it causes Moses to collapse thunderstruck.[113] *How, then, could Muḥammad remain unwavering during his intimate dialogue with the deity on the night of the ascension?*

Shiblī's response is surprisingly simple, namely that Muḥammad was able to bear the experience because he had been prepared for it. Compare this idea to the anonymous statement articulated in saying 20, namely that Muḥammad was "strengthened." In the above saying, the manner of Muḥammad's preparation is never specified. The reference to preparation could represent an allusion to the importance of Sufi training and discipline prior to a mystical experience. Alternately, it could point to the need for divine grace in order to achieve exalted states. In other words, God prepared Muḥammad to bear the experience. Without any further context, it becomes difficult to know how the petitioner might have understood Shiblī's brief and ambiguous answer.

46 - THE FALTERING TONGUE

I once found in a book of hadith by Ismāʿīl b. Nujayd that Abū ʿUthmān [Ḥīrī] was asked about the saying of the Prophet, "I cannot enumerate the praise of you as you have praised yourself."[114] He said: The Prophet ﷺ had unceasingly invoked and praised his Lord. When he was made to ascend on the night of the night journey, he witnessed what he witnessed of the grandeur of his Lord, being ashamed of how he had praised and invoked. So his faltering tongue returned. He said, "I cannot enumerate the praise of you. . . ."[115]

Once again the subject is the Prophet's reticence to praise his Lord in his own words at the culmination of the ascension, an idea discussed in sayings 39, 40, and 43. Here the main issue revolves around the hadith itself: "I cannot enumerate the praise of you as you have praised yourself." The petitioner merely "asked about" the hadith, seemingly wanting to know how it should be understood in a general sense. Abū ʿUthmān, who is Ibn Nujayd's teacher Abū ʿUthmān Saʿīd b. Ismaʿīl Ḥīrī (d. 298/910-11), connects the hadith to the events of the Prophet's ascension as the previous sayings had done. Unlike previous sayings, however, this one provides a narrative context for the hadith, describing Muḥammad's shame at realizing that his prior expressions of praise and petition had been inadequate in light of the divine grandeur (ʿaẓama). *This shame, according to Abū ʿUthmān, leads directly to Muḥammad's reluctance to express his own words of praise. The saying thus explains Muḥammad's "faltering tongue"* (lisān al-ʿajaz), *but does not explore its implications for the claim of some Sufis that their mystical experiences are similarly ineffable. Perhaps this omission could be attributed to the fact that the source for this saying was not a work on mysticism but a work on hadith.*

This reference to a written source, "a book on hadith by Ismāʿīl b. Nujayd," deserves some comment. It remains the only explicit textual reference in this entire collection of Sufi sayings. The author of the hadith work mentioned, Ismāʿīl b. Nujayd Sulamī (d.

365/976-77), is Abū ᶜAbd al-Raḥmān's maternal grandfather. This same grandfather served as Abū ᶜAbd al-Raḥmān's guardian upon the death of the latter's father. It is not surprising, then, that the author of The Subtleties of the Ascension *would refer to Ibn Nujayd's work as a source. The fact that the author refers to a work by the latter rather than quoting him directly, however, suggests that* The Subtleties of the Ascension *probably was compiled some time after the death of Ibn Nujayd in 365/976-77.*

47 - APPROACHING THE COMPANION

Abū ᶜUthmān [Ḥīrī] also said, "The kindness of his Lord that he saw on the night journey made the pangs of death easy for him. He said, 'The most exalted companion,' when he chose. That is, 'Would one who witnessed what I witnessed choose anything but the most exalted companion, who caused me to approach and brought me near?'

As in saying 31, this saying alludes to a hadith of the Prophet in which he was said to have chosen to die out of his desire for the most exalted companion, the divinity. In one version of this hadith, Muḥammad addresses the dead in a cemetery and tells them that they are better off than the people who are still living.[116] *The above saying, which like saying 46 may have originated in Ibn Nujayd's book on hadith, postulates that Muḥammad's calm attitude toward his death derived from his experiences on the night journey and ascension. Abū ᶜUthmān underscores the connection by offering an interpretive gloss on Muḥammad's concise remark in the hadith, "Rather, the most exalted companion." Abū ᶜUthmān essentially states that anyone who had witnessed such bounties awaiting him or her in the afterworld, and anyone who had been brought as close as Muḥammad had been brought to the divine presence, would similarly have been unafraid to die. Indeed, such a person might even have been eager to choose death over life, if given such a choice.*

48 - RAISING HIS MENTION IN THE HEAVENS

I heard Abū Bakr [Muḥammad b. ᶜAbd Allāh Ibn Shādhān] Rāzī (may God be compassionate to him) say that he heard Abū al-ᶜAbbās Ibn ᶜAṭāʾ say, "When the Real (be he exalted) desired that his chosen one and beloved should become the best of creatures in mention, the greatest of them in ability, the loftiest of them in glory, the noblest of them in destiny, and the highest of them in rank, he caused him to ascend to the heavens and to look down upon the angelic realm."

"He beautified him with the necklace of the approach, causing him to approach the carpet of nearness, something for which the angels and prophets lacked the strength. [He did all this] in order to elevate his mention in his heavens just as he *raised his mention*[117] on his earth."

Numerous sayings in The Subtleties of the Ascension *discuss the purpose behind the night journey and ascension. The above saying offers a perspective that we have seen previously, namely that its purpose was to honor the Prophet and to prove his superiority to all other beings. It elaborates upon the idea that God's demonstration of the Prophet's exalted rank was aimed at all creation, not only human beings but also angels. One thinks of the qurʾānic account of the creation of Adam, in which the angels question the creation of one who will sow dissension, and Iblīs refuses to prostrate to Adam out of pride.*[118] *In order to prove Muḥammad's unparalleled status, he was caused to ascend. During the ascension, Muḥammad was made to look down upon* (ashrafu ᶜalā) *the angelic realm* (al-malakūt)[119]*, proclaiming the Prophet's exalted nobility* (sharaf) *and superiority over this realm. He was given the gift of approaching the divine presence, something that neither angel nor prophet besides him was given, in order to "raise his mention in the heavens." Unlike many other discussions of the night journey and ascension which focus on how the human audience responds to Muḥammad's journey, the above saying shifts focus from* *the human audience to the reception of the events by the angelic audience, and to Muḥammad's subsequent fame in that heavenly realm.*

The metaphors used to symbolize Muḥammad's unparalleled approach to the divine presence, the "necklace of approach" (ḥalqat al-danaww) *and the "carpet of nearness,"* (bisāṭ al-qurb) *recall similar metaphors that appear in the dream ascension attributed to Abū Yazīd Bisṭāmī.*[120] *For instance, at the culmination of Abū Yazīd's journey, God addresses him saying, "O my chosen one* (ṣafī), *come near to me and look upon* (ashrif ᶜalā) *the plains of my splendor and the domains of my brightness. Sit upon the carpet of my holiness until you see the subtleties of my artisanship* [*in*] *I-ness. You are my chosen one, my beloved, and the best of my creatures."*[121] *Metaphorical phrases linking a concrete object to an abstract concept, such as the "carpet of nearness," are relatively common in this type of Sufi discourse. The numerous parallels between the Abū Yazīd text and the above saying show that such mystical language was applied to both prophetic and non-prophetic ascension narratives at a relatively early date.*

49 - ASK AND BE GIVEN

> Ḥusayn b. Manṣūr [Ḥallāj] said, "When the most exalted mediator approached the Real on the night journey, he commanded him saying, 'Ask and be given.' He replied, 'What shall I ask for, since I have been given? What should I request, since I have been satisfied?'"
>
> "A voice called out, '*You have indeed a magnificent character,*[122] having distanced our carpet from the request of needs.' Upon that he gave [him] the proof, and he made him free in the judgment of one of the two abodes for whom he willed. He returned to the assembly of his companions, and he judged in favor of paradise for ten of the Quraysh."[123]

Although the official Jamāʿī-Sunnī hadith sources rarely report the specific dialogue between Muḥammad and his Lord on the night of the ascension, the ascension narrative attributed to Ibn ʿAbbās reports this dialogue at length.[124] *One of the standard elements of this dialogue is an intercessory scene in which God commands Muḥammad to "ask and be given," which is usually followed by a series of petitions by the Prophet to which God responds.*[125] *The above saying attributed to Ḥallāj draws upon but reinterprets this "ask and be given" trope. It subverts the trope's basic premises, claiming that the Prophet remains too noble to request anything of his Lord. God rewards Muḥammad for his noble response, implying that the "requesting of needs"* (ṭalab al-ḥawāʾij) *would have tainted God's sanctified abode. The anecdote illustrates the Sufi concept of* tawakkul *or "trust in God," for Muḥammad shows that he is content with all that God has given him and does not desire anything else. This saying can be read, therefore, as an appropriation and subversion of the scene from the popular ascension accounts in which Muḥammad makes numerous intercessory requests during the ascension.*

Despite this saying's subversion of the "ask and be given" trope, a key section in the Ibn ʿAbbās ascension narrative, the saying nevertheless shows that by refusing to ask for favors, Muḥammad proves himself worthy to receive favors. Here God ends up richly rewarding Muḥammad in ways that are standard in the Ibn ᶜAbbās accounts. For instance, in the latter God grants all or part of the Qurᵓān to Muḥammad on the night of the ascension. Ibn ᶜAbbās' version frequently mentions that God gives Muḥammad that night specific sūras, such as the chapter of the Opening, or specific verses, such as the final verses of the chapter of the Cow.[126] *In the saying above, the allusion to Muḥammad being given "the proof"* (al-burhān, *one of the names for the Qurᵓān) suggests that he was presented with the entire Qurᵓān on the night of the ascension.* [127]

Similarly, the reference in the above saying to Muḥammad being given the power to decree the eschatological fate of anyone he wished presents a higher degree of intercession than that which appears in the majority of the ascension texts, for God usually reserves the ultimate authority to judge humanity for himself.[128] *In the face of this boon, here Muḥammad shows restraint in selecting only ten among the Quraysh to receive his immediate indulgence. This last anecdote, which is unknown in the majority of the extant Arabic ascension narratives, must have been relatively familiar to Ḥallāj's contemporaries, since the idea is mentioned here only in passing without giving further explication.*

The above saying illustrates how Muḥammad's unselfishness in asking for divine favors results in him receiving some of the ultimate divine gifts. It clearly depicts Muḥammad as "the most exalted mediator" between the divine and human realms. It furthermore demonstrates how Muḥammad's behavior on the night of the ascension embodies the Sufi values of humility, trust in God, and contentment.

50 - FROM FANCY TO REALIZATION

> Abū Saᶜīd Kharrāz (may God be compassionate to him) said, "Before he was caused to journey by night, the Prophet ﷺ used to imagine and suppose. But when he was caused to journey by night, he realized [the truth] about what he had imagined, and he witnessed what he had supposed. The Real also does this when he overcomes the attributes of the servant."

The above saying attributed to Kharrāz conveys two main ideas: first, that one of the purposes of the ascension was to give the Prophet an experiential rather than a theoretical or conjectural knowledge of the afterlife and otherworld; and second, that the mystical experience of the ordinary servant also provides a similar type of experiential knowledge. On its surface, the first idea does not offer any startling insights, for it stands to reason that the night journey and ascension presented Muḥammad with a more complete and concrete image of the otherworld than he had previously possessed. The two key verbs that Kharrāz uses to describe what Muḥammad got out of the experience, however, namely "he realized" (taḥaqqaqa) *and "he witnessed"* (shāhada), *present a more subtle insight into the resulting mystical state in which the divine Real became "realized."*

Such a mystical understanding of Kharrāz's saying gains support from the second and more controversial idea it offers, namely that "the servant" (al-ᶜabd) *also gains this level of insight when the Real overcomes* (ghalaba) *his or her attributes* (ṣifāt). *According to Kharrāz, it seems that the mystical state of* fanāʾ *is analogous to a heavenly ascension. Although nowhere in his work does Sulamī explicitly discuss the idea of mystical ascensions of non-prophetic individuals, the final statement in this saying leaves open the possibility for Sufis to claim to have obtained experiential knowledge of the otherworld and the divine reality through their own mystical experiences. A related idea appears in the text of Qushayrī's contemporary, Hujwīrī (d. ca. 469/1076), whose Per-*

sian treatise preserves the one of the earliest extant records of the alleged link between ritual prayer (ṣalāt) *and the experience of ascension.*[129]

51 - BURĀQ'S BEHAVIOR

I heard Ḥusayn b. [Yakhtar] say that he heard Ja^cfar Khuldī say that Jurayrī was asked, "Why was Burāq hard upon the Prophet ﷺ on the night of the night journey?" He replied, "Out of dread of him, and out of gladness for his riding upon him, honoring and blessing him."

Many narratives of the night journey contain an account of how Gabriel introduced Muḥammad to the fantastic riding beast Burāq, often described as a winged steed somewhat akin to the Greek Pegasus. Even some of the official narratives describe how Burāq shied away when Muḥammad first tried to touch the riding mount. The questioner here asks why Burāq behaved in such a manner, that is, why initially he acted difficult to control or ride. The response attributed here to Jurayrī claims that Burāq's behavior could be explained in two main ways, both of which focus upon Burāq's recognition of Muḥammad's exalted station.

Notably absent from Jurayrī's response is any sense that Burāq may initially have mistakenly believed that Muḥammad was not worthy of riding him. One finds the latter idea in both sound hadith reports and popular ascension narratives. A few of the popular accounts even describe a scene in which Burāq speaks with Gabriel about Muḥammad. In these scenes, Burāq either does not recognize Muḥammad as a prophet of God, or he suspects Muḥammad of being somehow tainted with a hint of impurity (e.g. complaining that Muḥammad recently touched an idol).[130] *Whatever the reason for Burāq's suspicion, Gabriel scolds Burāq, assuring him that Muḥammad is the most noble human being ever to ride upon him. In some of the sound hadith reports, Burāq begins to sweat after Gabriel scolds him, perhaps out of shame for not recognizing Muḥammad's exalted station from the outset.*

The idea that Burāq shied out of ignorance of Muḥammad's station is so well known that the above saying might be seen as a deliberate inversion of the standard interpretation of Burāq's behavior, attempting to emphasize how the Prophet's high status and Burāq's immediate recognition thereof led to his excited behavior.

This reverent attitude ascribed to Burāq in his first introduction to the Prophet becomes even more pronounced in a few popular texts from the middle and later periods of Islamic history. One narrative goes so far as to state that the Burāq was chosen out of thousands of possible other "Burāqs" to serve as the Prophet's mount on the night of the ascension, because its love of the Prophet was more intense than that of any other candidates.[131]

Figure 9: Riding Burāq.

52 - SPECIAL VIRTUES OF THE PROPHET

I heard Muḥammad b. ᶜAbd Allāh [Ibn Shādhān] say that he heard Abū ᶜUmar Dimashqī when he was asked what special virtues were given to the Prophet ﷺ on the night journey. He responded, "He showed his precedence over the totality, and he elucidated his correctness in dialoguing and witnessing."

Regarding the things that distinguish the Prophet on the night of the ascension, this saying suggests that the Prophet's special virtues (khaṣāʾiṣ) *were demonstrated that night by his unparalleled status and his ability to gaze upon and converse with the divinity. The reference above to Muḥammad's dialogue* (muḥāwara) *is left ambiguous. It could refer to the proper manner in which the Prophet conversed with the angels and the other prophets he encountered, but it also could refer to Muḥammad's intimate conversation with the deity on the night of the ascension. The phrase "his precedence over the totality"* (sabquhu ᶜalā al-kull) *in this saying is noteworthy. Whereas saying 44 portrays Muḥammad as a "witness to the totality," here Abū ᶜUmar Dimashqī portrays his "precedence over the totality," invoking the idea that the Prophet is the first being among all of creation, the best of all creatures. As in previous sayings, this saying distinguishes Muḥammad from the other prophets, who unlike him were not allowed to look directly at the divinity.*

53 - MASTER OF THE FOREFATHERS

Someone said, "Since the station of the Prophet ﷺ was more elevated than those of the other prophets عليهم السلام, he was hastened to types of abodes and bounties in the present that were delayed for other prophets until the afterlife. He was caused to journey by night, and he was shown [both] his station as distinct from their station, as well as his approach [to the divinity] as distinct from their approach."

"Through the reports about himself, he commanded the realities that he did not embellish. Thus he returned and said, 'I am the master of the children of Adam, which is no boast.'[132] That is, how could one whose glory is in his master boast about anything himself?"

The recurring theme of the Prophet's superiority to the other prophets forms the central focus of this saying. Similar to saying 44, the anonymous saying above claims that Muḥammad was given an early taste of the experience that other prophets will receive only later, either after their deaths or on the day of judgment. Muḥammad was shown how his station (maqām) *and his approach* (dunuww) *to the divinity contrast with, i.e. are superior to, those of the other prophets. The saying claims that Muḥammad did not embellish upon the realities* (ḥaqāʾiq), *meaning both that he told the truth about the realities (which he did not expand upon in an attempt to boast), and also that he genuinely experienced something of the divine realities that result from mystical experience.*

The above saying closes with reference to a hadith in which Muḥammad states upon his return, "I am the master (sayyid) *of the children of Adam, which is no boast* (fakhr)*." Only a few ascension narratives include a reference to this hadith in their accounts. Nevertheless, the anonymous speaker draws upon it here in order to support the idea that the ascension demonstrates Muḥammad's superiority to the rest of humanity, and to suggest that the reports about the Prophet's superiority do not mean that the Prophet was boasting. Although the Prophet is said to be the* *master of all humanity, the saying concludes with the message that the Prophet himself drew all his glory from his true master, namely the divinity. In contrast to the sayings that suggest that the ascension leads to union or divinization, this saying insists that Muḥammad's high status is merely the status that his divine master has granted him, a status that continually remains separate from and subordinate to that of the divinity.*

54 - THE REAL'S UNIQUE POWER

I heard ᶜAbd al-Wāḥid b. ᶜAlī [Sayyārī] say that he heard [Qāsim b. al-Qāsim] Sayyārī say that he heard Wāsiṭī say, "The Prophet ﷺ was uncertain about praise when the magnificent power and loftiness of God was unveiled to him and to no other. He knew that his praise would not correspond with the description of the Real, and that when the sayings of creatures exalt, they exalt the station of their [own] powers. So he restored the praise to the Real, and in the whole it returned to him in order to teach him that he alone had the power of his power."

That the presumed question here has to do with why the Prophet was ambiguous or uncertain about praising the divinity on the ascension becomes clear when one notices that the beginning of this saying closely resembles the response attributed to Ḥallāj in saying 40: "When he knew that praise, even if pure and plentiful, falls short of reaching the Real, that it returns nobility to the praiser not to the one praised, and that it shows the ability of its speaker and no other, his tongue once again faltered. Thus he said, 'I cannot enumerate the praise of you.'"[133] *The similarity between these two sayings is not all that surprising, especially since Wāsiṭī was said to have been one of those individuals who transmitted the teachings of Ḥallāj.*

Unlike in saying 40, however, here the emphasis lies not upon the idea of articulation but upon the idea of ability or power (qadr). *Muḥammad is said to have experienced the unveiling* (kashf) *of "the power of God"* (qadr Allah), *and this unveiling makes him realize that all human praise falls short of the Real. As in saying 40, here one finds the idea that praise reflects well on the one expressing the praising more than the one to whom the praise is addressed. Here there is an added mystical twist to the latter idea, however: insofar as the lover and the beloved have become one in mystical union, all praise ultimately returns to that one. The ambiguity of the third person singular masculine pronoun "he/it" once again plays a crucial role in this mystical reading of the text. In the totality of being or "the whole"* (al-kulliya), *it* (*the praise*) *or he* (*the lover*) *return to him* (*the one, the beloved, the Real*) *in order to teach a lesson.*

The final sentence of this saying heightens the tension introduced by the ambiguous pronouns, a tension allowing for multiple levels of interpretation. One who remains averse to the notion of mystical union can find in the final sentence an affirmation of Muḥammad's realization of the divine's utter transcendence and inaccessibility. On the other hand, one inclined to mystical speculation could understand the masculine pronouns in the final sentence to refer not to a multiplicity of subjects (*God teaching Muḥammad about divine power*) *but rather to the unity of the "Real." He alone, and none but he* (siwāhu), *has "the power of his power." To the degree that Muḥammad gives up praising, the power of the Real manifests itself. The final phrase of this saying thus underscores the theme of power that runs throughout this entire saying, implying that the unveiling of the power of the Real was not something witnessed from afar by an external created being, but something intimately experienced as he displayed it to him(self).*

55 - SPECIAL AND GENERAL VISION

> Abū Yazīd [Bisṭāmī] said, "The Prophet ﷺ guarded his glance during the night journey, so '*His sight did not waver nor did it exceed bounds*,'[134] because of his knowledge of what type of witnessing was worthy of him. In this [state] he did not witness a thing, nor did his glance wander toward anyone. Then when he was restored to the station of the teaching of propriety, he gazed at paradise, hellfire, the prophets, and the angels, [both] for the reports about them and the teaching of propriety to creatures through them. The first station is a special station, the second station is a general station."

Previous sayings have dealt with the issue of the Prophet's gaze on the night of the ascension. For instance, saying 42 draws upon the same qurʾānic verse quoted above in order to assert that the Prophet's gaze was unswerving, not attracted by created things. Approaching the issue from a different angle, saying 5 maintains that the Prophet was shown created things before his audience with the divinity in order to prepare him for the ultimate vision. The saying attributed to Abū Yazīd Bisṭāmī above discusses both the unswerving vision and the vision of created things as each forming a separate mystical station (maqām). *In contrast to saying 5, the above saying insists that Muḥammad was shown the created realms and beings only after his divine audience. The latter explains this second type of vision, which reflects a general rather than special station, through the Prophet's need to communicate something of his experience to humanity upon his return.*

The above saying discusses the idea that the Prophet, in addition to communicating to humanity through his hadith reports on the night journey and the ascension, teaches humanity moral lessons of propriety (adab) *through his narratives. This idea resembles a remark from saying 8 which states that the divinity "showed the Prophet in the station of servanthood in order that the proprieties* (ādāb) *of servanthood could be shown to the community." The above saying portrays the teaching of propriety* (taʾdīb) *as a sta-*

tion that is set apart from the mystical state of union in which no individuated created thing was witnessed.[135] *The idea of teaching propriety is also central to saying 5, which by contrast depicts the Prophet learning propriety through created things upon his ascent rather than the Prophet teaching propriety to humanity through created things after his descent. In each of these cases, however, the sayings explain the rationale behind the Prophet's depictions of his otherworldly visions by the value of these depictions for moral instruction.*

The exegetes distinguish this more general level of understanding of the night journey and ascension from a more specialized understanding which sees the journey as a process of mystical transformation, a process ultimately culminating with ecstatic union. In the latter station "he did not witness a thing," for there was nothing apart from the Real to witness. This station describes a special station (maqām khuṣūṣ) *that the uninitiated cannot comprehend.*

As in previous sayings, the saying above contains details that resemble the famous dream ascension that later becomes associated with Bisṭāmī himself.[136] *Here the resemblance can be seen in the way that the above saying describes how Muḥammad encountered the other prophets after his audience with the divinity, not before.*[137] *As the introduction to this work mentions,* The Subtleties of the Ascension *never explicitly discusses the idea that the Sufis could experience an ascension that resembles that of the Prophet, in a dream or otherwise. The fact that Sulamī relates a saying attributed to Bisṭāmī in this work without ever mentioning the notion that Bisṭāmī claimed to have had a similar experience could be explained in several ways: One might suppose that Sulamī was unaware of the claim attributed to Bisṭāmī, or that he was aware of the claim but disapproved of it, or that he was aware of the claim but felt that a reference to Bisṭāmī's account did not belong in a work devoted to the subtleties of Muḥammad's ascension.*

56 - AFTER THE NIGHT JOURNEY

Someone said, "He made little of new things after the night journey. When are the branches ever large in comparison with the roots? When is something new ever certain in comparison with something eternal?"

Although the night journey and ascension must have been transformative experiences for the Prophet Muḥammad, surprisingly few ascension narratives or prophetic hadiths discuss the manner in which the Prophet saw the world differently after returning from the journey.[138] *Most accounts instead detail how the journey served as a test of faith for the early Muslim community and as a controversial sign of Muḥammad's prophesy for the doubting Meccans, not as a transformative experience for the Prophet himself. In contrast, this saying suggests that the night journey and ascension served as a pivotal event in the Muḥammad's life, after which all other events appeared of little consequence in comparison.*

The above saying uses the opposition between small and large to juxtapose the relative value of several pairs of terms, the first such pair being the branches and the roots. New and passing events are analogous to branches, visible and wide-ranging, but ultimately less important than the foundational roots to the life of a tree. It is important to note that these two terms, branches (furūᶜ) *and roots* (uṣūl), *are key terms in the Islamic sciences and in Muslim systems of classification. Muslim scholars frequently reserve the term "roots" for the most basic and most critical matters in any particular system. With this metaphor, then, the anonymous commentator explains how the experience of ascension helped Muḥammad to get in touch with the beliefs and practices that matter most.*

The second pair of terms juxtaposed in the above saying comes in the opposition between the new or recent (ḥādith) *and the ancient or eternal* (qidam). *This pair had a significant technical meaning in Islamic science and philosophy, the former coming to represent an "accident," something created and contingent, the latter coming to represent a more essential quality, something "preexisting," necessary and eternal. This anonymous saying proposes that after Muḥammad was granted an experience of the foundational essence and eternity, the events of created existence no longer seemed so important to him.*[139] *The night journey taught the Prophet to give up the passing things of this world in favor of the eternal things of the next.*[140]

This final saying in The Subtleties of the Ascension *lacks any explicit reference to the Prophet. Certainly the "he" at the beginning of the saying will tend to be read as a reference to Muḥammad, the one whom Muslims understand as the "servant" referred to in the night journey verse, the one who was shown "some of the greatest signs of his Lord" (Q 17:1). The lack of an explicit and definite subject in this final saying, however, could convey the additional connotation that all who are touched by the events of the night journey, either through a familiarity with the Prophet's reports, or through their own mystical experiences, never see their worldly existence in the same way again.*

[CONCLUSION]

God's blessing and peace be upon Muḥammad
the pure prophet, and upon his family.

The end.

Praise be to God, Lord of the worlds.

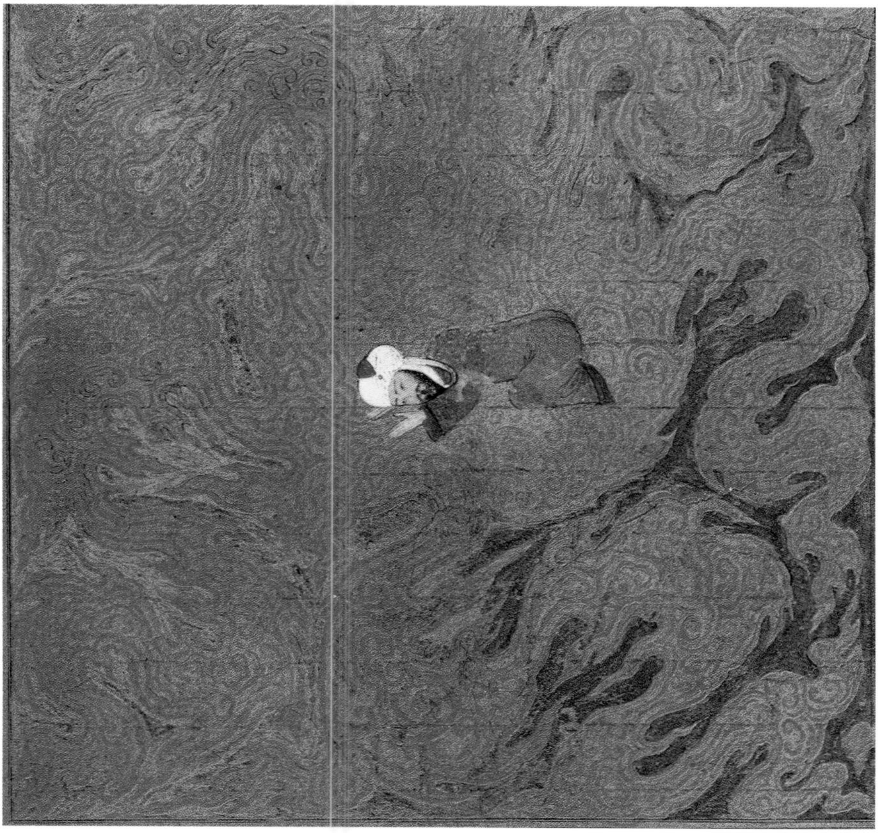

Figure 10: Muhammad bowing down at the Throne.

Arabic Text

of

The Subtleties of the Ascension

by

Abū ᶜAbd al-Raḥmān Sulamī

بسم الله الرحمن الرحيم حسبي ربي وبه توفيقي

مسألة بيان لطائف المعراج

الحمد لله رب العالمين أولاً وآخراً وصلى الله على محمد وآله وسلم كثيراً
سألت أسعدك الله بالتوفيق عن إفادة حكماء الأمة في مسرى النبي صلى الله عليه وسلم
ليلة المعراج من دقائق المعاني وحقائق الأحوال فجمعت لك من ذلك فصولاً
بقدر وسعي وطاقتي بعد أن استخرت الله تعالى فيه واستعنته عليه وهو حسبي ونعم المعين

قال الله سبحانه وتعالى سبحان الذي أسرى بعبده

قال الواسطي رحمه الله نزه نفسه أن يكون لأحد في تسييره بعبده صلى الله عليه وسلم
حركة أو خطرة فيكون شريكاً في الإسراء والتسيير وقال ابن عطاء نزه مكان القربة
وموقف الدنو عن أن يكون فيه تأثير لمخلوق بحال فأسرى بنفسه وسرى بروحه
وسيّر بسره فلا السر علم ما فيه الروح ولا الروح علم ما شاهد السر ولا النفس
عنده شيء من خبرهما وما هما فيه وكل واقف مع حده مشاهد للحق متلقٍ منه
بلا واسطة ولا بقاء البشرية بل حق تحقق بعد تحقيقه وأقامه حيث لا مقام
وخاطبه وأوحى إليه ما أوحى جل ثناؤه وتعالى ○ سمعت منصور بن عبد الله يقول
سمعت أبا القاسم البزاز يقول قال ابن عطاء في قوله ما كذب الفؤاد ما رأى قال ما اعتقد القلب خلاف
ما رأت العين وقيل قال ابن عطاء البشر كل من رأى منكر فؤاده إذ ذاك العيان قد
يظهر فيضطرب السر عن حمل الوارد عليه والرسول صلى الله عليه وسلم محمول
فيما في فؤاده عن غلبة حسه ونظره وهذا دال على صدق طويته وحمله لما
شهده به ○ سمعت أبا القاسم النصراباذي يقول أسقط الحق أدنى جميع الأغيار
والشواهد عن المعراج بقوله أسرى ولم يقل سرى إذ القدرة والربوبية لا
تحد فيها ولا للحق منها ○

وسئل بعضهم لم اري النبي صلى الله عليه وسلم ليلة المعراج الجنة والنار والانبيا
والملائكة قبل الدنو من الحق فقال ليتادب بها لمكان التمكين فان محمد
الكون ما يحجبه في عز ولا شئ وكرامتهما ولولا ذلك ما شغف لشئ ولكان
يرانيه شئ من جوانبه توهما فلما تفرد بشاهده عن الشواهد كان ما سواه
اقل من كل حسن حتى عرض على النبي صلى الله عليه وسلم الاكوان حتى كلم الانبيا
والملائكة صلوات الله عليهم فلما علم انه ليس المراد منه ذلك غمض البصر عن
الاكوان وما فيها واخذ في التزام ادب المشاهدة حتى دنا فتدلى فاوحى الى عبده
ما اوحى ۝ وقيل للواسطي ما الذي كانت همة النبي صلى الله عليه وسلم من ربه
ليلة المعراج فقال البشر لباس نعته واذن له في المشاهدة وخاطبه بالمكافحة
وقيل للنوري من الحشمين ما الذي اطاق النبي عليه السلم في المعراج المشاهدة فقال لم
يزل يشهد عليه من بر الحق به على الدوام فمكنه ذلك من مشاهدة البارئ ۝ لمعنى
محمد عبد الله وسئل بعضهم ما المعاني ما الحكمة في المعراج فقال ابو بكر ابن الله تعالى
ان يرفع حال الحبيب صلى الله عليه وسلم عن محل العبودية الى محل الازلية وينقله من محل الازلية
الى محل الربوبية فاظهر النبي صلى الله عليه وسلم في محل العبودية ليظهر اداب العبودية
للامة ثم نقله الى مقام الازلية ليتادب بها من هو دون ذلك المقام ثم نقله الى مقام
الربانية وهو المعراج الذي اسري به اليه فازيل عنه اذ ذاك المقامات والرسوم
ونقل الى المقام الذي حل فيه من الدنو والقرب ۝ وسئل بعضهم لم لم يسجد النبي صلى الله عليه وسلم
عند سدرة المنتهى فقال لان السجود رؤية النفس واظهار العبودية وتعظيم الحق
وكان هو في محل الفنا من اوصافه لم يبق له بقية الحقيقة عند مشاهدة الحق فاني
يكون له التفات الى السجود او فراغ له ۝ وسئل الحسين بن منصور لم لم يلتفت محمد
صلى الله عليه وسلم في المعراج الى الاكوان فقال لانه لاحظ الاشيا بعين الله تعالى
ومن لاحظها كذلك لا يرى شيا غير الله ۝

وقال الحسين المغربي لا يخبر عن مشاهدة بشكل الهام الحدث وإذا اظهر من الربانية
فبينا احكام البشرية الا ترى ان محمدا صلى الله عليه وسلم لما ظهر بلبسة الالهية كيف
يخرجه على السلام مع عظيم محله عن رؤيته وحجته فقال لو يدنو اعلمه اجاز فيه
وقال جعفر الصادق رضي الله عنه ادنى الحق الى حسبه محمدا صلى الله عليه وسلم من نفسه
بقوله دنا فتدلى بلا كيفية لانه اخرجه من حدود الكيف واواه في مواقف لا متشابه
وصف له والدنو من الحق لا حد له ولا نهاية به وقال ادناه الى ما اودع في قلبه
من المعرفة والايمان فتدلى فسكن قلبه الى ما ادناه وزال عن قلبه الشك والارتياب متشابه
وسئل بعضهم لم لم يسجد محمد صلى الله عليه وسلم عند سدرة المنتهى ويسجد في القيمة عند الشفاعة
للخلق فقال لاجل ان كان عوضا من ذلك السجود شفاعة فيما لا وزن له ولا قيمة ولان الحاجة
توجب التضرع الا ترى موسى عليه السلام كيف لم يسجد عند المخاطبة لما اظلته من شهود الموقف
فالقوم اداب العبودية ولان الجواد السخي بقوته استحي ان يسجدوا له متشابه
عن العلم في ذلك المقام عن العالم بشرط العبودية لذلك لم يسجد محمد صلى الله عليه وسلم
عند سدرة المنتهى ولا موسى عليه السلام عند الكلام ⊙ وقال الجنيد رحمه الله انما بلغ
النبي صلى الله عليه وسلم ليلة المعراج الى حد لا عبارة عنه ولا وصف له الجاد في ذكر المشهد ⊙
بالواحد الاحد والابهام ما جرى فيه ولسكون النبي صلى الله عليه وسلم وترك الاخبار عنه
وسئل الجنيد عن قوله فاستطال وما كنت بجانب الطور اذ نادينا اذ نادى موسى عليه السلام
لانه كان وراء الحجاب ونادى محمدا صلى الله عليه وسلم لانه خرق الحجب ومن كان وراء الحجاب
نودي ومن جاوز الحجاب نوجي ومن قطع عن كل المقامات اواه الله وانشرفه على
الاكوان الا ترى ان محمدا صلى الله عليه وسلم شغل فيما يختصم الملا الاعلى بقى فلما وقع عليه
انوار صفاته وعراه من صفته كيف ذاق عن الاماكن كلها واحتبت عنها ⊙
وقال ابو سعيد الخراز امر النبي صلى الله عليه وسلم بالدعا بقوله رب زدني علما
وكان فوادي من الهموم بالوسواس والشهوات فلما

اجرى على لسانه هذا الدعا استجيب له ذلك من غير غيبة منه لم ولا ظلمه بل لاظهار
فضله لعروجه به الى المحل الادنى والمقام الارفع حيث انقطع عنه علوم الخلق
اجمع وصار في محل الدنو لخاطب ويخاطب من غير واسطة بل كفاحا
فايد في ذلك المقام بالثبات واكرم بهذه العلوم التي لم تعلمه احد
من الخلق وذلك المقام اشبه شيء عندي بالمقام المحمود لانه مستور بين
ربه وبين حبيبه لم يطلع عليه احد ٥ وسئل الواسطي عن دنو النبي صلى الله عليه وسلم
في المستوى فقال حجبه عن نفسه ودنا به منه اليه فتدلى حماز الله الحجب تدلى
عن محمد صلى الله عليه وسلم حتى ادرك الحال اشار اليه من قوله فكان قاب قوسين او ادنى
وذلك بقوة الانوار التي البس محمدا صلى الله عليه وسلم في حال مسيره ولولا ما جلي
به من رفع الصفة عليه والباسه الانوار المخصوصة لاحرقته انوار ذلك المقام حتى
لم يمكنه ان يحمل عليه الى الدنو منها الا ما عبر عنه البشر الحبيب عليهما السلم ٥
وقال جعفر الصادق رضي الله عنه من توهم انه بنفسه دنا جعل ثم مسافة انما
التدلي انه كلما قرب منه بعده عن انواع المعارف اذ لا دنو ولا بعد وكلما دنا
بنفسه من الحق تدلى بعدا فاعلم في الحقيقة خاسئا وهو حسير اذ لا سبيل الى
مطالعة الحقيقة حقيقة واما الاخبار عن محل الكرامه والفضل فاز الحق
احد من انبيايه فاشهدوا اياه وكان في الحقيقة ذاته منشا هدا آيته وفي
الاخبار عن محمد صلى الله عليه وسلم لما وسمه به من المحل الشريف والموقف المنيف ٥
بعد الجسمين يقول بعد جعفر محمد يقول بعد الجنيد يقول لنبيه المعراج البشر محمد
صلى الله عليه وسلم لبشته خصه بها من بين الخلايق اجمع فعجز عنها حتى حل صلوات الله عليهما
نور اعلمه لاحترقت ٥ فتلك البشه انه عمرة في انوار ولطايف من جميع
صفاته فاطاق الهجوم على الكلام والمشاهده والمراجعه والتلقف من
ذي جلاله وزينته بانوار صفاته

الحق التحيات فقابله الحق بالتحيات اجمع لا التحية واحده ثم لقنه بان قابل
الحق بمثله فقال بل التحيات والمباركات والطيبات لله لانك اهل لذلك ٥
فهذا العصمه الفرق بين كلام محمد صلى الله عليه وسلم في السما السابعه وكلام
موسى عليه السلم على الطور ان موسى عليه السلم لم يبق من معانيه الا الصواعق فلم
يبق من القوه ما يحتمل اشارات الذات وايد محمد صلى الله عليه وسلم بروية
السموات والارضين ووضع الكف فما طاف بعدها كل وارد وورد على سره من امور ربه ٥
وقد فاق هو بجود صفات جبريل عليه السلم مع نقابها الحق عن صفات محمد صلى الله عليه وسلم
وهو فاني بالحق حين اخبر عنه بقوله لقد راى من ايات ربه الكبرى وانما عاد عليه كبرى لانه
مبالغه في الكبر وليس بعد المبالغه غايه وانما صادف آية لانه تجلى بكمال الجلال
فلما استوفاه نفت الجلال عن بقية غيبه مكتوب ومنع جبريل عليه السلم من النهوض اليه
لانه لم يمده بما حمله نبيه وايد محمد عليه السلم بما حمله فيما استوفاه وكان القامين
له وليه واحدهما اعانه والاخر كشف ٥ سمعت محمد بن عبد الله يقول قال
الحسين بن منصور قد الخليل عليه السلم منك الحق فابلاه بالنار وقد الكليم منك الملك
فابلاه بالبحر وقد محمد صلى الله عليه وسلم منك الملك فابلاه بالمسرى ٥ سمعت
النصراباذي يقول سمعت ابن عطاء يقول سمعت ابا سعيد القرشي يقول تجلى الله تعالى
لنبينا محمد صلى الله عليه وسلم بصفة الكرم والجمال وكلمه بالايناس عند سدره المنتهى
وقابله بالبر واللطف فزاد لطفا بالايناس وبرا ورافه وشفاعه ٥
وكشف لموسى عليه السلم بصفه الهيبه والاجلال فمن هناك بدا موسى عليه السلم
غلطا او شكا ٥ وسئل جعفر الصادق عن قوله ثم دنا فتدلى فقال المادح
الحبيب من الحبيب بغاية القرب بالشي غايه الهيبه والطف الحق بغايه
اللطف لانه لا يحتمل غايه الهيبه الا غايه اللطف وذلك قوله فاوحى الى عبده ما اوحى
اي كان ما كان وجرى ما جرى وقال الحسين للحبيب ما يقول الحبيب للحبيب والطف

[illegible] الكف
مسايله

به الطاف الحبيب بالحبيب واشار اليه ما يبهم الحبيب الى الحبيب

فاخفيا ولم يطلعا على سرهما احدا اشار اليهما لذلك قوله فاوحى الى عبده

ما اوحى ولم يعلم احد ما اوحى الا الذي اوحى واوحى اليه وذلك دلالة على

غاية البر ثم قال ما كذب الفواد ما راى بل صدق الفواد ما راى ولم

يعلم احد ما راى الا الذي ارى والذي راى فصار الحبيب الى الحبيب قريبا وله

نجيا وبه انيسا حتى صار والطاف الله عز وجل تهمع درجات من نيشان ○

وقال بعضهم قطع الحق سر محمد صلى الله عليه وسلم عن الاغيار اجمع فنظر الى ربه بعين

البصر وتحقق بانوار الحق حتى غاب له عين البصر حق البصر فتحمل مكافحة

المخاطبة بقوله اوحى الى عبده ما اوحى ولما ادناه فتدلى اراه هو بنفسه فانا عنه

انبيته واسقط عنه اثاره وحلاه بانواره واطاف شهود تلك المشاهده

ولم ير نورا يعلو فاوق نوره فيشغله فلذلك ما هاله شي ولا استوحش شيئا

بعد ما شاهد ما حكى الله تعالى عنه في قوله لقد راى من ايات ربه الكبرى وقوله تعالى

ما زاغ البصر وما طغى ان الحق نوره وصفاته ○ وقال ابو محمد الجريري رحمه الله

لما نظر المصطفى صلى الله عليه وسلم الى الحق بالحق راى الحق بالحق فبقي مع الحق بالحق بغير ظرف

ولا في مكان لانه حصل مع من لا زمان له ولا مكان فغيبوي عن اوصافه باوصاف

الحق فلم يكن له في تلك الحال تفقد ولا علم ولا اشارة ولا بيان حتى رده الحق الى صفته

وعيبوي ظاهره من الانوار التي ستر عليه واسترى اليه رد الشبح الى صفة

لقيامه بمفروض سالته وحمل الشر في العصره لذلك ستر ما جرى من ذلك المشهد

وقال واوحى الى عبده ما اوحى ○ وسئل الحسين بن منصور عن حقائق الصلوة فقال

خاطب الله تعالى نبيه صلى الله عليه وسلم بالصلوة في المشهد الاعلى فقال يا رب

ما الذي لي من اقامة الصلوة انما اتباع امري واجتناب نهيي فقال وما لي فيه

فهذا ثناء عليك في اتباع الامر وشكري لك في اجتناب النهي فقال ان اثنيت
اثنيت على خلقك وان شكرت شكرت احسانك وليس للعبد معك مقام في هذين
وسال بعضهم لما دار النبي صلى الله عليه وسلم في المعراج انا لك كان الجواب من جهة الحق
ان كنت لي فانا لك اذ اللام في الباء بمعنى قيام فمن كان الله نعته كان الباء صفته
وسال بعضهم لما ابقى الحق محمدا صلى الله عليه في الثناء عليه عما زحاف الشرايف
مشاهدات الاعيان صفا هو عن التمني والاعتراض والدعا فقابل محل الدعا بالسما
فقال سبحان الله وقابل محل طلب الاعواض بالاشيا والى المستوحض وذلك المقام
في الدهور والاوساط الفنا عنها والبقا بموجدها فلما كان هذا المحل قرب
وادنى وتدلى عليه من انوار الصفات ما هو غيبة لبساط التمكين فشاهد الحق مشاهدة
وقرب حتى افنى بالقرب عن محل القرب ورحمن اذن له في العروج فشارك الدهش
الروح بما لم يزل به مختصا من بين الارواح وابصرت النفس ما لم تزل القلب فيما
والسر له مستبرا وصعق له عن محل ما كذب الفواد ما راى لم يكذب الفواد الدهش
شاهد ان بعض عبد الله محمد الدمشقي يقول سالت بعض مشايخنا من اهل الاشام
هل يرى ان مرتبة محمد صلى الله عليه وسلم في الفضل مرتبة غيره من الانبيا عليهم السلام
فقال ابو ادرى مرتبة محمد صلى الله عليه وسلم مرتبته مالك معرفة ولا سبيل لها
لا تدري مرتبته مرتبتهم وهو في الحضرة في المشاهدة ولم يبرح على مشاهدة
الروح والسر حتى ادني وكلم ونوجي واسقط عنه التوقف والهموم وقام
مع الحق ادنى مقام يمكن القيام فيه والعبارة عنه ليلة المعراج فكان قاب قوسين او ادنى
وفي ما كذب الفواد ما راى لن يسل بعضهم ما كانت الفائدة في المعراج ولم بعث النبي صلى الله عليه وسلم
عن الحضرة بل شاهد المغيبات بحقايق الايمان فقال كان محمد صلى الله عليه وسلم
الحبيب وكان من اشد الخلق شوقا اليه حتى خلق محبته فعلمه الحق

شوقه اليه فلما صعد عن مشاهدته بتجلي ذلك قبل جميع الانبيا عليهم السلام
والرسل صلوات الله عليهم ما زاده ذلك الا شوقا اليه والانزعاج لما حصل
كبير اختيار وقال ابن الاخص الاعلى ۝ وسمعت ابا علي احمد بن علي الشاشي
يقول سمعت فارس البغدادي يقول سمعت قيمد يقول اقام الحق الخلق منه على مراتب فالاكثر
المحجوب منهم عليهم القبض وللانبيا صلوات الله عليهم عين القبض ولمحمد صلى الله عليه وسلم
حق القبض فتراهم اهل المعرفة على القبض وانقبضوا ما علموا و وصل الانبيا عليهم السلام
الى عين القبض وشاهدوا منها حقيقة القبض ونبي محمد صلى الله عليه وسلم عن اوصافه
وكشف له حقائق الحق في روح حق القبض وذلك المقام الذي لا وراه مقام ۝ وقال
الصوفي رحمه الله شاهد الحق الخلق فلم ير قلبا اشوق اليه من قلب محمد عليه السلام
فاكرمه بالمعراج بتعجيل الرويه والمكالمه فلما اوصل الى ذلك المشهد العظيم صغرت ۝
الاكوان في عينه حتى لم يلتفت الى شي ولم يستحسن شيا والعظمة للمقصود الذي قصده
وسئل بعضهم لم انبسط النبي صلى الله عليه وسلم في القبه اذا انقبضت الانبيا عليهم السلام
وانقبضوا فقال لانه ازال عنه الانقباض موقفه في المعراج ومكالمته مع الحق
ومخاطبته فلم يدهشه الموقف لما شاهد قبل ذلك من عظيم الجلال ولا الانبيا عليهم السلام
بشر جهوا فشكلوا وانقبضوا ۝ سمعت محمد بن عبد الله يقول سمعت علي بن محمد الطلبي
يقول قال ابو سعيد الخراز بلغ محمد صلى الله عليه وسلم من المحبة المنتهى فطلع به في الدنو
المنتهى والله تعالى فكان قاب قوسين او ادنى وذلك حين بلغ مقام القدر ورا
قدامه بخال لم يستوي عن جميع ما يلتبس به العوام والبشر خصائص الخلق ثم
اثنى عليه بقوله وانك لعلى خلق عظيم وسال العصيم ان الله تعالى اراد ان يشهد بانوار محمد
صلى الله عليه وسلم السموات كما اشرق بركاته الارضين فسرى به الى المعراج ۝ وسئل
ابو العباس الدينوري لم اسري بالنبي صلى الله عليه وسلم اولا الى بيت المقدس قبل ان
عرج به الى السما فقال عليه السلام الله تعالى

ان كفار قريش يكذبونه فيما يخبرهم من اخبار السما فاراد ان يخبرهم بخبر
من الارض قد بلغوها وعاينوها ليعلموا ان النبي صلى الله عليه وسلم لم يدخل بيت
المقدس قط فلما اخبرهم باخبار بيت المقدس لم يمكنهم ان يكذبوه في اخبار السما
بعد ان صدقوه في اخبار الارض ○ وسمعت منصور بن عبد الله يقول سمعت ابا القسم
يقول سئل الواسطي لم اسرى بالنبي صلى الله عليه وسلم الى بيت المقدس قبل المعراج فقال
اراد الحق تعالى ان الخلق يرونه فاضله عن مشهده ووطى قدمه بها فيتم تقديس
البيت المقدس بصلاة محمد صلى الله عليه وسلم فيه فلما تم تقديسه به اخبر
النبي صلى الله عليه وسلم انه لا تشد الرحال الا الى ثلاث مساجد مسجد الحرام لانه
مولده ومسقط راسه وموضع نبوته ومسجد المدينة لانه مسجد هجرته وموضع تربته
ومسجد الاقصى لانه ارض مسراه وموضع معجزته ذكر الله تعالى كمال الاسرى بعبده
ليلا من المسجد الحرام الى المسجد الاقصى ○ وسئل بعضهم لما بلغ محمد صلى الله عليه وسلم الى
المنتهى في الدنو من الحق لم يظهر الانبساط والجرأة فلم يحتشم بشيء مما عاين ولم
ينبسط به وما رجع رجوعه الا تعلمون ما اعلم واني في ذلك المشهد باظهار العجز
فقال اعوذ بك منك لا احصي ثناء عليك انت كما اثنيت على نفسك ○ وسئل الحسين بن منصور
لم ابهم المصطفى صلى الله عليه وسلم الثناء في المعراج ○ فقال لما علم ان الثناء
وان صفا وكثر يكون قاصرا عن بلوغ الحق وانه راجع الى المثني شرعه لا الى
المثنى عليه وان فيه اظهار قدر قائله لا غير رجع الى البيان بالعجز فقال لا
احصي ثناء عليك ○ وسئل بعضهم لم انبسط المصطفى صلى الله عليه وسلم ليلة
المعراج بالسؤال لله دون الكلام على بساط القرب اذ لم يغبه حيرة او
المشاهدة وانما حضر المكالمة فانبسط في الشفاعة والسؤال ○

وقال [illegible] لما أكرم محمد صلى الله عليه وسلم بأعظم الشهود والمسرى علت
همته عن الالتفات الى الآيات والكرامات والجنة والنار فما زاغ البصر أي
ما أعار طرفه شيئا من الألوان ومن شاهد البحر استقل الأودية والأنهار
وسئل الواسطي لم أبهم النبي صلى الله عليه وسلم الثناء فقال الثناء للإلهية [illegible]
لم يبلغ حقيقة الثناء فالعجز عن الثناء ثناء وبعد منصور عبد الله يقول
سئل أبو بكر طاهر عن عروج النبي صلى الله عليه وسلم دون سائر الأنبياء عليهم السلام
فقال لأحوال أحدها أنه كان صاحب الشفاعة في القيمة فشوهد قبل أن لا
يقع له حشمة البداهة كما يقع لغيره من الأنبياء والثاني كان صاحب المقام المحمود
فأراد الحق عز وجل أن يسكن عنه قبل ذلك مقام الانقباض ليتمكن في المقام المحمود
فأقله قبل الملأ الأعلى للمشاهدة والكلام ثم رفعه الى مكان لا مكان والثالث أنه
بعد مكانه ولا مقام وراء مقامه ليكون مشاهد الكل فينتصر عن المشهد
الأعلى للشفاعة والتمكن في المقام المحمود وبعد منصور عبد الله يقول
سئل الشبلي كيف ثبت النبي صلى الله عليه وسلم في المعراج للقاء والمخاطبة فقال إنه
هيئ لأمر فمكن فيه وقال في كتاب [illegible] الجنيد [illegible] سئل أبو عمرو
عن قول النبي صلى الله عليه وسلم لا أحصي ثناء عليك أنت كما أثنيت على نفسك فقال ما زال
النبي صلى الله عليه وسلم كان [illegible] غائبا ومثنيا على ربه فلما غاب به ليلة المسرى
فشاهد ما شاهد من عظمة ربه استحيا مما أثنى ودعا فرجع الى لسان
العجز فقال لا أحصي ثناء عليك وقال النوري [illegible] هون عليه سكرات الموت
ما رأى من لطف ربه في المسرى وقال [illegible] الأفق الأعلى لما اختير أي وهل المختار من
شاهد ما شاهد [illegible] إلا الأفق الأعلى المسرى أدناني وقربني

سمعت أبا بكر الرازي رحمه الله يقول سمعت أبا العباس بن عطاء لما أراد الحق تعالى أن يكون
صفيه وحبيبه أبعد الخلق ذكرا وأكرمهم قدرا وأرفعهم فخرا وأشرفهم
قدرا وأسناهم رتبة عرج به إلى السموات وأشرفه على الملكوت وزينه
بخلع الدنو فأدناه من بساط القرب حتى عجز عن ذكر الملك والأنبياء لنبوه
بذكره في سمواته كما جعل ذكره في أرضه ٥ قال الحسين منصور لما دنا الشخص
الأعلى من الحق المستتر امتنع فقال سل تعط فقال ماذا أسأل وقد أعطيت
وماذا أبتغي وقد كفيت [illegible] ولك على خلق [illegible] حتى [illegible] بساط [illegible]
طلب الحوائج وأعطى إذ ذاك البرهان وأطلق له في الحكم لمن شاء بإحدى الدارين
وجمع إلى شهود الإيجاد وحكم لعشرة من قريش بالجنة ٥ وقال أبو سعيد الخراز رحمه الله
إن النبي صلى الله عليه وسلم لما أسري به [illegible] ونطق فلما أسري به [illegible] فيما
توهم وشاهد ما نطق وكذلك [illegible] إذا عاد على صفات العبد ٥ سمعت
الحسن [illegible] يقول سمعت جعفر الخلدي يقول سمعت الجنيد [illegible] البراق على النبي صلى الله عليه
[illegible] المسرى فقال هيبة له [illegible] إياه [illegible] سمعت محمد بن عبد الله
يقول سمعت أبا عمر الدمشقي يقول ما كان للنبي صلى الله عليه وسلم من الخصائص في المسرى فقال
أظهر شرفه على الكل وبين له استطالته للمجاورة والمشاهدة ٥ وقال
بعضهم لما كان مقام النبي صلى الله عليه وسلم أرفع من مقامات الأنبياء عليهم السلام
عجل له من أنواع المبار والكرامة في العاجل ما كان مدخرا لغيره من الأنبياء
في الآجل فأسري به وأري مقامه من مقاماتهم ودنوه من دنوهم وأمره بالأخبار عن
نفسه بحقائق ما زين به وجمع فقال أنا سيد ولد آدم ولا فخر أي ولكن يفتخر بمن
كان فخره بسيده ٥ سمعت عبد الواحد بن علي يقول سمعت الشيباني يقول سمعت
قول شيخ الشيباني يقول سمعت الواسطي يقول إن النبي صلى الله عليه وسلم

الثناء لما كوشف له من عظيم قدر الله وجلاله ما لم يكشف لغيره

فعلم أن ثناءه لا يقابل بصفة الحق وأن أقوال الخلق وإن علت فعلى

قدر أقدارهم فرد الثناء إلى الحق ورجع في الكلية إليه لعلمه بأن قدره

لا يقدر سواه ٥ قال أبو بكر حفظ النبي صلى الله عليه وسلم طرفه في المسرى

فما زاغ ولا طغى لعلمه بما يؤهل له من المشاهدة فلم يشاهد في ذلك شيئا ولم

يعر طرفه أحدا ثم لما رد إلى العالم للتأديب نظر إلى الجنة والنار

والأنبياء والملائكة للإخبار عنها وتأديب الخلق بها فالمقام الأول مقام

خصوص والمقام الثاني مقام عموم ٥ قال بعضهم استصغر الحوادث بعد

المشهد ومتى تعظم الفروع في مقابلة الأصول ومتى يلتفت الحدث في مقابلة

القدم وصلى الله على محمد النبي المصطفى وآله وسلم تسليما

آخره والحمد لله رب العالمين

[illegible]

قال الحكيم رحمة الله عليه

إن الله سبحانه وتعالى جعل لكل شيء سببا وجعل الأسباب معادن الوجود

فمن شهد السبب انقطع عن المسبب ومن شهد صنع المسبب في السبب

أوصله مشاهدة صنع المسبب في السبب إلى المسبب ٥

بسم الله الرحمن الرحيم حسبي ربي وبه توفيق

مسألة بيان لطائف المعراج

الحمد لله رب العلمين اولا واخرا وصلى الله على محمّد واله وسلم كثيرا

[المقدمة]

سألت أسعدك الله بالتوفيق عما قالة حكماء الأمة في مسرى النبي صلى الله عليه وسلم ليلة المعراج من دقائق المعاني وحقائق الاحوال فجمعت لك من ذلك فصولا بقدر وسعي وطاقتي بعد أن إستخرت الله تعالى فيه وإستنعمته عليه وهو خير ونعمة للمؤمن.

(١)

قال الله سبحانه وتعالى
«سبحان الذي أسرى بعبده».

قال الواسطي رحمه الله نزه نفسه أن
يكون لأحد في تسيير نبيه صلى الله عليه وسلم
حركة او خطرة فيكون شريكا في الإسراء
والتسيير.

(٢)

قال ابن عطاء [طهر] مكان القربة
وموقف الدنو عن أن يكون فيه تأثير لمخلوق بحال
فأسرى بنفسه وسرى بروحه وسير بسره فلا السر
علم ما في الروح ولا الروح علم ما شاهد السر ولا
النفس عند[ها] شيء من خبرهما وما هما فيه
وكل واقف مع حده مشاهد للحق متلقف [عنه]
بلا واسطة ولا بقاء البشرية بل حق تحقق بعبده
فحققه وأقامه حيث لا مقام وخاطبه وأوحى إليه
ما أوحى جل ربنا وتعالى.

(٣)

سمعت منصور[بن] عبد اللّه يقول سمعت
أبا القسم البزاز يقول قال إبن عطاء في قوله ما
كذب الفؤاد ما رأى قال ما إعتقد القلب خلاف ما
[رأته] العين قال و قال إبن عطاء ليس كل من
رأى مكّن فؤاده [من ادراكه] اذ بالعيان قد يظهر
فيضطرب السرّ عن حمل الوارد عليه والرسول
(صل) محمول فيها في فؤاده و عقله وحسّه
ونظره وهذا يدل على صدق طويته وحمله فيما
شوهد به.

(٤)

سمعت أبا القسم النصراباذي يقول أسقط الحق تعالى جميع الإعتراضات والشبهات عن المعراج بقوله أسرى ولم يقل سرى اذ القدرة والربوبية لا عجب فيها ولا تعجب منها.

(٥)

وسئل بعضهم لم أرى النبي (صل) ليلة
المعراج الجنة والنار والانبياء والملائكة قبل الدنوّ
من الحق فقال لتأدب بها بمكان التمكين فإنّه حجب
الكون بما حجب به في عرش وكرسي وعمدهما ولو
لا ذاك ما ثبت له شيء ولكان يدانيه شيء في
معاينة توهما فلما تفرد بشاهده عن الشواهد كان
ما سواه اقل من كل حس لحسس فعُرض على
النبي (صل) الاكوان حتى كلم الانبياء والملائكة
(صلوات الله عليهم) فلما علم أنه ليس المراد منه
ذلك غمض البصر عن الاكوان وما فيها وأخذ في
إلتزام أدب المشاهدة حتى «دنا فتدلى واوحى الى
عبده ما اوحى».

(٦)

وقيل للواسطي ماذا كانت هدية النبي (صل) من ربّه ليلة المعراج فقال ألبسه لباس نعته وأذن له في المشاهدة وخاطبه بالمكافحة.

(٧)

وقيل ليوسف بن الحسين بماذا أطاق النبي (عليه السلام) في المعراج المشاهدة فقال لم يزل [يريد] عليه من برّ الحقّ به على الدوام فمكّنه ذلك من مشاهدة البار.

(٨)

سمعت محمد بن عبد الله قال سئل محمد بن موسى [بن] الفرغاني [الواسطي]: ما الحكمة في المعراج فقال أراد الله تعالى أن يرفع حال الحبيب (صل) عن محل العبودية الى محل الازلية ومن محل الازلية الى محل الربوبية فأظهر النبي (صل) في محل العبودية ليظهر آداب العبودية للأمة ثم نقله الى مقام الازلية ليتأدب بها من هو في ذلك المقام ثم نقله الى مقام الربانية وهو المعراج الذي أسرى به اليه فأزيل عنه إذ ذاك المقامات والرسوم ونقل الى المقام الذي خلق من الدنو والقرب.

بسم الله الرحمن الرحيم حسبي ربي وبه توفيق

مسألة بيان لطائف المعراج

الحمد لله رب العلمين اولا واخرا وصلى الله على محمّد واله وسلم كثيرا

(١٠)

سئل الحسين بن منصور لِم لم يلاحظ محمد (صل) في المعراج الاكوان فقال لأنه لاحظ الاشياء بعين الله تعالى ومن لاحظها كذا لا يرى شيئا غير الله.

(١ ١)

وقال الحسين: البشرية لا تعجز عن مشاهدة شكلها من الحدث واذا أظهرت الربانية فنيت أحكام البشرية ألا ترى أن محمدا (صل) لما ظهر بلبسة الالهية كيف عجز جبريل (عليه السلام) مع عظم محله عن رؤيته وصحبته فقال لو دنوت أنملة لاحترقت.

(١٢)

وقال جعفر الصادق (رضي الله عنه) أدنى الحق تعالى حبيبه محمدا (صل) من نفسه بقوله دنى فتدلى بلا كيفية لأنه أخرجه من حدود الكيف واواه في [موقف] لا وصف له والدنو من الحق لا حد له ولا نهاية وقال أدناه الى ما اودع في قلبه من المعرفة والايمان فتدلى فسكن قلبه الى ما ادناه وزال عن قلبه الشك والإرتياب.

(١٣)

وسئل بعضهم لِما لم يسجد محمد (صل) عند
سدرة المنتهى، ويسجد في القيامة عند الشفاعة
للخلق فقال لا جرم كان عوض ذاك السجود شفاعة
فيما لا وزن له ولا قيمة ولأن الحاجة يوجب
التضرع ألا ترى موسى (عليه السلام) كيف لم
يسجد عند المخاطبة لما أظله من شهود الموقف
فإلتزم آداب العبودية ولأن الحق اذا ألبسهم نعوته
إستحال أن يسجدوا له لأنه عراهم في ذلك المقام
عن الرسم برسوم العبودية لذلك لم يسجد محمّد
(صل) عند سدرة المنتهى ولا موسى عليه السلام
عند الكلام.

(١٤)

وقال الجنيد (رحمه اللّه) انما بلغ النبي (صل) ليلة المعراج الى حد لا عبارة عنه ولا وصف له لاتحاده في ذلك المشهد بالواحد الأحد ولإبهام ما جرى فيه، ولسكوت النبي (صل) وترك الاخبار عنه.

(١٥)

وسئل الجنيد عن قوله عز وجل وما كنت بجانب الطور اذ نادينا قال نادى موسى (عليه السلام) لأنه كان وراء الحجاب وناجي محمد (صل) لأنه خرق الحجب ومن كان وراء الحجاب نودي ومن جاوز الحجاب نوجي ومن فنى عن هذه المقامات اواه اليه واشرفه على الاكوان الا ترى إن محمد (صل) سيل فيما يختصم الملاء الاعلى بقى فلما وقع عليه أنوار صفاته وعراه من صفته كيف نطق عن الأماكن كلها وأخبر عنها.

(١٦)

وقال ابو سعيد الخراز أمر النبي (صل) بالدعاء بقول رب زدني علما وكان قد أوتي من العلوم بالوسائط والسفراء فلما أجرى على لسانه هذا الدعاء إستجيب له ذاك من غير تمييز منه له ولا طلب بل لإظهار فضله فعرج به الى المحل الأدنى والمقام الأرفع حيث إنقطع عنه علوم الخلق اجمع وصار في محل الدنو يخاطب ويخاطب من غير واسطة بل كفاحا فأيد في ذلك المقام بالثبات وأكرم بزيادة [العلم] الذي لم يعلمه أحد من الخلق وذلك المقام اشبه شيء عندي بالمقام المحمود لأنه سر بينه وبين حبيبه لم يطلع عليه أحد.

(١٧)

وسئل الواسطي عن دنو النبي (صل) في المسرى فقال خرج من نفسه ودنا به منه اليه فتدلى فما زالت الحجب تدلى عن محمد (صل) حتى وصل الى ما أشار إليه من قوله فكان قاب قوسين او أدنى.

وذلك بقوة الانوار التي ألبس محمد (صل) في حال مسيره ولو لا ما حلى به من وقع الصفة عليه وإلباس الانوار المخصوصة لإحرقته أنوار ذلك المقام حيث لم [يمكن] لجبريل (عليه السلام) الدنو منها لما عري عما ألبس الحبيب (عليهما السلام).

(١٨)

وقال جعفر الصادق (رضي الله عنه) من توهم أنه بنفسه دنا جعل ثم مسافة انما التدلى إنه كلما قرب منه بعده عن أنواع المعارف اذ لا دنو ولا بعد فكلما دنا بنفسه من الحق تدلى بعدا فإنقلب في الحقيقة خاسئا وهو حسير اذ لا سبيل الى مطالعة الحقيقة حقيقة

وأما الأخبار عن محل الكرامة والفضل فإن الحق أخذ من أنيته فأشهده إياه فكان في الحقيقة ذاته مشاهدا ذاته وفي أخبار عن محمد (صل) لما وسمه به من المحل الشريف والموقف المنيف.

(١٩)

سمعت الحسين بن [يختر] يقول سمعت جعفر بن محمد يقول سمعت الجنيد يقول ليلة المعراج ألبس محمد (صل) لبسة خص بها من نفر الخلائق اجمع فعجز عنها جبريل (صلوات الله عليهما) فقال لو دنوت أنملة لإحترقت فتلك اللبسة أنه غمره في انواره و اخلاه من جميع صفاته وحلاه وزينه بانوار صفاته فأطاق الهجوم على الكلام والمشاهدة والمراجعة والتلقف من الحق التحيات فقابله الحق بالتحيات اجمع لا تحية واحدة ثم لقنه بأن قابل الحق مثله فقال بل التحيات والمباركات والطيبات لله لأنك أهل لذلك.

(٢٠)

وقال بعضهم الفرق بين كلامه محمد (صلى) في
السماء السابعة وكلامه موسى (عليه السلام)
على الطور إن موسى (عليه السلام) لم ير من
معانية إلا الصواعق فلم ينل من القوة ما إحتمل
إشارات الذات و ايد محمد (صل) برؤية السموات
والارضين ووضع الكف فأطاق بعدها كل وارد ورد
على سره من أمر ربه.

(٢١)

وقال فارس عجزت صفات جبريل (عليه السلام)
مع بقائها بالحق عن صفات محمد (صل) وهو
فاني بالحق حين أخبر عنه بقوله لقد رأى من أيات
ربه الكبرى وانما عاد عليه كبرى لأنه مبالغة في
الكبر وليس بعد المبالغة غاية وانما صارت أية لأنه
تجلي بكمال الجلال فلما إستوفاه نعت الجلال غيّر
غير مكترث ومنع جبريل (عليه السلام) من
الترقى إليه لأنه لم يمده بما حمله فيه و أيد محمد
(عليه السلام) بما حمله فيما استوفاه وكلا
المقامين له وبه واحدهما إغانة والآخر كشف.

(٢٢)

سمعت محمد بن محمد بن غالب يقول قال الحسين
بن منصور قال الخليل (عليه السلام) منك الي
فابلاه بالنار وقال الكليم مني اليك فابلاه بالبحر
فقال محمد (صل) منك اليك فابلاه بالمسرى.

(٢٣)

سمعت النصراباذي يقول سمعت إبن عائشة يقول
سمعت أبا سعيد القرشي يقول تجلي الله تعالى
لنبينا محمد (صل) بصفة الكرم والجمال وكلمه
بالإيناس عند سدرة المنتهى وقابله بالبر واللطف
فزاد لطفا بالناس وبرا ورأفة وشفاعة وكشف
لموسى (عليه السلام) بصفة الهيبة والجلال فمن
هنا زيد موسى (عليه السلام) غلظا وشدة.

(٢٤)

وسئل جعفر الصادق عن قوله عز وجل ثم دنا فتدلى فقال لما قرب الحبيب من الحبيب بغاية القرب نالته غاية الهيبة فألطفه الحق بغاية اللطف لأنه لا يحمل غاية الهيبة إلا غاية اللطف وذلك قوله فأوحى إلى عبده ما أوحى اي كان ما كان وجرى ما جرى وقال الحبيب للحبيب ما يقول الحبيب للحبيب وألطف به إلطاف الحبيب بالحبيب وأسر إليه ما يسر الحبيب إلى الحبيب فأخفيا ولم يطلعا على سرهما أحدا سواهما لذلك قال فأوحى إلى عبده ما أوحى ولم يعلم أحد ما أوحى إلا الذي أوحى وأوحي إليه وذلك دلالة على غاية البر بم قال ما كذب الفؤاد ما رأى بل صدق الفؤاد ما رأى ولم يعلم أحد ما رأى إلا الذي أرى والذي رأى فصار الحبيب إلى الحبيب قريبا وله نجيا وبه أنيسا حتى صار والها قال الله عز وجل نرفع درجات من نشاء.

(٢٥)

وقال بعضهم قطع الحق سر محمد (صل) عن الأغيار اجمع نظر إلى ربه بعين اليقين وتحقق بأنوار الحق حتى عاد له عين اليقين حق اليقين فجمل مكافحة المخاطبة بقوله أوحى إلى عبده ما أوحى ولما ادناه فتدلى أراه هويته فازال عنه أنيته وأسقط عنه أثاره و حلاه بأنواره فأطاق شهود تلك المشاهدة ولم ير نورا مخلوقا فوق نوره فيشغله فلذلك ما هاله شيء ولا إستحسن شيئا بعدما شاهد ما حكى الله تعالى عنه في قوله لقد رأى من أيات ربه الكبرى وقوله تعالى ما زاغ البصر وما طغا لعلو نوره وصفا أثره.

(٢٦)

وقال أبو محمد الجريري (رحمه الله) لما نظر المصطفى (صل) إلى الحق بالحق رأى الحق بالحق فبقى مع الحق بالحق بغير زمان ولا في مكان لأنه حصل مع من لا زمان له ولا مكان فعري عن أوصافه بأوصاف الحق فلم يكن له في تلك الحال نفس ولا علم ولا لسان ولا بيان حتى رده الحق إلى صفته وعري ظاهره من الأنوار التي سدل عليه وأسدي إليه رد الشبح إلى وصفه لقيامه بحقوق رسالته وحصل السر في الحضرة لذلك ستر ما جرى من ذلك المشهد فقال وأوحى إلى عبده ما أوحى.

(٢٧)

وسئل الحسين بن منصور عن حقائق الصلوة فقال
المشهد خاطب الله تعالى نبيه (صل) بالصلاة في
الاعلى فقال يا رب ما الذي لي في من اقامة
الصلاة فقال اتباع أمري وإجتناب نهيي قال وما
لي فيه فقال ثناي عليك في اتباع الأمر وشكري
لك في اجتناب النهي فقال إن أثنيت أثنيت على
خلقك وإن شكرت شكرت إحسانك وليس للعبد
معك مقام في شيء.

(٢٨)

وقال بعضهم لما قال النبي (صل) في المعراج أنا بك كان الجواب من جهة الحق إن كنت بي فأنا لك إذ اللام والباء يتعاقبان فمن كان اللام نعته كان الباء صفته.

(٢٩)

وقال بعضهم لما صفى الحق محمد (صل) في أزليته عن ممازجات السرائر ومشاهدات الأغيار صفاه عن التمنى والإعتواض والدعاء فقابل محل الدعا بالله فقال التحيات لله وقابل محل طلب الاعواض بالاشتياق إلى المعوض وقابل المقام في الدهور والأزمان بالفناء عنها والبقاء بموجدها فلما كان بهذا المحل قرب وأدنى وتدلى عليه من أنوار الصفات ما جذبه لبساط التمكين فشاهد الحق مشاهدة وقرب حتى أفنى بالقرب عن محل القرب وذاك حين أذن له في المعراج شارك النفس الروح بما لم يزل به مختصا من نفس الارواح وأبصرت النفس ما لم يزل القلب والسر له مبصرا وهو قوله عز وجل ما كذب الفؤاد ما رأى لم يكذب الفؤاد للنفس فيما شاهد.

(٣٠)

سمعت عبد الله بن محمد الدمشقي يقول سألت
بعض مشايخنا من اهل الشام هل يداني مرتبة
محمد (صل) في الفضل مرتبة غيره من الأنبياء
(عليهم السلام) قال لا يداني مرتبتة محمد
(صل) مرتبة ملك مقرب ولا نبي مرسل كيف
يدانى مرتبته مرتبتهم و هو في الحضرة والمشاهدة
ولم يترك على مشاهدة الروح والسر حتى لدني
وكلم ونوجى وأسقط عنه التوقيفات والرسوم وقام
مع الحق في أدنى مقام تمكن القيام فيه والعبارة
عنه ليلة المعراج فكان قاب قوسين او أدنى و قوله
ما كذب الفؤاد ما رأى.

(٣١)

سئل بعضهم ما كانت الفائدة في المعراج ولم يغب النبي (صل) عن الحضرة بل شاهد الغيبات بحقائق الايمان فقال كان محمد (صل) الحبيب وكان من أشد الخلق شوقا إلى ربه لخلوص محبته فعلم الحق شوقه إليه وقلة صبره عن مشاهدته فعجل له ذلك قبل جمع الأنبياء (عليهم السلام) والرسل (صلوات الله عليهم) وما زاده ذلك إلا شوقا إليه. ألا تراه لما خير كيف إختار وقال بل الرفيق الأعلى.

(٣٢)

وسمعت أبا علي أحمد بن علي الشامي يقول سمعت فارس البغدادي بسمرقند يقول أقام الحق الخلق منه على مراتب فلأهل المعرفة منهم علم اليقين وللأنبياء (صلوات الله عليهم) عين اليقين ولمحمد (صل) حق اليقين فترسم أهل المعرفة بعلم اليقين وأيقنوا ما علموا ووصل الانبياء (عليهم السلام) الى عين اليقين وشاهدوا منها حقيقة اليقين وفنى محمد (صل) عن أوصافه ويحقق بحقائق الحق فرزق حق اليقين وذلك المقام الذي لا وراءه مقام.

(٣٣)

وقال النوري (رحمه الله) شاهد الحق القلوب فلم
يرَ قلبا أشوق إليه من قلب محمد (عليه السلام)
فأكرمه بالمعراج تعجيلا الرؤية والمكالمة فلما أهل
لذلك المشهد العظيم صغرت الأكوان في عينه
حتى لم يلتفت إلى شيء ولم يستحسن شيئا ولم
يعظمه للمقصود الذي قصده.

(٣٤)

وسئل بعضهم لم إنبسط النبي (صل) في القيمة،
إذا سكت الأنبياء (عليهم السلام) وإنقبضوا قال
لأنه أزال عنه الإنقباض موقفه في المعراج ومكالمته
مع الحق ومخاطبته فلم يرعه الموقف لما شاهد قبل
ذلك من عظيم المحل والأنبياء (عليهم السلام)
بدهوا فسكتوا وإنقبضوا.

(٣٥)

سمعت محمد بن عبد الله يقول سمعت علي بن هند الفارسي يقول قال أبو سعيد الخراز بلغ محمد (صل) من المحنة المنتهى فبلغ به في الدنو المنتهى قال الله تعالى فكان قاب قوسين او أدنى وذلك حين لا مقام لقدم فرأى قدمه بحال ثم عري جميع ما يتلبس به العوام وألبس خصائص الخلع ثم أثنى عليه بقوله وإنك لعلى خلق عظيم.

(٣٦)

وقال بعضهم إن الله تعالى أراد أن يشرق بأنوار محمد (صل) السموات كما أشرق ببركاته الارضين فسرى به إلى المعراج.

(٣٧)

فسئل أبو العباس الدينوري لِم أسرى النبي
(صل) أولا إلى بيت المقدس قبل ان عرج به إلى
السماء فقال علم الله تعالى أن الكفار قريش
يكذبونه فيما يخبرهم به من أخبار السماء فأراد
أن يخبرهم بخبر من الأرض قد بلغوها وعاينوها
وعلموا أن النبي (صل) لم يدخل بيت المقدس قط
[فلما] أخبرهم بأخبار بيت المقدس لم يمكنهم أن
يكذبوه في أخبار السماء بعد أن صدقوه في
أخبار الأرض.

(٣٨)

وسمعت منصور بن عبد الله يقول سمعت القسم بن القسم السياري يقول سئل الواسطي لِمِ أسرى النبي (صل) الى بيت المقدس قبل المعراج فقال أراد الحق تعالى أن لا يخلي تربة فاضلة عن مشهده ووطئ قدمه بها فتم تقديس البيت المقدس بصلاة محمد (صل) فيه فلما تم تقديسه به أخبر النبي (صل) أنه لا تشد الرجاء إلا إلى ثلاث مساجد مسجد الحرام لأنه مولده ومسقط رأسه وموضع نبوته ومسجد المدينة لأنه مسجد هجرته وموضع تربته ومسجد الأقصى لأنه أرض مسراه وموضع معجزته قال الله تعالى سبحان الذي أسرى بعبده ليلا من المسجد الحرام إلى المسجد الأقصى.

(٣٩)

وقال بعضهم لما بلغ محمّد (صل) إلى المنتهى في الدنوّ من الحقّ لزم طريقة الذهول والخمود فلم يخبر بشيء مما عاين ولم يفتخر به وقال في رجوعه لو تعلمون ما أعلم وأثنى في ذلك المشهد بإظهار الفجر فقال أعوذ بك منك لا أحصى ثناء عليك انت كما إثنيت على نفسك.

(٤٠)

وسئل حسين بن منصور لِم أبهم المصطفى (صل) الثناء في المعراج فقال لما علم أن الثناء وإن صفا و كثر يكون قاصرا عن بلوغ الحق وأنه راجع إلى المثني شرفه لا إلى المثنى عليه وأن فيه إظهار قدر قائله لا غير رجع إلى لسان العجز فقال لا أحصي ثناء عليك.

(٤١)

وسئل بعضهم لِم إنبسط المصطفى (صل) ليلة المعراج بالمشاهدة والكلام على بساط القرب [قال] أزيل عنه حيرة اوان المشاهدة وإنقباض حين المكالمة فإنبسطه في الشفاعة والسؤال.

(٤٢)

وقال رويم لما أكرم محمد (صل) باعظم الشرف في المسرى علت همته عن الإلتفات الى الأيات والكرامات والجنة والنار فما زاغ البصر اي ما أعار طرفه شيئا من الأكوان ومن شاهد البحر إستقل الأودية والأنهار.

(٤٣)

وسئل الواسطي لِمَ أبهم النبي (صل) الثناء فقال الثناء للأكفاء ومن لم يبلغ حقيقة الثناء فالعجز عن الثناء ثناء.

(٤٤)

سمعت منصور بن عبد الله يقول سئل أبو بكر بن طاهر لِم عرج النبي (صل) دون سائر الانبياء (عليهم السلام) فقال لأحوال أحدها إنه كان صاحب الشفاعة في القيمة فيوسط قبلها ليلا يقع له حشمة البديهة كما يقع لغيره من الأنبياء ولأنه كان صاحب المقام المحمود فأراد الحق عز وجل أن يزال عنه قبل ذلك مقام الإنقباض ليتمكن في مقام المحمود فأهله قبل الملاء الأعلى للمشاهدة وللكلام ثم رفعه الى مكان لا مكان بعد مكانه ولا مقام وراء مقامه ليكون مشاهدا للكل فيتضرع في المشهد الأعلى للشفاعة والتمكن في المقام المحمود.

(٤٥)

وسمعت منصور بن عبد الله يقول سئل الشبلي كيف ثبت النبي (صل) في المعراج للقائ المخاطبة فقال إنه هيء لأمر فمكن فيه.

(٤٦)

ووجدت في كتاب حديث إسماعيل بن نجيد لحظة سئل أبو عثمان عن قول النبي (صل) لا أحصى ثناء عليك انت كما إثنيت على نفسك فقال ما زال النبي (صل) كان داعيا ومثنيا على ربه فلما عرج به ليلة المسرى فشاهد ما شاهد من عظمة ربه إستحيا مما أثنى ودعا فرجع إلى لسان العجز فقال لا أحصى ثناء عليك.

(٤٧)

وقال أبو عثمان هوّن عليه سكرات الموت ما رأى
من لطف ربّه في المسرى فقال الرفيق الأعلى لما
خير أي وهل يختار من شاهد ما شاهدت إلاّ
الرفيق الأعلى الذي أدناني وقرّبني.

(٤٨)

سمعت أبا بكر الرازي (رحمه الله) يقول سمعت أبا العباس بن العطاء [يقول] لما أراد الحق تعالى أن يكون صفيه وحبيبه أبعد الخلق ذكرا وأكبرهم قدرا وأرفعهم فخرا وأشرفهم قدرا وأسناهم رتبة عرج به إلى السموات وأشرفه على الملكوت وزينه بحلقة الدنو فأدناه من بساط القرب حين عجز عن ذلك الملايكة والانبياء لينوّه بذكره في سمواته كما رفع ذكره في أرضه.

(٤٩)

وقال الحسين بن منصور لما دنا السفير الأعلى من الحق في المسرى أمره فقال سَلْ تُعْطَ فقال ماذا أسأل وقد أعطيت وماذا أبتغي وقد كفيت فنودي وإنّك لعلى خلق عظيم حيث نزّهت بساطنا عن طلب الحوائج وأعطى إذ ذاك البرهان وأطلق له في الحكم لمن شاء بإحدى الدارين فرجع إلى مشهد الأصحاب وحكم لعشرة من قريش بالجنّة.

(٥٠)

وقال أبو سعيد الخراز (رحمه الله) كان النبي (صل) قبل أن أسرى به يتوهم ويظنّ فلما أسرى به تحقّق فيما توهم وشاهد ما ظنّ وكذلك فعل الحق إذا غلب على صفات العبد.

(٥١)

سمعت الحسين بن [يختر] يقول سمعت جعفر الخلدي يقول سئل الجريري لِم إستصعب البراق على النبي (صل) ليلة المسرى فقال هيبة له وفرحا بركوبه إياه شرفا به وتبرّكا.

(٥٢)

سمعت محمد بن عبد الله يقول سمعت أبا عمر الدمشقي وسئل ما كان للنبي (صل) من الخصائص في المسرى فقال أظهر سبقه على الكل وبيّن له إستصلاحه للمحاورة والمشاهدة.

(٥٣)

وقال بعضهم لما كان مقام النبي (صل) أرفع من مقامات الأنبياء (عليهم السلام) عجل له من أنواع المقارّ والكرامة في العاجل ما كان مأخرا لغيره من الأنبياء في الأجل فأسرى به وأرى مقامه من مقامهم ودنوّه من دنوّهم وأمر بالأخبار عن نفسه بحقائق ما زيّن [بها] فرجع فقال أنا سيّد ولد ادم ولا فخر اي وكيف يفخر بشيء من كان فخره بسيّده.

(٥٤)

سمعت عبد الواحد بن علي يقول سمعت السياري
يقول سمعت الواسطي يقول أبهم النبي (صل)
الثناء لما كوشف له من عظيم قدر الله وجلاله ما
لم يكشف لغيره فعلم أنّ ثنائه لا يقابل بصفة الحقّ
وانّ أقوال الخلق وإن علت فعلي محلّ إقدارهم فردّ
الثناء الى الحقّ ورجع في الكليّة إليه لعلمه بأن
قدره لا يقدر سواه.

(٥٥)

وقال أبو يزيد حفظ النبي (صل) طرفه في المسرى فما زاغ [بصره] و[ما] طغى لعلمه بما يؤهّل له من المشاهدة فلم يشاهد في ذلك شيئا ولم يعر طرفه أحدا ثم لما ردّ إلى محلّ التأديب نظر إلى الجنّة والنار والأنبياء والملائكة للأخبار عنها وتأديب الخلق بها فالمقام الاول مقام خصوص والمقام الثاني مقام عموم.

(٥٦)

وقال بعضهم إستصغر الحوادث بعد المسرى

ومتى تعظم الفروع في مقابلة الاصول ومتى يثبت الحدث في مقابلة القدم.

[خاتم الكتاب]

وصلى الله على محمد النبي المصطفى وآله وسلّم تسليما.

آخره والحمد لله رب العلمين.

APPENDIX: BIOGRAPHICAL NOTES

This appendix gives very brief notices on the individuals mentioned in the text and other select individuals mentioned in the notes to Sulamī's *Subtleties of the Ascension*, where it has been possible to identify these individuals and find information about them. Bibliographical references mention resources in European languages when available, but they are primarily for those who wish to access further information about these individuals in the Arabic sources.

The abbreviations used in this appendix are as follows:

EI^2 = *Encyclopaedia of Islam*. New Edition. Leiden, E. J. Brill: 1960- .

Hilya = Abu Nu^{c}aym Isbahānī. *Hilyat al-awliyā$^{\circ}$*. 10 volumes. Beirut: Dār al-Fikr, [1980].

Lum^{c}a = Abū Naṣr Sarrāj Ṭūsī. *al-Lum^{c}a*. Edited by ^{c}Abd al-Ḥalīm Maḥmūd and Ṭaha ^{c}Abd al-Bāqī Surūr. Cairo: Dār al-Kutub al-Ḥadītha, 1960.

Nuṣūṣ = Paul Nwyia. *Nuṣūṣ ṣūfiyya ghayr manshūra* [Trois oeuvres Inédites de Mystiques Musulmanes]. Beirut: Librairie Orientale, 1986.

Risāla = Abū al-Qāsim Qushayrī, *al-Risāla al-qushayriyya*. Edited by ^{c}Abd al-Ḥalīm Maḥmūd and Maḥmūd b. al-Sharīf. Cairo: Dār al-Sha^{c}b, 1989.

Ṣifa = Abū al-Faraj ^{c}Abd al-Raḥmān Ibn Jawzī. *Ṣifat al-ṣafwa*. 2 vols. in 4. Edited by ^{c}Abd al-Salām Muḥammad Hārūn. Beirut: Dār al-Fikr, 1991.

Ta^{c}arruf = Abū Bakr Muḥammad b. Ishāq Kalābādhī, *al-Ta^{c}arruf li-madhhab ahl al-taṣawwuf*. Edited by Aḥmad Shams al-Dīn. Beirut: Dār al-Kutub al-^{c}Ilmiyya, 1993.

Ṭabaqāt = Abū ^{c}Abd al-Raḥmān Sulamī. *Ṭabaqāt al-ṣūfiyya*. Edited by N. Sharība. Cairo: 1953. In references to this work below, the page number in brackets refers to the Arabic text in the edition and translation of the work by Johannes Pederson, *Kitāb Ṭabaqāt al-Ṣūfīyah* (Leiden: E.J. Brill, 1960).

ᶜAbd Allāh b. Muḥammad Dimashqī (no. 30) = Abū al-Qāsim ᶜAbd Allāh b. Muḥammad al-Dimashqī (d. ?). Transmitted from Ṭāhir Muqaddisī, Abū ᶜAmr Dimashqī, and other teachers from Syria. His name is similar to an individual known as Abū Muḥammad ᶜAbd Allāh b. Muḥammad Naysabūrī Murtaᶜsh, an important companion of Junayd, but this is probably not the same person. See *Ṭabaqāt*, 275–77 [271–73], s.v. Ṭāhir al-Maqdisī.

ᶜAbd al-Wāḥid b. ᶜAlī Sayyārī (no. 54). Nephew of Qāsim b. al-Qāsim Sayyārī (see under Qāsim b. al-Qāsim), transmitted sayings from him. Mentioned in *Ṭabaqāt* in the biography of the latter.

Abū al-ᶜAbbās Dīnawarī (no. 37) = Abū al-ᶜAbbās Aḥmad b. Muḥammad al-Dīnawarī (d. ca. 340/951–2). A longtime resident of Nishapur, died in Samarqand, said to have been a companion of Kharrāz, Yusuf Rāzī, Jurayrī, Ruwaym, and Ibn ᶜAṭāʾ. See *Ṭabaqāt*, 475–8 [500–504]; *Risāla*, 122–23; *Hilya* 10: 383.

Abū al-ᶜAbbās Ibn ᶜAṭāʾ (nos. 2, 3, 48) = Abū al-ᶜAbbās Aḥmad b. Sahl Ibn ᶜAṭāʾ al-Adamī Baghdādī (d. ca. 309/921). One of the companions of both Junayd and Ḥallāj. He was said to be a specialist on the Qurʾān, one who was eloquent in explaining it. See *Taᶜarruf*, 27; *Ṭabaqāt*, 265–272 [260–68]; *Risāla*, 97; *Hilya*, 10: 302–305; *Ṣifa*, vol. 2, 268–69; *Nuṣūṣ*, 23f.; Böwering, "From Word of God to Vision of God," 217; Louis Massignon, *La Passion de Husayn Ibn Manṣūr Ḥallāj* (New ed., Paris: Gallimard, 1973).

Abū ᶜAlī Aḥmad b. ᶜAlī (no. 32) = Abu ᶜAlī Aḥmad b. ᶜAlī b. Jaᶜfar al-Karkhī al-Shāmī. Other than what we learn from *The Subtleties of the Ascension*, namely that this individual transmitted Sufi sayings from Fāris Baghdādī, I have not been able to find information about him.

Abū Bakr b. Ṭāhir (no. 44) = Abū Bakr ᶜAbd Allāh b. Ṭāhir b. Ḥātim al-Ṭāʾī al-Abharī (d. ca. 330/941–2), one of the companions of Shiblī and of Yusuf b. al-Ḥusayn Rāzī. See *Taᶜarruf*, 26; *Ṭabaqāt* 391–95 [406–410]; *Risāla*, 113; *Hilya*, vol. 10, 351–52.

Abū Bakr Rāzī (nos. 8, 35, 48, 52). See Ibn Shādhān (Abū Bakr Muḥammad b. ᶜAbd Allāh).

Abū Muḥammad Jurayrī (no. 26, 51) = Abū Muḥammad Aḥmad b. Muḥammad al-Jurayrī (or in some sources, Ḥarīrī or Hurayrī, d. ca. 311/923). One of the oldest companions of Junayd, reportedly seated after Junayd in his assemblies as a sign of his high station. He was also a companion of Sahl Tustarī. See *Ṭabaqāt*, 259–64 [253–59]; *Riṣāla*, 96; *Hilya*, vol. 10, 347–48; *Ṣifa*, vol. 2, 270–71; EI², vol. 8, 840b, sv. "Sahl al-Tustarī."

Abū al-Qāsim al-Bazzāz (no. 3) = Abū al-Qāsim al-Bazzāz, possibly Muḥammad b. Ibrahīm (d. 348/960), discussed by Pederson, 86. See Nwyia's remark on his inability to identify this individual in *Nuṣūṣ*, 28, n. 11.

Abū al-Qāsim Naṣrābādhī (nos. 4, 23). Abū al-Qāsim Ibrāhīm b. Muḥammad Naṣrābādhī (d. 367/977–78). One of Sulamī's most important teachers, whom he calls "the shaykh of Khurasan in his time." Born and raised in Nishapur, companion to Shiblī and others, he was said to have written and transmitted many hadiths. He is mentioned by name only twice in this text; also mentioned in the notes to saying 27 as a source for a Sulamī hadith in Qushayrī. See *Ṭabaqāt*, 484–88 [511–515]; *Risāla*, 124–25.

Abū Saᶜīd Kharrāz (nos. 16, 35, 50) = Abū Saᶜīd Aḥmad b. ᶜĪsā al-Kharrāz (or in some sources: al-Khazzāz) al-Baghdādī (d. ca. 279/892), a companion of Dhū Nūn, Sarī Saqaṭī, and other early Sufis. Said to have been one of the earliest to speak of the science of *fanāᵓ* and *baqāᵓ*, and called by some "the spokesperson of Sufism." See *Taᶜarruf*, 27; *Ṭabaqāt*, 228–32 [223–228]; *Risāla*, 93; *Hilya*, vol. 10, 246–49; *Ṣifa*, vol. 2, 262–64.

Abū Saᶜīd Qurashī (no. 23) = Abū Saᶜīd al-Qurashī (d.?). The only biographical information in the short notice on this individual in *Hilya* 10:342 states that Abū Saᶜīd was an expert at perceiving and doing away with illnesses and pests.

Abū ᶜUmar Dimashqī (no. 52) = Abū ᶜUmar al-Dimashqī (d. 320/931–2). Companion of Dhū Nūn, master of the "sciences of the realities," according to Sulamī. See *Ṭabaqāt,* 277–79 [274–77]; *Hilya*, vol. 10, 346f.

Abū ᶜUthmān Ḥīrī (nos. 46, 47) = Abū ᶜUthmān Saᶜīd b. Ismāᶜīl Ḥīrī (or in some sources: Jabrī) Nīsābūrī (d. 298/910–11), originally from Rayy. He was a companion of Yaḥyā b. Muᶜādh Rāzī and Shāh Kirmānī before traveling to Nishapur. He became a teacher of Ismāᶜīl b. Nujayd (q.v.), who was Sulamī's maternal grandfather. See *Ṭabaqāt*, 170–175 [159–165]; *Risāla*, 81–83.

Abū Yazīd Bisṭāmī (no. 55) = Abū Yazīd ᶜĪsā b. Tayfūr Bisṭāmī, sometimes known as Bayezīd (d. ca. 261/875). From the town of Bisṭām, Abū Yazīd's grandfather had been a Magian who converted to Islam. Many ecstatic utterances have been attributed to him. References to the dream of mystical ascension attributed to Bisṭāmī (see Sells, *Early Islamic Mysticism*, chapter 7) appear in the commentary to sayings 5, 33, 42, 55 above. On Abū Yazīd's sayings and biography, see *Lumᶜa*, 459–77; *Taᶜarruf*, 25; *Ṭabaqāt*, 67–74 [60–67]; *Risāla*, 63–64; *Hilya*, vol. 10, 33–40; EI^2, vol. 1, 162a–163a.

ᶜAlī b. Hind Fārisī (no. 35) = Abū al-Ḥusayn ᶜAlī b. Hind al-Fārisī al-Qurashī (d.ca.330?/941–42?). One of the eldest sages of the eastern lands, companion to ᶜAmr Makkī, Junayd, and other teachers from Persia. See *Ṭabaqāt*, 399–401 [414–417]; *Hilya*, vol. 10, 362f.

Bazzāz (no. 3). See under Abū al-Qāsim al-Bazzāz.

Bisṭāmī (no. 55). See under Abū Yazīd Bisṭāmī.

Dimashqī. See either under ʿAbd Allāh b. Muḥammad or Abū ʿUmar.

Dīnawarī (no. 37). See under Abū al-ʿAbbās Dīnawarī.

Fāris Baghdādī (no. 21, 32) = Fāris al-Baghdādī. Mentioned in *Ṭabaqāt*, 309, as someone who asked questions of Ḥallāj and transmitted what he heard to ʿAbd al-Wāḥid Sayyārī. See the discussion in Lumʿā, 73; Louis Massignon, *La Passion de Husayn Ibn Manṣūr Ḥallāj* (New ed., Paris: Gallimard, 1973).

Fārisī. See ʿAlī b. Hind or Qāsim b. Qāsim.

Ḥallāj (nos. 10, 11, 22, 27, 40, 49) = Ḥusayn b. Manṣūr al-Ḥallāj (d. 309/922). Famous ecstatic and martyr. He was originally from the village of Bayḏā in Persia, but he grew up in Wāsiṭ and Iraq. A companion of Junayd, Nūrī, ʿAmr Makkī, and others, Ḥallāj was subsequently rejected by many Sufis, but accepted by the likes of Ibn ʿAṭāʾ, Naṣrābādhī, Wāsiṭī, and Ibn Khafīf Shīrāzī. See *Ṭabaqāt*, 307–11 [308–313]; EI^{2}, vol. 3, 99b–104b. See also the works of Louis Massignon, especially *La Passion de Husayn Ibn Mansur Hallaj* (New ed., Paris: Gallimard, 1975), translated and abridged as *The Passion of Hallaj*, trans. Herbert Mason (Princeton, NJ: Princeton University Press, 1994).

Ḥīrī (nos. 46, 47). See under Abū ʿUthmān.

Ḥusayn b. Manṣūr, or simply Ḥusayn (nos. 10, 11, 22, 27, 40, 49). See under Ḥallāj.

Ḥusayn b. [Yakhtar] (nos. 19, 51). I have not been able to identify this individual.

Ibn ʿĀʾisha (no. 23), likely an individual who was related to a famous female named ʿĀʾisha, as in the case of the prolific hadith transmitter Abū ʿAbd al-Raḥmān ʿUbayd Allāh b. Muḥammad b. Hafs (d. 228/843), known as "Ibn ʿĀʾisha the younger" after his father who was also called "Ibn ᶜĀʾisha" because of one of his relatives (see EI^2, vol. 3, 698b). Sulamī's reference could not be to either of these individuals, however, since it must refer to someone from whom Abū al-Qāsim Naṣrābādhī (d. 367/977–78), who lived considerably later, might plausibly have heard sayings.

Ibn ᶜAṭāʾ(nos. 2, 3, 48). See under Abū al-ᶜAbbās Ibn ᶜAṭāʾ.

Ibn Farghānī (nos. 1, 6, 8, 17, 38, 43, 54). See under Wāsiṭī.

Ibn Khafīf Shīrāzī = Abū ᶜAbd Allāh Muḥammad Ibn al-Khafīf al-Shīrāzī (d. 371/981–2). A near contemporary of Sulamī's who composed a work on the Prophet's night journey and ascension, significantly not mentioned at all in The Subtleties of the Ascension. Sulamī mentions him in his *Ṭabaqāt*, calling Ibn Khafīf the "teacher of teachers in his time." See *Ṭabaqāt*, 462–66 [485–90]; *Risāla*, 120–21; *Hilya*, vol. 10, 385–89; EI^2, vol. 3, 823a–824a, sv. "Ibn Khafīf."

Ibn Shādhān (nos. 8, 35, 48, 52). Abū Bakr Muḥammad b. ᶜAbd Allāh b. Muḥammad b. ᶜAbd al-ᶜAzīz Ibn Shādhān al-Bijālī (or al-Bajalī) al-Rāzī (d. 376/986), one of Sulamī's teachers. He wrote a history of Sufism that Sulamī supposedly drew upon heavily in his own works. According to Dhahabī, Ibn Shādhān arrived in Khurasan in 340/951–52. He is cited in numerous quotes in *Ṭabaqāt*, but it contains no biography of him. See the editor's note "jīm" on his life in *Ṭabaqāt*, 18–19. See also *Nuṣūṣ*, 27. Saying 48 includes the epithet "may God be compassionate to him" after his name, suggesting that this collection may have been compiled after Ibn Shādhān's death. The phrase may instead reflect the insertion of a later copyist, however, so it does not offer strong proof in and of itself.

Ismāᶜīl Ibn Nujayd (no. 46) = Abū Amr Ismāᶜīl b. Nujayd al-Sulamī (d.ca. 365/976–77), maternal grandfather of the compiler of *The Subtleties of the Ascension*. Said to have been a companion of Jurayrī, and said to have met Junayd. He was the author of a work on hadith mentioned in saying 46. See *Risāla*, 119.

Ja^{c}far b. Muḥammad Khuldī (nos. 19, 51) = Ja^{c}far b. Muḥammad b. Naṣīr al-Khuldī al-Baghdādī (d. 348/959–60), grew up in Baghdad. A companion of Junayd, Nūrī, Jurayrī, and others, said to have collected many of their writings. *Ṭabaqāt*, 434–39 [454–461]; *Hilya* 10: 381–82.

Ja^{c}far al-Ṣādiq (nos. 12, 18, 24) = Ja^{c}far b. Muḥammad b. Ḥusayn al-Ṣādiq (d. 148/765). Sixth Shī^{c}ī Imām, claimed by the Sufis. Sulamī's "Ja^{c}far" has sometimes been called "pseudo-Ja^{c}far." See Nwyia, "Le Tafsīr Mystique Attribué a Ga^{c}far Ṣadiq: Édition critique"; idem, *Exegesis coranique*, passim; Böwering, 219–220; Sells, 84; EI^2, vol. 2, 374a–375a, s.v. "D̲ja^{c}far al-Sādik."

Junayd (nos. 14, 15, 19) = Junayd b. Muḥammad al-Baghdādī (d. 297/910), the most famous of the early Baghdādī Sufis who wrote extensively about technical issues such as tawḥīd, and who advocated a "sober" approach to Sufism. See *Ta^{c}arruf*, 27; *Ṭabaqāt*, 155–63 [141–150]; *Risāla*, 78–81; *Hilya* 10: 255–87; *Ṣifa*, vol. 2, 251–56; EI^2, vol. 2, 600a–600b, s.v. "D̲junayd."

Jurayrī (nos. 26, 51). See under Abū Muḥammad Jurayrī.

Kharrāz (nos. 16, 35, 50). See under Abū Sa^{c}īd Kharrāz.

Manṣūr b. ^{c}Abd Allāh (nos. 3, 38, 44, 45) = Manṣūr b. ^{c}Abd Allāh al-Dimartī and/or al-Iṣfahānī, a contemporary of Sulamī. Mentioned in passing in *Lum^{c}a*, 171.

Muḥammad b. ^{c}Abd Allāh (nos. 8, 35, 48, 52). See Ibn Shādhān.

Muḥammad b. Muḥammad b. Ghālib (no. 22). I have not been able to identify this individual, but he was apparently an acquaintance of Sulamī's who had heard Sufi sayings from Ḥallāj.

Muḥammad b. Mūsā (nos. 1, 6, 8, 17, 38, 43, 54). See under Wāsiṭī.

Naṣrābādhī (nos. 4, 23). See under Abū al-Qāsim Naṣrābādhī.

Niffarī = Muḥammad b. ᶜAbd al-Jabbār Niffarī (d. 354/965). Sufi author of the famous work *Kitāb al-mawāqif*. Mentioned in the notes to saying 2. See *Nuṣūṣ*, 182 f.; EI^2, vol. 8, 13b–14a, s.v. "al-Niffarī."

Nūrī (no. 33) = Aḥmad b. Muḥammad al-Nūrī, also known as Ibn al-Baghawī (d. 295/907). Born in Baghdad, his family was originally from Khurasan. A disciple and companion to Sarī Saqaṭī and to Muḥammad b. ᶜAlī Qassāb. A famous early ecstatic Sufi, said to have been fond of music and poetry. He was also, according to Sulamī, one of the greatest of the early Sufis. See *Lumᶜa*, 492–94; *Taᶜarruf*, 27; *Ṭabaqāt*, 164–69 [151–58]; *Risāla*, 83–84; *Hilya*, vol. 10, 249–55; *Ṣifa*, vol. 2, 264–265; EI^2 vol. 8, 139b–140a, sv. "al-Nūrī."

Qāsim b. al-Qāsim (nos. 38, 54). Abū al-ᶜAbbās al-Qāsim b. al-Qāsim Fārisī Sayyārī (d. 342/953–4), maternal uncle of ᶜAbd al-Wāḥid b. ᶜAlī Sayyārī. A faqīh and hadith transmitter from Marv, known as a companion of Wāsiṭī who transmitted his sayings. See *Ṭabaqāt* 440–448 [462–68]; *Hilya*, vol. 10, 380–81.

Qushayrī, Abū al-Qāsim ᶜAbd al-Karīm (d. 465/1072). Famous Sufi scholar from Nishapur, a student of Sulamī. Author of a famous treatise on Sufism known simply as "The Treatise" (*al-Risāla*), as well as a lesser known work devoted entirely to Muḥammad's night journey and ascension. One section of the latter work draws upon a large number of the sayings from *The Subtleties of the Ascension* and often includes Qushayrī's commentary upon them. See the discussion of this work in the introduction and the notes.

Rāzī. See either under Yūsuf b. Ḥusayn Rāzī or Ibn Shādhān (Abū Bakr Rāzī).

Ruwaym (no. 42) = Abū Muḥammad Ruwaym b. Aḥmad al-Baghdādī (d. 303/915–16), a Ẓāhirī faqīh and a member of the circle of Baghdādī Sufis. See *Taᶜarruf*, 27; *Ṭabaqāt*, 180–84 [170–74]; *Risāla*, 85–86; *Hilya*, 10: 296–302; *Ṣifa*, vol. 2, 266–67.

Sayyārī (nos. 38, 54). See either under Qāsim b. al-Qāsim or ᶜAbd al-Wāḥid b. ᶜAlī.

Shāmī (no. 32). See under Abū ᶜAlī Aḥmad b. ᶜAlī.

Shiblī (no. 45) = Abū Bakr Dulaf b. Jaᶜfar al-Shiblī al-Baghdādī (d. 334/946), originally from Khurasan, but grew up in Baghdad. Became a Malikī faqīh, and was remembered as a restless and ecstatic figure. He was an important companion of Junayd, and stories of Junayd rebuking Shiblī for his excesses became a type of convention or trope. See *Lumᶜa*, 477–91; *Taᶜarruf*, 28; *Ṭabaqāt* 337–48 [340–55]; *Risāla*, 105–106; *Hilya*, vol. 10, 366–75; *Ṣifa*, vol. 2, 276–79; EI^2, vol. 9, 432a–433a, s.v. "al-Shiblī."

Ṭabarī = Muḥammad b. Jarīr al-Ṭabarī (d. 310/923). Famous compiler, author of *Tārīkh al-Imam wa 'l-mulūk* and the famous early tafsīr entitled *Jāmᶜ al-bayān ᶜan taᵓwīl ay al-qurᵓān*. Mentioned in notes to sayings 1, 3, etc.

Wāsiṭī (nos. 1, 6, 8, 17, 38, 43, 54) = Abū Bakr Muḥammad b. Mūsā al-Wāsiṭī (d.ca. 320/932), known as Ibn Farghānī. Wāsiṭī was a companion of Junayd, who spent a number of years (and died) in Marv. He composed one of the earliest Sufi Qurᵓān commentaries, but unfortunately it only survives in the citations of later works. He is known for his provocative mystical utterances and his difficult and uncompromising statements of divine oneness. See *Lumᶜa*, 506–515; *Taᶜarruf*, 28; *Ṭabaqāt*, 302–306 [302–307]; *Risāla*, 100; *Hilya*, vol. 10, 349–50. See also Richard Gramlich, *Alte Vorbilder des Sufitums*, Zweiter Teil: *Scheiche des Ostens* (Weisbaden: Harrassowitz, 1996), 267–411; and especially Laury Silvers, "Tawhid in early

Sufism: The Life and Work of Abū Bakr al-Wasiṭī" (Ph. D. diss., State University of New York at Stony Brook, 2002).

Yūsūf b. Ḥusayn Rāzī (no. 7) = Abū Ya^{c}qūb Yūsuf b. al-Ḥusayn Rāzī (d. 304/916–17), a Sufi who transmitted sayings from the early Sufi master Dhū Nūn Miṣrī. He was also said to have been a friend of Kharrāz, and to have heard hadith from Ibn Ḥanbal. See *Lum^{c}a*, 20; *Ṭabaqāt*, 185–191 [175–82]; *Risāla*, 91; *Hilya*, vol. 10, 238–43.

NOTES

Introduction

1. A short biographical sketch of the compiler and an explanation of the dual system of dating used in this work will be given later in this introduction. Very brief biographical notices on most of the Sufis mentioned in this work can be found in the appendix to the translation.

2. The literature on otherworldly journey narratives is vast. I. P. Couliano offers an accessible introduction to these narratives in his work *Out of this World: Otherworldly Journeys from Gilgamesh to Albert Einstein* (Boston and London: Shambhala, 1991); those interested in more specialized studies may wish to consult the collection of essays dedicated to Couliano's memory, edited by John J. Collins and Michael Fishbane and entitled *Death, Ecstasy, and Other Worldly Journeys* (Albany, NY: State University of New York Press, 1995), as well as Claude Kappler's *Apocalypses et Voyages dans l'Au-Dela* (Paris: Editions of CERF, 1987).

3. For those unfamiliar with Sufism, a very brief discussion of Sufis and Sufism appears later in this Introduction.

4. While the earliest written records of Muḥammad's night journey and ascension, such as the biography of the Prophet by Ibn Isḥāq in the recension of Ibn Hishām or the Qur'ān commentary by Muqātil b. Sulaymān, identify the "furthest place of prayer" (*al-masjid al-aqṣā*) mentioned in the Qur'ān with the site of the holy temple in Jerusalem, some other early accounts, including some of the sound hadith reports cited by such trusted authorities as Bukhārī and Muslim, identify this location with a site in the heavens. Reports of the latter type have led some Islamicists, including those who studied the night journey and ascension narratives in the early twentieth century such as Bevan ("Mohammad's Ascension to Heaven" in *Studien zur semitischen Philologie und Religionsgeschichte*, ed. Karl Marti, 49–61 (Giessen: Alfred Töpelman, 1914)) and Schrieke ("Die Himmelsreise Muhammeds," *Der Islam* 6 (1916): 1–30) to postulate that the heavenly interpretation of the "furthest place of prayer" represents the earliest versions of the story. Alfred Guillaume offers a different theory altogether, locating the "furthest place of prayer" in the Arabian Penninsula; see his article "Where was al-Masyid al-Aqṣā?" *Andalus* 18 (1953): 323–36.

5. Unlike the contemporary English usage of the word "heaven" in the singular to refer to a place of eternal bliss, the premodern Arabic

usage of the term *al-samāʾ* ("sky") comes to stand for a sphere of existence apart from and above the earthy realm that is not necessarily the final pleasure-filled abode promised to the blessed in the Qurʾān. In fact, in some versions of Islamic otherworldly journey narratives, some of the lower heavens serve as the site where the evil-doers receive the torture corresponding to their particular misdeeds. This understanding of the term "heaven" in the singular (*al-samāʾ*) and "heavens" in the plural (*al-samawāt*) appears to have been indebted to Hebrew (*shama / shamayim*), and ultimately can be traced back to the ancient Babylonian system of the celestial spheres. In this work, the abode of final bliss often associated with the English word "heaven" will be translated by the technical term "paradise" (*al-janna*), which evokes the lush garden imagery used to describe this locale in the Qurʾān.

6. While a number of article-length discussions of the night journey and ascension literature have appeared within the last century, a comprehensive study of this vast literature has only just begun. My study entitled "Constructing an Islamic Ascension Narrative" (Duke University Ph. D. Dissertation (2002)) surveys one strand of the web of oral narratives. Brooke Olson Vuckovic's study, recently published as *Heavenly Journeys, Earthly Concerns: The Legacy of the Miʿrāj in the Formation of Islam* (New York: Routledge, 2005) takes a thematic approach to the early Arabic material. Christiana Gruber's study entitled "The Prophet Muḥammad's Ascension (*Miʿrāj*) in Islamic Art and Literature, ca. 1300–1600" (University of Pennsylvania Ph. D. Dissertation (2005)) traces the development of the illustrated Islamic ascension texts and their Arabic, Persian, and Turkish contexts. These recent studies reflect a promising beginning, but they also reveal how much more work lies ahead.

7. Qurʾān, sūra 17 (*al-Isrāʾ*): 1. All translations from the Qurʾān in this work are my own unless otherwise stated. In the text, references to the Qurʾān will often be indicated by the shorthand "Q" followed by surā number, a colon, and the verse number. Notes on issues of translation, such as the reason for using lower case letters in adjectives and pronouns that refer to the divinity, appear near the end of this Introduction. The "place of ritual prayer" (*masjid*, literally "mosque") mentioned in the above verse need not be physical structures, because the word *masjid* in Arabic designates any place where one touches his or her head to the ground in the performance of ritual prayer. The entire chapter of the Qurʾān (*sūra*) in which this verse appears is frequently called the chapter of the "Night Journey" after this famous first verse. The sūra is also known by the name "The Children of Israel" (*Banī Isrāʾīl*).

8. Qurʾān, sūra 53 (*al-Najm*): 1–18.

9. Some commentators deny that the opening section of "the Star" refers to the night journey and ascension, rather they interpret it in terms of Muḥammad's vision of the angel Gabriel when the latter appeared to him in his "true form." Nevertheless, scholars are virtually unanimous that the locations specified in the second half of the passage, the "lote tree of the boundary" and the "garden of the refuge," refer to places in the heavens. Therefore, at the very least, the second of the two visions mentioned in the passage, Qurʾān 53 (*al-Najm*): 13–18, frequently becomes collated with the events of Muḥammad's heavenly ascension.

10. The proper transliteration of this term is *ḥadīth* in the singular, *aḥādīth* in the plural. Throughout this work I will use the forms that have become common in Islamic studies, hadith (or hadith report) in the singular and hadiths (or hadith reports) in the plural.

11. The Shīʿī movement was still in its early stages during this period, but the proto-Shīʿīs tended to look to other sources, especially the teachings of the first Shīʿī leaders known as the Imams, for their oral reports on Muḥammad and his close companions. A useful survey of early Imāmī ("Twelver") and Ismāʿīlī ("Sevener") Shīʿī anecdotes on the night journey and ascension can be found in the collection of essays edited by Mohammad Ali Amir-Moezzi, *Le Voyage initiatique en Terre d'Islam* (Leuven and Paris: Peeters, 1996), especially the essay by the editor himself (*ibid.*, 99–116) and that by Y. Marquet (ibid., 117–132).

12. This study will not consider the question of the origins of these narratives, nor will it explore in detail the various components that make up any given composite narrative. For one approach to the latter issue, see the case treated in my "Constructing an Islamic Ascension Narrative," chapters 2–3.

13. This "cup test" is depicted as a trial to choose the true Islamic path over paths that lead to destruction. Some narratives seek to trace the prohibition of wine in the Islamic tradition to Muḥammad's refusal of the wine during this test. Muḥammad's embracing of "natural disposition" (*fiṭra*) receives little comment in the ascension narratives other than the fact that it symbolizes his devotion to his innate and natural religious path that is none other than the religion of Islam. The metaphor implies that Islam nurtures the soul, just as a mother's milk nurtures a baby's body.

14. The exact same questions given at the gate to the first heaven are repeated at this and all subsequent heavenly gates. For the sake of brevity, I will skip these interrogations at each gate and replace them with ellipses.

15. Qurʾān, sūra 19 (*al-Maryam*): 57.

16. An allusion to the Qurʾān, sūra 53 (*al-Najm*): 16.

17. An allusion to the Qurʾān, sūra 53 (*al-Najm*): 10.

18. Drawing upon the idea in the Qurʾān, sūra 6 (*al-Anʿām*): 160.

19. Muslim, *Ṣaḥīḥ*, *al-Īmān*, hadith 259, adapted from my translation in "Constructing an Islamic Ascension Narrative," 117–118; compare Michael Sells, *Early Islamic Mysticism* (New York: Paulist Press, 1996), 49–51, from which the phrase "House of Life" was borrowed.

20. The House of Life, *al-bayt al-maʿmūr*, is mentioned explicitly in the Qurʾān only once, and this only in passing, sūra 52 (*al-Ṭūr*): 4. Within ascension narratives, however, the phrase is often understood as a reference to a type of celestial temple in the seventh heaven that mirrors the earthly Kaʿba in Mecca. Such a notion draws upon the Jewish concept of a heavenly temple that mirrors the earthly Temple in Jerusalem.

21. Those interested in investigating the hadith reports on Muḥammad's night journey and ascension in greater detail are directed to examine the first chapters of my "Constructing an Islamic Ascension Narrative" and the work of Brooke Olson Vuckovic and Christiana Gruber, cited above.

22. Ibn Saʿd, al-Ṭabaqāt al-kubrā, vol. 1 (Beirut: Dār al-Ṣādir, 1957), 213; for a translation of the passage, see my "Constructing an Islamic Ascension Narrative," 103–104.

23. Ibn Isḥāq, *Sīrat rasūl allāh*, ed. Wüstenfeld, vol. I/1, 263 f.; see the translation by Alfred Guillaume, *The Life of the Prophet Muḥammad* (Lahore: Oxford University Press, 1955), 185. See also Vuckovic, *Heavenly Journeys, Earthly Concerns*, 38; also my "Constructing an Islamic Ascension Narrative," 101. As I discuss there, evidence suggests that this portion of the narrative may not have appeared in Ibn Isḥāq's version of the night journey and ascension, but may instead have been added by a subsequent editor such as Ibn Hishām.

24. Sulamī, *The Subtleties of the Ascension*, saying 5. This and all other sayings from *The Subtleties of the Ascension* are translated below in the body of this work, and the saying numbers refer to those numbers that I have included in my edition and translation.

25. A few of the hadiths in Bukhārī and Muslim do mention a visit to paradise, but such references are given in passing and few details are included. See, for example, Muslim, *Ṣaḥīḥ*, *al-Īmān*, hadith 263. It also should be noted that Ibn Ḥanbal's *Musnad* and other important hadith collections do in fact discuss the individuals who will receive reward or punishment in the afterlife. A number of these hadiths are discussed by Vuckovic in *Heavenly Journeys, Earthly Concerns*, chapter 4.

26. Tirmidhī, *Jāmiʿ al-ṣaḥīḥ*, transmitted in *al-ʿĀriḍa*, vol. 12, 111–113, no. 3247 (*tafsīr* to sūrat *Ṣad*, no. 2). The anecdote springs from an

exegesis of sūra 38 (*Ṣad*), 67–70, a passage that contains a reference to "knowledge of the heavenly host debate" (*ᶜilm biʾl-malāʾi ʾl-aᶜlā idh yakhtaṣimūn*) in verse 69. Daniel Gimaret traces the spread of this anecdote in his article "Au coeur du Miᶜrāğ, un hadith interpolé," in *Le Voyage Initiatique*, ed. Amir-Moezzi, 67–82. For further discussion of the anecdote, see my dissertation, "Constructing an Islamic Ascension Narrative," 135 f.

27. Sulamī, *The Subtleties of the Ascension*, sayings 15 and 20. The notion of God touching Muḥammad with his hand raises the whole problem of anthropomorphism, the idea that God takes a human form. While this idea was unequivocally rejected by the vast majority of Muslim theologians, during the early period it appears that some anthropomorphic beliefs were in circulation (see the examples cited by van Ess, "The Youthful God: Anthropomorphism in Early Islam," Ninth Annual University Lecture in Religion, Arizona State University, 1988).

28. On popular ascension narratives in general and the Ibn ᶜAbbās ascension narratives in particular, see my "Constructing an Islamic Ascension Narrative."

29. For an early example, see *ibid.*, Appendix 1, 414–39.

30. The italicized portions of this paragraph are all allusions to passages in the Qurʾān: sūra 4 (*al-Nisāʾ*): 125; sūra 4 (*al-Nisāʾ*): 164; sūra 19 (*Maryam*): 57; sūra 38 (*Ṣad*): 35; sūra 4 (*al-Nisāʾ*): 163; and sūra 17 (*al-Isrāʾ*): 55.

31. The Arabic text is based upon Suyūṭī, *al-Lālī al-maṣnūᶜa fī aḥādīth al-mawḍūᶜa*, ed. Abū ᶜAbd al-Raḥmān Ṣalāḥ b. Muḥammad b. ᶜUwayḍa, vol. 1 (Beirut: Dār al-Kutub alᶜIlmiyya, 1996), 69–70, in consultation with other recensions, including by Sulamī's student Qushayrī (d. 465/1072) in his *Kitāb al-miᶜrāj*; see the translation of this passage in my "Constructing an Islamic Ascension Narrative," 428–32.

32. Qurʾān, sūra 53 (*al-Najm*): 11, 17.

33. For a discussion of how the ascension narratives serve to create a discourse seeking to legitimate Muḥammad's prophetic career, both comparing him to previous prophets and distinguishing him from them as their superiors, see Vuckovic, *Heavenly Journeys, Earthly Concerns*, chapters 2.

34. The brief discussion I offer in this introduction can hardly do justice to the vast and complex subject of Sufism. Those readers who are unfamiliar with Sufism are encouraged to consult one or more of the many excellent introductions to the subject, including the following: Michael Sells, *Early Islamic Mysticism*; Carl Ernst, *The Shambhala Guide to Sufism* (Boston and London: Shambhala, 1997); William Chittick, *Sufism: A Short Introduction* (Oxford: Oneworld, 2000).

35. For a comparative study of this type of mystical discourse, see Michael Sells, *Mystical Languages of Unsaying* (Chicago: University of Chicago Press, 1994).

36. See Ernst, *The Shambhala Guide to Sufism*, 98–106, which offers a chart of the "stations" according to Sufi treatises by Qushayrī and Ansarī; see also Chittick, *Sufism: A Short Introduction*, 85–96, where the "stations" and "states" are discussed in the context of the "ascent of the soul."

37. See Sells, *Early Islamic Mysticism*, chapter 7.

38. Vuckovic argues convincingly that this moral didacticism serves as one of the major factors that shapes the development of the ascension narratives more generally. See, for instance, *Heavenly Journeys, Earthly Concerns*, chapter 4.

39. For a useful biography of Sulamī's life and times, as well as a discussion of his major works, see the introduction by Rkia Cornell, *Early Sufi Women* (Louisville KY: Fons Vitae, 1999), 20–42; see also the introduction by Kenneth Honerkamp to Sulamī's works "Stations of the Righteous" and "The Stumbling of those Aspiring" in *Three Early Sufi Texts*, Translated by Nicholas Heer and Kenneth Honerkamp (Louisville, KY: Fons Vitae, 2003), 87–92.

40. Cornell, *Early Sufi Women*, 37–38, drawing upon the concept of "uṣūlization" as articulated by Vincent Cornell, *Realm of the Saint* (Austin: University of Texas Press, 1998), 12 f. In contrast to this usulization thesis, Laury Silvers argues that the early Sufis were by and large in step with the scholarly "Hadith Folk" from the very beginning. See her article "The Teaching Relationship in Early Sufism: A Reassessment of Fritz Meier's Definition of the *shaykh al-tarbiya* and the *shaykh al-taᶜlīm*," *The Muslim World* 93 (January 2003): 73–76.

41. For an Arabic edition and brief scholarly introduction to this important work, see the edition by Johannes Pederson, *Kitāb Ṭabaqāt al-ṣūfiyya* (Leiden: E. J. Brill, 1960).

42. See Rkia Cornell, *Early Sufi Women*, passim.

43. Regarding his shorter works, Sulamī has an important treatise on the antinomian Sufis known as the *Malāmatiyya* and a treatise on the concept of Sufi chivalry known as *Futuwwa*. For readers of Arabic, two collections of Sulamī's treatises deserve special mention: *Tisᶜa kutub fī uṣūl al-taṣawwuf wa 'l-zuhd*, ed. Sulaymān Ibrahīm Ātesh (N.p.: al-Nāshir, 1993); *Majmūᶜa-yi asār-i Abū ᶜAbd al-Raḥmān Sulamī*, ed. Naṣr Allāh Pūrjavādī (Tehran: Markaz-i Nashr-i Dānishgāhī, 1990-).

44. On this important work, see Gerhard Böwering, "The Qurᵓān Commentary of al-Sulamī," in Islamic Studies Presented to Char*les J.*

Adams, ed. Wael Hallaq and Donald Little (Leiden: E. J. Brill, 1991), 41–56; *idem*, *Encyclopaedia of Islam*, New Edition, s.v. "al-Sulamī."

45. As mentioned in my article, "The subtleties of the Ascension: al-Sulamī on the Miʿrāj of the Prophet Muḥammad," *Studia Islamica* 94 (2002): 169, of the fifty-six sayings in *The Subtleties of the Ascension*, four sayings (1, 2, 4, 18) are nearly or exactly identical to passages in Sulamī's *Ḥaqāʾiq al-tafsīr*, and six sayings (3, 9, 12, 13, 17, 24) are similar or closely related to passages in *Ḥaqāʾiq al-tafsīr*.

46. Sulamī, *The Subtleties of the Ascension*, preface, from the translation presented in this text, based upon the Arabic text of "The Subtleties of the Ascension (*Laṭāʾif al-miʿrāj*)," Ms. 2118 Muḥammad b. Saʿūd. Note that the Arabic word "*masrā*" ("journey") comes from the exact same root as the word "*isrāʾ*" ("night journey"), and the two terms appear interchangeably in some early texts, e.g. Ibn Isḥāq's *Sīra*.

47. One possible exception comes in a passing reference in sayings 18 and 35 to the "choice of cups" scene, which in some versions of the ascension narrative takes place in Jerusalem, but in other versions takes place in the heavens.

48. I first discussed these four major themes in "The subtleties of the Ascension: al-Sulamī on the Miʿrāj of the Prophet Muḥammad," *Studia Islamica* 94 (2002): 167–83. This article contains more details on these four themes than the present context allows.

49. Sulamī, *The Subtleties of the Ascension*, sayings 11, 17, and 19.

50. *Ibid.*, saying 30; see my discussion of saying 30 in my article, "The subtleties of the Ascension," 172–73.

51. Qurʾān, sūra 53 (*al-Najm*): 8.

52. Qurʾān, sūra 53 (*al-Najm*): 9.

53. Sulamī, *The Subtleties of the Ascension*, saying 17.

54. See especially Uri Rubin, "Pre-existence and light: Aspects of the concept of *Nūr Muḥammad*," *Israel Oriental Studies* 5 (1975): 62–119; the article "Nūr Allāh," *Encyclopedia of Islam* (New Edition); Carl Ernst, *Teachings of Sufism* (Boston: Shambhala, 1999), 15–20.

55. In the early period this trope only appears, as far as I have been able to determine, in select versions of the ascension narrative attributed to Ibn ʿAbbās and in Shīʿī discussions of Muḥammad's cloak. The trope may have originated in Shīʿī circles. See Mohammed Ali Amir-Moezzi, *The Divine Guide in Early Shiʿism*, 48 f.; *idem*, "L'Imām dans le ciel," in *Le Voyage initiatique en Terre d'Islam*, ed. *idem*, 99–116 (Leuven and Paris: Peeters, 1996); Colby, "The subtleties of the Ascension," 174; *idem*, "Constructing an Islamic Ascension Narrative," 203. Despite Sulamī's concern for upholding Sunnī norms, therefore, one has to look beyond

the official Sunnī hadiths on the night journey and ascension of the Prophet in order to understand some of the sayings in *The Subtleties of the Ascension*. This fact provides further support for the thesis that the boundaries drawn by the early Sufi authors to describe what was acceptable Sufi belief and practice appear to have been relatively broad (see Silvers, "The Teaching Relationship in Early Sufism," 76). In the later period, the idea of the "light of Muḥammad" became much more widespread; see Gruber, "The Prophet Muḥammad's Ascension (*Miʿrāj*) in Islamic Art and Literature, ca. 1300–1600," Chapter 5.

56. See my article, "The subtleties of the Ascension," 175–77; on the vision of God more generally, see the article "Ruʾyat Allāh," *Encyclopedia of Islam* (New Edition); Chittick, *Sufism: A Short Introduction*, chapter 8. Readers of Persian will want to consult Nasrollah Pourjavady, *Ruʾyai'ī māh dar asmān* (Tehran: Markaz-i Nashr-i Danishgahi, 1996).

57. For example, recall the qurʾānic statement that "sight will not comprehend him" (sūra 6 (*al-Anʿām*): 103), a verse that Muḥammad's wife ʿĀʾisha supposedly cited in order to dispute the idea that Muḥammad claimed to have seen God. Also recall the qurʾānic account of Moses' request to see God on Mount Sinai (sūra 7 (*al-Aʿrāf*): 143), to which God replies, "*You will not see me*." See the discussion of this latter qurʾānic passage attributed to Jaʿfar Ṣādiq, preserved in Sulamī's *Tafsīr* and translated by Sells, *Early Islamic Mysticism*, 79–81.

58. Qushayrī, [*Kitāb al-miʿrāj*], Ms. Bankipore 1891, 37v-38r; *idem*, *Kitāb al-miʿrāj*, ed. ʿAlī Ḥusayn ʿAbd al-Qādir (Cairo: Dār al-Kutub al-Ḥadītha, 1964), 75–76. The printed edition must be used with caution, and ideally in comparison with the manuscript.

59. Qushayrī's work contains a section that imports many of the sayings from Sulamī's *The Subtleties of the Ascension* wholesale. Compare *The Subtleties of the Ascension* to Qushayrī's [*Kitāb al-miʿrāj*], Ms. Bankipore 1891, 54v-61v; *idem, Kitāb al-miʿrāj*, ed. ʿAbd al-Qādir, 107–116. All but one of the sayings in Qushayrī's work is based upon a saying in *The Subtleties of the Ascension*, and that is a saying that Qushayrī attributes to Sulamī himself at the end of the chapter. See [*Kitāb al-miʿrāj*], Ms. Bankipore 1891, 61v; *idem*, *Kitāb al-miʿrāj*, ed. ʿAbd al-Qādir, 116. Also it is interesting to note that the chapter preceding these sayings in Qushayrī's work is entitled "Mention of the Subtleties of the Ascension" (*Dhikr laṭāʾif al-miʿrāj*); see [*Kitāb al-miʿrāj*], Ms. Bankipore 1891, 50v; *Kitāb al-miʿrāj*, ed. ʿAlī Ḥusayn ʿAbd al-Qādir, 100. The reference could be understood as an allusion to Sulamī's work.

60. For example see Sulamī, *The Subtleties of the Ascension*, saying 15.

61. Sulamī, *The Subtleties of the Ascension*, sayings 16, 24. The lovers trope also appears in saying 30.

62. *Ibid.*, preface. On the subtleties and nuances of the word "meaning" (*maʿnā*), see William Chittick, *The Sufi Path of Love: The Spiritual Teachings of Rumi* (Albany, NY: State University of New York Press, 1983), 15 and 19–21.

63. I discuss these issues in "Constructing an Islamic Ascension Narrative." See especially Chapter 3, 215–243, which examines the situation in Nishapur immediately before and after the period in which Sulamī lived.

64. See Brockelmann, *GAL*, rev. ed., vol. 1 (1943), 218–219; *idem*, *GAL*, suppl. 1 (1937), 361–62; Sezgin, *GAS*, vol. 1, 671–74; Shams al-Dīn Muḥammad Dhahabī, *Siyar aʿlām al-nubalāʾ*, ed. Shuʿayb Arnaʾūt, vol. 17 (Beirut: al-Resalah, 1996-), 247–55. See also Nasr Allāh Pūrjavādī, *Majmūʿa-yi asār-i Abū ʿAbd al-Raḥmān Sulamī*, vols. 1- (Tehran: Markaz-i Nashr-i Danishgāhi, 1990-).

65. Dhahabī, *Siyar aʿlām al-nubalāʾ*, 247, quoted in Cornell, *Early Sufi Women*, 38; Böwering, EI^2 s.v. "al-Sulamī, Abū ʿAbd al-Raḥmān," lists the number of full works by Sulamī as "more than a hundred titles."

66. Over one-sixth of the sayings in the first half of *The Subtleties of the Ascension* are either identical or very similar to passages in *Ḥaqāʾiq al-tafsīr*. See note 45, above.

67. Honorific phrases such as "peace be upon him" (hereafter replaced by the following symbol: ﷺ) appear frequently in Muslim texts as a sign of respect after the name of a prophet or an individual considered especially holy. Although removing such phrases in translation tends to ease the flow of the text (see, for instance, the justification of Kugle, *The Book of Illumination*, 43), I have decided to include the formulae in this text since they are sometimes important in supplying a definitive referent to an otherwise ambiguous pronoun.

68. Up to this point, compare saying 6 in Sulamī's *The Subtleties of the Ascension*. The question posed to Wāsiṭī is slightly different in Qushayrī's text, but the answer Wāsiṭī gives is identical in both texts.

69. Qushayrī, [*Kitāb al-miʿrāj*], Ms. Bankipore 1891, fol. 56v.; *idem.*, ed. ʿAbd al-Qādir, 110. The reference to the Prophet's family, which could be construed as a sign of ʿAlīd loyalty, appears out of place in a "Sunnī internationalist" such as Qushayrī. In any case, the phrase here for "what he attributed exclusively to him and his family" is *mā khaṣṣahu bihi wa ahlihi*. Granted the Arabic in this phrase is not exactly elegant, but the editor of the printed text of Qushayrī's *Kitāb al-miʿrāj* mistakenly seeks to correct the original, leaving out the first of the possessive suffixes "*hu*" in this phrase, without any indication of the change. The editor makes similarly minor but even more significant changes throughout

his printed edition of Qushayrī's text, one of the several reasons that the printed edition needs to be used only in consultation with the original manuscript.

70. Sulamī, *The Subtleties of the Ascension*, sayings 4 and 23.

71. Gerhard Böwering, "The Qurān Commentary of al-Sulamī," in Wael Hallaq and Donald Little, eds., *Islamic Studies Presented to Charles J. Adams* (Leiden: E. J. Brill, 1991): 45; *idem*, *EI*[2] s.v. "al-Sulamī."

72. Sulamī, *The Subtleties of the Ascension*, saying 48. Variations on Ibn Shadhān's name appears in three other sayings, however, without this honorific formula: sayings 8, 35, and 52.

73. See my article, "The Subtleties of the Ascension," 180, in which I first discussed these issues, and I furthermore examined other ascension works relatively contemporary with Sulamī to investigate the literary milieu in which *The Subtleties of the Ascension* was written.

74. Böwering, "The Qurān Commentary of al-Sulamī," 49.

75. The manuscript, Ms. 2118 Muḥammad ibn Saᶜūd Islamic University, Riyadh, was called to the attention of modern scholars by Maḥmūd Muḥammad Ṭanāḥī, editor of an Arabic edition of *Dhikr al-niswa al-mutaᶜabbidāt al-ṣūfiyyāt* (Cairo: Maktabat al-Khānjī, 1993).

76. Cornell, *Early Sufi Women*, 44.

77. A number of key issues in current translation theory are surveyed by Hussein Abdul-Raof in *Qurān Translation: Discourse, Texture and Exegesis* (Richmond, Surrey: Curzon Press, 2001), 5f. See also the insightful comments of Scott Kugle to his translation of Ibn ᶜAṭā Allah al-Iskandarī's *Book of Illumination* (Loiusville, KY: Fons Vitae, 2005), 41–47 and 370–80.

78. On the mystical meaning potentially generated by ambiguous pronouns, see Michael Sells, *Mystical Languages of Unsaying* (Chicago: The University of Chicago Press, 1994), *passim*, but especially 1–13 and specific textual examples such as the apophatic nuances of Ibn ᶜArabī's polished mirror discussed on 72–76.

79. Other translators decide to use an abbreviation of the entire phrase such as "p.b.u.h.," and yet others use an Arabic shorthand that appears in many Arabic texts: (*ṣal*). I find replacing the phrase with the calligraphic symbol to be more elegant. I therefore do something similar with the phrase "upon him be peace" that often follows the name of a prophet or angel, replacing it too with a calligraphic symbol. For the reasoning behind including such formulae in the text, see note 67 above.

80. For an example of a saying that might consist of two separate anecdotes, see saying 12.

81. Sells, *Early Islamic Mysticism*, 8–9.

82. The manuscript is Ms. Sup Turc 190, Bibliothèque Nationale de France, partially published in *The Miraculous Journey of Mahomet* (New York: George Braziller, 1977) and recently published in a more complete German edition by Max Scherberger, *Das Mi^{c}ragname: Die Himmel- und Höllenfhart des Propheten Muhammad in der osttükischen Überlieferung* (Würzburg, Ergon, 2003). Compare the discussion of this manuscript by Wheeler Thackston, "The Paris *Mi^{c}rājnāma*," *Journal of Turkish Studies* 18 (1994): 263–99; Christiane Gruber, "L'Ascension (Mi^{c}rāj) du Prophète Mohammad dans la peinture et la littérature islamiques," *Luqmān* 39 no. 1 (Fall and Winter 2003–4): 64f; see also *idem*, "The Prophet Muḥammad's Ascension (*Mi^{c}rāj*) in Islamic Art and Literature, ca. 1300–1600," Chapter 4. Gruber is preparing a work in English devoted to this famous text, forthcoming in 2007 by Patrimonio Ediciónes (Valencia, Spain).

83. See my "Constructing an Islamic Ascension Narrative," chapter 4, and especially 317–321 where the *Mi^{c}rājnāma* is compared to the Ibn ^{c}Abbās ascension narrative.

84. In a modest way, my use of illustrations here follows the more ambitious project of Jamel-Eddine Bencheikh in his creative work of translation and interpretation entitled *Le Voyage nocturne de Mahomet* (Paris: Gallimard, 1988).

Notes to the English Translation of *The Subtleties of the Ascension*

English Translation, Preface and Sayings 1–9

1. The final sentence of the preface begins with the third person masculine singular pronoun "*huwa*," which could be translated as either "he" or "it." I have chosen above to interpret it as referring to Sulamī's project in writing the book, the nearest referent. It may instead, however, be read as a reference to God: "He is a good and a blessing for the believer." I find the final word of the preface especially difficult to decipher. Instead of "believer" (*muʾmin*), it may read something closer to the word "certainty" (*yaqīn*).

2. For brief notices about the individuals mentioned in Sulamī's text, see the Appendix.

3. As mentioned in the introduction, the symbol ﷺ following the name of the Prophet Muḥammad stands for the Arabic honorific phrase "God's blessings and peace be upon him" (*ṣallā allāhu ^{c}alayhi wa-sallam*).

4. Abū ᶜAbd al-Raḥmān Sulamī, "*Ḥaqāʾiq al-tafsīr*," Ms. 9433 Or., British Library, fols. 151r-151v; *ibid.*, Ms. 261 Fatih, Süleymaniye Kütüphanesı, Istanbul, fol. 133v.

5. Muḥammad Ṭabarī, *Tafsīr al-Ṭabarī*, vol. 8 (Beirut: Dār al-Kutub al-ᶜIlmiyya, 1992), 3.

6. Gerhard Böwering understands this saying somewhat differently. See his paraphrase of the saying (as it appears in Sulamī's "*Ḥaqāʾiq al-tafsīr*") in Böwering's essay, "From the Word of God to the Vision of God: Muḥammad's Heavenly Journey in Classical Ṣūfī Qurʾān Commentary," in *Le Voyage initiatique en Terre d'Islam*, ed. Mohammad Ali Amir-Moezzi (Louvain: Peeters, 1996), 214: "Because of His absolute transcendence, God, in Wāsiṭī's view, is above being an actual participant in the Prophet's night journey (*isrāʾ*)."

7. Qurʾān, sūra 53 (*al-Najm*): 10.

8. As discussed in the introduction, 24, the temptation to capitalize pronouns and verbs believed to refer to the divinity remains strong in modern English, but no such distinction appears in the Arabic (a language in which there are no capital letters). This passage illustrates a major problem with such a system of capitalization when translating mystical texts: the semantic openness of the original becomes reduced to a rigid duality imposed by the translator. Compare my translation of the passage with that of Gerhard Böwering: "Each of them was confined to its own limit, beholding the Real One (*al-ḥaqq*) and apprehending something of Him without any mediation and without anything human supporting it. The Real One dealt in reality with His servant and made him real, making him stand where there is no station, addressing him, and revealing to him what He revealed" (Böwering, "From the Word of God to the Vision of God," 218). The subject-object duality that this translation maintains through the use of capital letters represents one, but only one, possible way to read this mystical passage.

9. Niffarī, *The Mawāqif*, ed. and trans. by A. J. Arberry (London: Luzac, 1935). More recently, portions of this work have been translated by Michael Sells in chapter 10 of his *Early Islamic Mysticism* (New York: Paulist Press, 1996).

10. Qurʾān, sūra 53 (*al-Najm*): 11.

11. This additional phrase appears in the majority of versions of the saying in Sulamī's work *Ḥaqāʾiq al-tafsīr*. For specific references, see the notes to the Arabic text.

12. Ṭabarī, *Tafsīr Ṭabarī*, vol. 11, 510–11.

13. Qurʾān, sūra 17 (*al-Isrāʾ*): 1.

14. Qurʾān, sūra 53 (*al-Najm*): 8, 10.

15. Compare saying 55.

16. Compare saying 10.

17. See the translation of Abū Yazīd's dream ascension by Michael Sells in chapter 7 of *Early Islamic Mysticism*, 244–50.

18. Unlike Vuckovic, I do not consider the tortures witnessed during certain versions of the night journey to represent full-fledged tours of hell, but rather didactic visions that depict the tortures in store for various classes of evil-doers. For Dr. Vuckovic's position and insightful analysis of these scenes, however, see her *Heavenly Journeys, Earthly Concerns*, chapter 4.

19. Here one finds the phrase "upon him be peace" (*ᶜalayhi al-salām*) after a reference to the Prophet Muḥammad instead of the more conventional honorific for him, "God's blessings and peace be upon him" (*ṣallā allāhu ᶜalayhi wa-sallam*).

20. One who wishes to pursue the concept of allegory further is encouraged to consult Peter Heath's fascinating study of the use of Neoplatonic philosophical allegory in the *Miᶜrājnāma* of Sulamī's near contemporary Ibn Sīnā (d. 428/1038): *Allegory and Philosophy in Avicenna (Ibn Sīnā)* (Philadelphia: The University of Pennsylvania Press, 1992). A later Sufi figure who interprets the night journey and ascension allegorically is the grand Andalusian master Ibn ᶜArabī (d.638/1240). See James Morris, "The Spiritual Ascension: Ibn ᶜArabī and the Miᶜrāj," *Journal of the American Oriental Society* (107): 629–652 and (108): 63–77; Ibn ᶜArabī, *Kitāb al-isrāʾ ilā ʾl-maqām al-asrā*, ed. Suᶜād al-Ḥakīm (Beirut: Dandara li'l-Ṭibāᶜa wa'l-Nashr, 1988); Vuckovic, *Heavenly Journeys, Earthly Concerns*, Epilogue.

English Translation, Sayings 10–19

21. See Carl Ernst, *Words of Ecstasy in Sufism* (Albany, NY: State University of New York Press, 1985).

22. Qurʾān, sūra 53 (*al-Najm*): 8.

23. A slightly different version of the second half of this saying, preserved in Sulamī's Qurʾān commentary to 53: 8, has been translated into English previously by two different scholars: Michael Sells, *Early Islamic Mysticism*, 84; Gerhard Böwering, "From the Word of God to the Vision of God," 220. The chief differences between the versions in the Qurʾān commentary and in *The Subtleties* lie in the distinct ways that they present the verb forms.

24. Böwering refers these sayings to a "pseudo-Jaᶜfar" (Böwering, "From the Word of God to the Vision of God," 219), while Sells refers to the "Sulamī-Jaᶜfar" (Sells, *Early Islamic Mysticism*, 77). A few manu-

scripts of Sulamī's work present sayings that offer more overtly Shīʿī overtones. See the extended discussion of the Jaʿfarian sayings in Sulamī's Qurʾān commentary by Paul Nwyia, "Le Tafsīr Mystique Attribué à Gaʿfar Ṣādiq: Édition critique," *Mélanges de l'Université Saint-Joseph* 43 (Beirut, 1968): 181–230; *idem*, *Exégèse coranique et language mystique* (Beirut: Dār al-Machreq, 1970), 156–208.

25. The repetition of the word "he said" (*qālā*) suggests that a second saying is being joined to the first. Sulamī's Qurʾān commentary the *The Realities of Exegesis* preserves no direct parallel to the first half, but as mentioned above, the second half does appear there with only slight variations between the extant versions. Despite the fact that standard convention would suggest that the two sayings should be treated separately, I have decided to include them together here since the editor/copyist of the Sulamiyyāt manuscript himself chose to do so. Breaks between sayings in the manuscript are unambiguously indicated by a circular symbol with a dot in the middle of it, and no such symbol appears between the two halves of this saying in the text. Furthermore, the continuity in the theme of the two halves — an interpretation of Qurʾān 53:8 — justifies keeping the two together as one.

26. See Harris Birkeland, *The Legend of the Opening of Muhammad's Breast* (Oslo: I Kommisjos Hos Jacob Dybwad, 1955); Uri Rubin, *The Eye of the Beholder: The Life of Muhammad as Viewed by the Early Muslims* (Princeton: The Darwin Press, 1995), 59 f.; these approaches to the "splitting open of the breast" (*shaqq al-ṣadr*) trope are discussed by Vuckovic, *Heavenly Journeys, Earthly Concerns*, 18–25. See also Christiana Gruber, "The Prophet Muḥammad's Ascension (*Miʿrāj*) in Islamic Art and Literature, ca. 1300–1600," Chapter 2.

27. See below, saying 20; see also my "Constructing an Islamic Ascension Narrative," 429, as well as *ibid.*, chapter 3.

28. See Meir Bar-Asher, *Scripture and Exegesis in Early Imāmī Shiism* (Leiden: E. J. Brill, 1999), 224–232, and specifically 230, where Bar-Asher explains how three early Imāmī commentators all understand the meaning of sūra 10 (*Yūnus*):94 in this fashion.

29. Qurʾān, sūra 28 (*al-Qiṣaṣ*): 46.

30. An allusion to the Qurʾān, sūra 38 (*Ṣad*): 69, "*I had no knowledge of the heavenly host when they were debating.*" See the discussion in the introduction, as well as the commentary below.

31. See the introduction above. Variations of this "heavenly host debate" hadith appear in *Jāmīʿ ṣaḥīḥ* of Tirmidhī (d. 279/892), found in the commentary or Ibn ʿArabī Mālikī entitled *ʿĀriḍat al-aḥwazī bi-sharḥ Ṣaḥīḥ al-Tirmidhī*, ed. Hishām Samīr Bukhārī, vol. 12 (Beirut: Dar Iḥyāʾ

al-Turāth al-ᶜArabī, 1995), 111–15 (section on *Tafsīr sūrat Ṣad*). See also references in the following works: Suyūṭī, *al-La᾿ālī al-maṣnūᶜa fī aḥādīth al-mawḍūᶜa*, ed. Abū ᶜAbd al-Raḥmān Ṣalāḥ b. Muḥammad b. ᶜUwayḍa, vol. 1, 70; Qushayrī, "[*Kitāb al-miᶜrāj*]," Ms. 1891 Bankipore, fol. 27v; *idem*, *Kitāb al-miᶜrāj*, ed. ᶜAlī Ḥasan ᶜAbd al-Qādir (Cairo: Dār al-Kutub al-Ḥadītha, 1964), 59. Daniel Gimaret offers a study of this "heavenly host debate" scene in his article "Au coeur du *Miᶜrāǧ*, un hadith interpolé," published in *Le Voyage Initiatique en Terre d'Islam*, ed. Mohammad Ali Amir-Moezzi (Louvain-Paris: Peeters, 1996), 67–82.

32. Mālikī, *ᶜĀriḍat al-aḥwazī*, vol. 12, 112.

33. Qur᾿ān, sūra 20 (*Ṭa Ha*): 114.

34. Qur᾿ān, sūra 17 (*al-Isrā᾿*): 79.

35. See the translation of the "Primitive Version" of the Ibn ᶜAbbās ascension narrative in Appendix 1 of my "Constructing an Islamic Ascension Narrative," 429.

36. See, for instance, the two hadith commenting on this verse transmitted by Bukhārī in his Ṣaḥīḥ, Bāb al-Tafsīr, nos. 4718–19 (hadith on Qur᾿ān 17:79).

37. See Ibn Diḥya Kalbī, *al-Ibtihāj fī aḥādīth al-miᶜrāj*, ed. Rifᶜat Fawzī ᶜAbd al-Muṭṭalib (Cairo: Maktabat al-Khānjā, 1996), 142.

38. Qur᾿ān, sūra 53 (*al-Najm*): 8.

39. Qur᾿ān, sūra 53 (*al-Najm*): 9. The parallel passage in the *The Realities of Exegesis* ends at this point.

40. While the first half of the saying appears in Sulamī's Qur᾿ān commentary (e.g. "*Ḥaqā᾿iq al-Tafsīr*," Ms.. 261 Fatih, fol. 267r), this second half of the saying does not appear in the latter work.

41. Compare sayings 11 and 19 which refer to the hadith that had Gabriel approached the length of a fingertip he would have burned up.

42. Qur᾿ān, sūra 53 (*al-Najm*): 8.

43. Qur᾿ān, sūra 67 (*al-Mulk*): 4, referring to the sight of one who attempts to view all of God's creation.

44. The text of "*Ḥaqā᾿iq al-Tafsīr*" (Ms. 261 Fatih, fol. 267r; Ms. 9433 Or., fol. 318r) replaces the word "his vessels," *aniyatahu*, with the word "to him," *iyāhu*. It thus reads the verb as "to take" (*akhadha*) rather than "to cause to take" (*akhkhadha*). *The Subtleties of the Ascension* gives no indication that the verb should read this way, nor does it contain the personal pronoun necessary for reading the passage "he took him from him" as in the version from the *The Realities of Exegesis*.

45. In my dissertation, "Constructing an Islamic Ascension Narrative," p. 98f., I discuss this "choice of cups narreme"; see also Vuckovic, *Heavenly Journey, Earthly Concerns*, 26–29.

46. Böwering's translation of this saying replaces the ambiguous pronouns with unambiguous nouns, sacrificing original openness and mystical play with a perhaps clearer yet more "closed" text where all sense of ambiguity disappears: ". . . God took Muḥammad away from himself and made him witness God. Therefore, in reality, it was God's essence witnessing His own essence. . . ." (Böwering, "From the Word of God to the Vision of God," 215).

English Translation, Sayings 20–29

47. See Vuckovic, *Heavenly Journey, Earthly Concerns,* Chapter 1.

48. These passages are most common in the ascension narratives transmitted in the name of Ibn ᶜAbbās, as discussed in the introduction above.

49. See Qushayrī, "[Kitāb al-miᶜrāj]," Ms. 1891 Bankipore, fols. 25v-30r; *idem, Kitāb al-miᶜrāj*, ed. ᶜAbd al-Qādir, 56–62. Near the beginning of the report, Qushayrī explicitly states that he transmits those additions to the narrative that do not reach what he considers "the limit of objectionable things" (*ḥadd al-manākīr*). For a discussion of the treatment of the Ibn ᶜAbbās version of the ascension narrative by the early Sufis, see chapter 3 of my dissertation "Constructing an Islamic Ascension Narrative."

50. Qurʾān, sūra 53 (*al-Najm*): 18.

51. For an example of the *rafraf* raising Muḥammad and leaving Gabriel behind, see the "Reshaped Version" ascribed to Aḥmad Bakrī and translated in Colby, "Constructing an Islamic Ascension Narrative," 452.

52. Moses' nickname "the Speaker" (*al-kalīm*) derives from the story of how Moses spoke with God as described in the following verse: "*And God spoke* (kallama) *to Moses directly* (taklīman)" (Qurʾān 4:164).

53. A number of ascension narratives end with the scenes in which the doubting Meccans question Muḥammad about his journey in order to ascertain the truth of his account, and some report that a certain number of people converted or apostatized as a result of what they heard. See Vuckovic, *Heavenly Journey, Earthly Concerns*, chapter 3.

54. Interestingly, according to Qushayrī's version of this saying, the journey serves not as Muḥammad's "trial" but rather as Muḥammad's "bounty." See Qushayrī, "[*Kitāb al-miᶜrāj*]," fol. 60v; *idem*, *Kitāb al-miᶜrāj*, 115: "*fa-akrāmahu bi-'l-miᶜrāj*." Significantly the Arabic term for trial, *balāʾ*, can also be used in a positive sense of a "favor" or "blessing."

55. Qurʾān, sūra 53 (*al-Najm*): 14.

56. Such systems became highly developed in the western Islamic lands in the Middle Period of Islamic history, for instance in the writings

of Muḥyī al-Dīn Ibn ᶜArabī (d. 638/1240). For references to the latter's writings on the *miᶜrāj,* see the citations given above, note 20.

57. Qurʾān, sūra 53 (*al-Najm*): 8.

58. Qurʾān, sūra 53 (*al-Najm*): 10.

59. Up to this point, compare the following translations, based upon the text of Nwyia: Gerhard Böwering, "From the Word of God to the Vision of God," 220; Michael Sells, *Early Islamic Mysticism*, 84.

60. Qurʾān, sūra 53 (*al-Najm*): 11.

61. This sentence and the first two phrases that follow it, i.e. the next sentence with the exclusion of the phrase "until he became bewildered," are also included in the text of Nwyia and the English translations of Böwering and Sells that are based upon it.

62. Qurʾān, sūra 6 (*al-Anᶜām*): 83; sūra 12 (*Yūsuf*): 76.

63. Muḥammad never displays such an intense terror in the official accounts of the ascension narratives, but in several of the popular versions he becomes increasingly terrified as he witnesses the seas of fire, the torments of hellfire, and the wonders of God in the heavens. In the narratives ascribed to Ibn ᶜAbbās, Muḥammad is too terrified to come into the divine presence until God comforts him and puts him at ease. For an example, see Colby, "Constructing an Islamic Ascension Narrative," 424f.

64. In addition to this saying, see also saying 16.

65. Qurʾān, sūra 53 (*al-Najm*): 10.

66. Qurʾān, sūra 53 (*al-Najm*): 8.

67. Qurʾān, sūra 53 (*al-Najm*): 18.

68. Qurʾān, sūra 53 (*al-Najm*): 17.

69. Up to this point one can compare the translation of Qassim Samarrai, *The Theme of Ascension in Mystical Writings*, 210. Unfortunately Samarrai changes the meaning by erroneously inserting a negative: "He was not stripped of his attributes by the attributes of the Real...." (*ibid.*, emphasis added).

70. Qurʾān, sūra 53 (*al-Najm*): 10.

71. See, for example, the saying ascribed to the divinity (*hadith qudsī*) discussed by Mahmoud Ayoub, *The Qurʾān and its Interpreters*, vol. 1, 43; Ṭabasī, *Tafsīr Ṭabarī*, vol. 1, 117.

72. The penultimate sentence may be read this way, which seems to be the reading favored by whoever inserted sporadic vocalization into the text. Alternately, given that short vowel markings are optional in an Arabic text, there is no way to know if the verbs in the beginning of the final speech are first person singular (e.g. ithnaytu) or second person masculine singular (e.g. *ithnayta*). As a result, the passage could be read as

follows: "He said, 'If I praise, I praise your good character, and if I thank, I thank your beneficence. The servant has no station with you in anything.'" One could imagine reading the statement this way as a speech delivered by Muḥammad, telling the divinity that all praise and thanks defers to him. While this interpretation appears to be less problematic than the above interpretations, it is contradicted by the few short vowels that appear in the text, it contradicts the sentiment of the hadith given in sayings 39, 40, 46, and 54 (see above), and it conveys the strange idea that Muḥammad would praise God's "character" (*khulq*; one could vowel this word differently, such as khalq, "creation" or "creatures," but that raises other problems). To complicate matters further, it is possible, albeit unlikely, that the verb-subject could switch between the two verbs in each pair. For example, "If I praise, you praise your good character, and if I thank, you thank your beneficence" OR "If you praise, I praise your good character, and if you thank, I thank your beneficence." All these combinations and more remain potential ways to interpret the unvoweled text at the end of saying 27, found in Sulamī, *Laṭāʾif al-miʿrāj,* fol. 15v lines 1–2.

73. The hadith is cited or alluded to in sayings 39, 40, 46, and 54. Its full text is given in saying 39.

74. The ambiguity and confusion can be detected in the text itself, for the initial verb stem *ithnat-* seems to have both a short a (*fatḥa*, rendering *ithnayta*) and a short u (*dhamma*, rendering *ithnaytu*) written above it. See the last word on line 1 of Sulamī, *Laṭāʾif al-miʿrāj,* fol. 15v.

75. Qushayrī, ["Kitāb al-miʿrāj,"] Ms. 1891, fol. 61r; Qushayrī, *Kitāb al-miʿrāj*, ed. ʿAbd al-Qādir, 116.

76. For further details suggesting the authenticity of Sulamī's text, see the introduction, above.

77. Here we find an interesting allusion to the Qurʾān sūra 53 (*al-Najm*): 8, which I have translated "he approached and he descended" (*fa-danā wa tadallā*). As in saying 17, this saying interprets the verb *tadallā* (often understood as "he descended") as a feminine verb form ("she/they descend"). Unlike saying 17, where the subject of the verb was "the veils," here the feminine subject of the verb is "the lights." Thus this saying offers another example of the various ways in which the Qurʾānic phrase *danā wa tadallā* can be interpreted.

78. Qurʾān, sūra 53 (*al-Najm*): 11.

79. In addition to the discussion in the introduction, see sayings 15, 17, 19, and especially 25.

80. The carpet is one of the types of objects that symbolizes the proximity of the divine presence. Cf. the ascension vision attributed to Abū Yazīd Bisṭāmī, translated by Sells, *Early Islamic Mysticism*, 249.

81. Cf. *ibid.*, where Abū Yazīd Bisṭāmī claims to have been brought "nearer to him than the spirit is to the body." Subsequently Bisṭāmī encounters the spirits of the prophets.

English Translation, Sayings 30–39

82. Qur'ān, sūra 53 (*al-Najm*): 9.

83. Qur'ān, sūra 53 (*al-Najm*): 11.

84. This final expression, as will be discussed in the commentary, refers to an anecdote told about the choice that God grants Muḥammad just before the latter's death.

85. Ibn Hishām's recension of Ibn Isḥāq's *Sīra*, translated by A. Guillaume, *The Life of Muḥammad*, 680. See also a variation on this same hadith reported in *ibid.*, 678.

86. Qur'ān, sūra 53 (*al-Najm*): 17.

87. The base Arabic text was first published in Reynold Nicholson, "Early Arabic Version of the Miʿrāj of Abū Yazīd al-Bisṭāmī," *Islamica* 2 no. 3 (1926): 402–415. For a reliable translation of the extensive ascension dream vision ascribed to Abū Yazīd Bisṭāmī that forms part of the larger work "Quest to God" ("*Qaṣd ilā Allāh*"), see Sells, *Early Islamic Mysticism*, chapter 7.

88. See for instance the hadiths from Tirmidhī's hadith collection, transmitted in *al-ʿĀriḍa*, vol. 11, 305–307, no. 3160 (from the section *Tafsīr* on Qur'ān 17:1, no. 18), translated in Colby, "Constructing an Islamic Ascension Narrative," 133–134. Tirmidhī transmits numerous reports about intercession in the section of his collection entitled "Description of Resurrection ..." (*Ṣifat al-Qiyāma*). On intercession in Sulamī's *The Subtleties of the Ascension*, compare the above saying to sayings 41 and 44.

89. Compare the phrase "boundary in the approach to the Real" that appears in saying 39.

90. Qur'ān, sūra 53 (*al-Najm*): 9.

91. Qur'ān, sūra 68 (*al-Qalam*): 4. The same verse is quoted in saying number 49.

92. See Colby, "Constructing an Islamic Ascension Narrative," 98 f.; Vuckovic, *Heavenly Journey, Earthly Concerns*, 26–29; Christiana Gruber, "The Prophet Muḥammad's Ascension (Miʿrāj) in Islamic Art and Literature, ca. 1300–1600," Chapter 2.

93. See, for example, saying 17, discussed above in the introduction in the section devoted to the garment of light theme.

94. See Jamal Elias, "The Sufi Robe (*Khirqa*) as a Vehicle of Spiritual Authority," in *Robes and Honor: The Medieval World of Investiture*, edited by Stewart Gordon (New York: Palgrave, 2001), 275–289.

95. The primary meaning of the word *miʿrāj* is a stair or ladder, something by which one ascends. See Vuckovic, *Heavenly Journey, Earthly Concerns,* 2. In Islamic literature, the word comes to be used most commonly as a type of synecdoche, standing for the entire heavenly journey, and that is how I have translated the term throughout *The Subtleties of the Ascension.* The word *miʿrāj* appears at the end of this saying, however, in a context that suggests that it needs to be understood in its concrete rather than symbolic sense. The idea of Muḥammad journeying by night (*sarā*) to the *miʿrāj* requires that the latter term be read in its primary meaning, as a physical ladder or stair upon which one ascends. I have therefore chosen to translate the term *miʿrāj* here as "ascension-ladder" rather than simply "ascension."

96. On the light of Muḥammad, see Ḥallāj's chapter "The TS [Ṭa Sīn] of the Lamp," translated by Carl Ernst, *Teachings of Sufism*, 17–20.

97. On anthropomorphism in the early Islamic period, again see the writings of Josef van Ess: "The Youthful God: Anthropomorphism in Early Islam," Ninth Annual University Lecture in Religion, Arizona State University, 1988; *idem.*, "Le Miʿrāǧ et la Vision de Dieu," in *Le Voyage Initiatique en Terre d'Islam*, ed. Mohammad Ali Amir-Moezzi (Louvain-Paris: Peerters, 1996), 27–56; *idem.*, "Vision and Ascension: Surat al Najm and its Relationship with Muhammad's Miʿraj," *Journal of Qurʾanic Studies* 1 (1999): 47–62.

98. See, for example, Ibn Diḥya Kalbī (d.633/1236), *al-Ibtihāj fī aḥādīth al-miʿrāj*, ed. Rifʿat Fawzi ʿAbd al-Muṭṭalib (Cairo: Maktabat al-Khanjā, 1996), 107.

99. Qurʾān, sūra 17 (*al-Isrāʾ*): 1.

100. For a later interpretation that rejects the identification between the "furthest mosque" and Jerusalem, see the Shīʿī narrative recorded by ʿAlī Qummī (d.ca. 307/919) in his exegesis to Qurʾān 38: 67–70; see *Kitāb tafsīr ʿAlī b. Ibrāhīm Qummī* (Tabriz: n.p., 1895), 572–73, translated in Colby, "Constructing an Islamic Ascension Narrative," 213–214.

101. This hadith was the subject of an interesting article by M. J. Kister, "You Should Only Set Out for Three Mosques," *Le Muséon* 82 (1960): 173–96.

102. Compare the phrase "approach boundary" that appears in saying 35.

103. This is a reference to a hadith, recorded in many sections of Bukhārī as well as in other major hadith collections, in which the Prophet reportedly said, "Were you to know what I know, you would laugh little and cry much." See, for example, Bukhārī, *Ṣaḥīḥ*, Kusūf, 2, no. 1044. For a full list of references to this hadith, see A. J. Wensinck, *Concor-*

dance et Indices de la Tradition Musulmane, 2nd ed. (Leiden: E. J. Brill, 1992), vol. 4, 319.

104. This final phrase represents a widely recorded hadith report, found in the collections of Muslim, Abū Dawūd, Nasāʾī, Tirmidhī, Ibn Māja, and Ibn Ḥanbal, in addition to Mālik's *Muwaṭṭaʾ*. See, for example, *Ṣaḥīḥ Muslim*, the section on *Ṣalāt*, no. 222. For other references, see Wensinck, vol. 1, 304. In *The Subtleties of the Ascension,* sayings 40, 46, and 54 also refer to this same hadith either directly or indirectly; compare also saying 27.

English Translation, Sayings 40–49

105. This final reference presents an abbreviated version of the hadith quoted more extensively in saying 39.

106. This same pair of terms also appears in saying 34, and they are implied in saying 44; see the commentary to these sayings for a discussion of these terms and their connection to the concept of intercession in this text.

107. In some popular ascension narratives, often bargaining takes place not only over the forgiveness of Muslims to spare a certain number or percentage of them from hellfire but also over the ritual obligations. For an example, see Colby, "Constructing an Islamic Ascension Narrative," 459–460. Later versions describe this intercession scene in detail, some continuing at length to recount how Muḥammad secures forgiveness for a greater and greater proportion of Muslims, and how he gets the number of fasting months reduced to one (the month of Ramadan only). Compare texts as diverse as the Iberian Latin translation of the *Liber Scale*, the Arabic ascension narrative of the Anatolian Mūsā Iznīkī, and the Paris Timurid Chaghatay-language illustrated *Miʿrājnāma*, all discussed in *ibid.*, 271, 317, and 319–20.

108. Qurʾān, sūra 53 (*al-Najm*): 17.

109. On Abū Yazīd's vision, see especially the commentary to saying 33.

110. For examples of this trope within the visionary ascension of Abū Yazīd, see Sells, *Early Islamic Mysticism*, 245 and 248.

111. The hadith introduced in saying 39 is also alluded to in sayings 40 and 46. Note that the connection between saying 43 and the night journey and ascension narrative remains implicit rather than explicit.

112. Recall that in Tirmidhī's hadith, with the touch of the cold palm Muḥammad "knew what was in the heavens and what was in the earth," (Colby, "Constructing and Islamic Ascension Narrative," 136). Some popular ascension narratives expand upon this idea to describe Muḥammad's comprehensive power of vision at this stage.

113. Qurʾān, sūra 7 (al-*Aʿrāf*): 143.

114. For the sources of this hadith, see saying 39.

115. The end of this saying, with its reference to the "faltering tongue" and its abbreviated quotation of the hadith, appears in a form nearly identical to portions of sayings 40 and 54.

116. Ibn Hishām, *Sīra*, trans. A. Guillaume, *The Life of Muḥammad*, 678; see also the commentary to saying 31.

117. An allusion to Qurʾān, sūra 94 (*al-Inshirāḥ*): 4, in which God states, "*[Did we not] raise for you your mention?*"

118. For instance, see Qurʾān 38:71–75; Sells, *Early Islamic Mysticism*, 33.

119. This term can also be rendered simply as "dominion" or "empire," and need not have a direct connection to the term angel (*malak*), which like the term kingdom (*mamlaka*), shares the same Arabic root: *m-l-k*. Nevertheless, the term *malakūt* in ascension narratives always relates to the upper heavens, often found together with the term *jabarūt*. I would argue that the concept of "angelic realm" thus embraces this concept in the present context more precisely than the general idea of dominion does.

120. On Bisṭāmī''s narrative, also see sayings 33, 42, and 55.

121. Sells, *Early Islamic Mysticism*, 249; see the Arabic text in Nicholson, "Early Arabic Version," 407.

122. Qurʾān, sūra 68 (*al-Qalam*): 4.

123. The final sentence refers to the popular tradition in which Muḥammad is said to have listed the names of ten Muslims who will be admitted to paradise without first having to pass through judgment. A certain Muḥibb al-Dīn Ṭabarī (d. 694/1295) composed an entire work, entitled *al-Riyāḍ al-naḍra fī faḍāʾil al-ʿashara*, devoted to the biographies of these ten individuals. In this work, the first four of the ten individuals are the so-called "rightly guided caliphs": Abū Bakr, ʿUmar, ʿUthmān, and ʿAlī.

124. For details regarding the Ibn ʿAbbās ascension narrative, see Colby, "Constructing an Islamic Ascension Narrative," *passim*.

125. One of the earliest dateable examples of this "ask and be given" trope appears in the hadith collection of Tirmidhī (d. 279/892), section on tafsīr of Qurʾān 17:1, in a hadith attributed to Abū Saʿīd Khudrī. See, for example, Tirmidhī's text as edited by Ibn ʿArabī Mālikī in *al-ʿĀriḍa al-aḥwazī bi-sharḥ ṣaḥīḥ al-tirmidhī*, vol. 11, 305–307, no. 3160; cf. *ibid.*, section on tafsīr of Qurʾān 38: 67–71, vol. 12, 115, no. 3249. See also the *Tafsīr* of Ṭabarī, tafsīr of Qurʾān 17:1 in a hadith attributed to Abū Hurayra, vol. 8, 11; this latter passage is translated in John Renard, ed., *Windows on the House of Islam* (Berkeley, CA: University of California Press, 1998), 336–45 (the "ask" reference appears on 343–44).

126. Qur'ān, sūra 1 (*al-Fātiḥa*); sūra 2 (*al-Baqara*): 285–86, often called the "seals of *sūrat al-baqara*" and sometimes turned into a dialogue between Muḥammad and the divinity. See chapter 2 of my "Constructing an Islamic Ascension Narrative," 131f.

127. This idea appears in the Latin translation known as *Liber scale*. The notion that Muḥammad receives the Qur'ān during the night journey and ascension also can be seen in the earliest extant illustration of the Prophet's journey in Rashīd al-Din's *Jāmiᶜ al-tawārīkh*, dated ca. 706/1306, in which Burāq is depicted holding a codex which is probably the Qur'ān (Gruber, "L'Ascension (Miᶜrāj) du Prophète Mohammed dans le peinture et la littérature islamiques," *Luqmān* 39 no. 1 (Fall and Winter 2003–4): 59–60). See also *idem*, "The Prophet Muḥammad's Ascension (*Miᶜrāj*) in Islamic Art and Literature, ca. 1300–1600," Chapter 2.

128. See for example Colby, "Constructing an Islamic Ascension Narrative," 459; in later versions, Muḥammad asks God for the power to intercede on behalf of all humanity, to judge them mercifully in a manner that he would prefer, but God refuses this request.

English Translation, Sayings 50–56 and Conclusion

129. Hujwīrī, *Kashf al-Maḥjub of Al Hujwīrī*, trans. Reynold Nicholson, new ed. (London: E. J. W. Gibb Memorial, 1976), 302. Later Sufis expand upon this idea to the notion that ritual prayer gives every believer the access to the ascension experience, conveyed in the hadith, "Ritual prayer *(ṣalāt)* is the ascension of the believers *(al-mu'minīn)*."

130. The notion that the smallest amount of impurity could disqualify one from traveling in the celestial realms recalls the famous Jewish account of the recall of Rabbi Neḥuniah from his visionary "Merkabah" journey when his onlookers place a cloth with an imperceptibly impure cloth onto his lap. See Gershom Scholem, *Jewish Gnosticism, Merkabah Mysticism, and Talmudic Tradition* (New York: Jewish Theological Seminary, 1965), 10; Lawrence Schiffman, "The Recall of Rabbi Neḥuniah Ben ha-Qanah from Ecstasy in the *Hekhalot Rabbati*," 269–281.

131. See the Arabic manuscript catalogued as "*Risale fī Mevlīd al-Nabī ve Mi'rāc*" attributed to Muṣṭafā Maḥmūd (d.?), Ms. 257 H. Hüsnü Paṣa, Süleymaniye Kütüphanesı, Istanbul, fol. 367v.

132. This hadith appears in Abū Dāwūd Sijistānī, *Sunan*, Sunna, no. 13; Ibn Māja Qazwīnī, *Sunan*, Zuhd, no. 37; and Aḥmad Ibn Ḥanbal, *Musnad*, vol. 1, no. 5. It closely resembles a hadith in which the Prophet proves his superiority to other prophets by the fact that only he is allowed to intercede on behalf of humanity on the day of judgment. One version of this hadith appears in Bukhārī, *Ṣaḥīḥ*, Tafsīr sūra 17, no. 4712; cf. Muslim, *Ṣaḥīḥ*, Īmān, no. 327; Tirmidhī, *Sunan*, Tafsīr sūra 17, no. 18.

133. Sulamī, *The Subtleties of the Ascension*, Saying 40. Also compare the other sayings that allude to the hadith, "I cannot enumerate the praise of you...," sayings 39 and 46.

134. Qurʾān, sūra 53 (*al-Najm*): 17.

135. On the latter idea compare saying 8, and see also saying 10.

136. See also sayings 5, 33, 42, 48.

137. For this detail in the dream ascension attributed to Bisṭāmī, see Sells, *Early Islamic Mysticism*, 249. The same concept also appears in the much later text composed ca. 1036/1627 by Ismāʿīl b. Maḥmūd Sindhī Shattarī Qādirī of Burhanpur, translated in Ernst, *Teachings of Sufism*, 75–76.

138. One possible exception appears in the hadith that states how after Muḥammad witnessed hellfire, he says to his followers, "Were you to know what I know, you would laugh little and cry much" (see saying 39).

139. Compare the end of saying 42, which draws metaphorically upon rivers and oceans to illustrate how created things appear insignificant next to the divine reality.

140. Recall Muḥammad's final "choice," alluded to in sayings 31 and 47.

NOTES TO THE ARABIC TEXT OF *LAṬĀʾIF AL-MIʿRĀJ*

IMPORTANT: The notes that follow are numbered according to the number of the saying in the printed edition of the text, rather than by any footnote or endnote symbol given in the text itself. That is, all of the notes, cross references, and comments that I wish to add for a particular saying will be found together under its saying number, below. As mentioned in the introduction, the Arabic parenthetical *ṣal* is shorthand for the phrase *ṣalla allāhu ʿalayhi wa ʿs-sallam*, "God's prayers and peace be upon him," on honorific phrase following a reference to a holy figure such as the Prophet. The shorter honorific, *ʿalayhi as-salām*, "upon him be peace," I often replace with the first letters of each word of the phrase: (ʿa s). As a general rule, I have tried to add little by way of punctuation and voweling, especially as the original text was largely free of such devices. The Arabic text was typed in "Baghdad" font on a Macintosh computer using version 5.1.1 of the "Nisus Writer" wordprocessing program.

Saying 1. Sulamī, *Laṭāʾif al-miʿrāj*, fol. 12v (corresponding to the start of this copy of the Arabic text, according to the information given to me by Dr. Kenneth Honerkamp), lines 8–9. Compare Sulamī, "*Ḥaqāʾiq al-tafsīr*," Ms. 261 Fatih, Süleymaniye Kütüphanesı, Istanbul (hereafter, Ms. 261 Fatih), fol. 133v; Ms. 9433 Or., British Library, London (hereafter, Ms. 9433 Or.), fols. 151r–151v.

Saying 2. Sulamī, *Laṭāʾif al-miʿrāj,* fol. 12v, lines 8–14. The words in brackets in the text are either difficult to make out in the original and thus represent my proposed reading when no other sources for comparison are available, or else represent a correction in the text made by the copyist himself (the first case here) or through comparison with other manuscripts that preserve the saying (the second and third case here). For parallel versions of this saying, compare Sulamī, "*Ḥaqāʾiq al-tafsīr*," Ms. 261 Fatih, fol. 133v; Ms. 9433 Or., fol. 151v; Paul Nwyia, *Nuṣūṣ ṣūfiyya ghayr manshūra* [*Trois oeuvres inédites de mystiques musulmans*] (Beirut: Dār al-Machreq, 1973), 75–76; Qushayrī, ["*Kitāb al-miʿrāj*"], Ms. 1891, Kahuda Bakhsh Oriental Public Library, Bankipore (photostat, Institut Français des Études Arabes de Damas, hereafter Ms. 1891), fols. 54r–55r; Qushayrī, *Kitāb al-miʿrāj*, ed. ʿAlī Ḥasan ʿAbd al-Qādir (Cairo: Dār al-Kutub al-Ḥadītha, 1964), 107–108. Nwyia's edition of the text contains a lengthy (approximately three line) insertion at the beginning of the saying after the words "*maqām al-qurba*."

Saying 3. Sulamī, *Laṭāʾif al-miᶜrāj*, fol. 12v, lines 14–19. Compare Sulamī, "*Ḥaqāʾiq al-tafsīr*," Ms. 261 Fatih, fol. 267v; Ms. 9433 Or., fol. 318v; Nwyia, *Nuṣūṣ*, 151. The phrase *min idrākihi* appears in most copies of the *Ḥaqāʾiq*. Although both *Laṭāʾif al-miᶜrāj* and *Ḥaqāʾiq al-tafsīr* give the word "knot" or "contract" (*ᶜaqd*) near the end of the saying instead of the word "intellect" (*ᶜaql),* I agree with Nwyia that "intellect" makes more sense in this context (Nwyia, *Nuṣūṣ*, 151). Böwering also reads the term as ᶜ*aql* (Böwering, "From the Word of God to the Vision of God," 218).

Saying 4. Sulamī, *Laṭāʾif al-miᶜrāj,* fol. 12v, lines 19–21. Compare Sulamī, "*Ḥaqāʾiq al-tafsīr*," Ms. 261 Fatih, fol. 133v; Qushayrī, ["*Kitāb al-miᶜrāj*,"] Ms. 1891, fol. 55r; Qushayrī, *Kitāb al-miᶜrāj,* ed. ᶜAbd al-Qādir, 108.

Saying 5. Sulamī, *Laṭāʾif al-miᶜrāj,* fol. 13r, lines 1–8.

Saying 6. Sulamī, *Laṭāʾif al-miᶜrāj*, fol. 13r, lines 8–9. Compare Qushayrī, ["*Kitāb al-miᶜrāj*,"] Ms. 1891, fol. 56v; Qushayrī, *Kitāb al-miᶜrāj,* ed. ᶜAbd al-Qādir, 110.

Saying 7. Sulamī, *Laṭāʾif al-miᶜrāj,* fol. 13r, lines 10–11. Compare Qushayrī, ["*Kitāb al-miᶜrāj,*"] Ms. 1891, fol. 56v; Qushayrī, *Kitāb al-miᶜrāj,* ed. ᶜAbd al-Qādir, 110.

Saying 8. Sulamī, *Laṭāʾif al-miᶜrāj,* fol. 13r, lines 11–17. Compare Qushayrī, ["*Kitāb al-miᶜrāj,*"] Ms. 1891, fols. 56v–57r; Qushayrī, *Kitāb al-miᶜrāj*, ed. ᶜAbd al-Qādir, 110.

Saying 9. Sulamī, *Laṭāʾif al-miᶜrāj,* fol. 13r, lines 17–20. Compare Qushayrī, ["*Kitāb al-miᶜrāj,*"] Ms. 1891, fols. 57v–58r; Qushayrī, *Kitāb al-miᶜrāj,* ed. ᶜAbd al-Qādir, 111. See also a similar saying attributed to Wāsiṭī in Sulamī, "*Ḥaqāʾiq al-tafsīr,*" Ms. 261 Fatih, fol. 268r; Ms. 9433 Or., fol. 318v.

Saying 10. Sulamī, *Laṭāʾif al-miᶜrāj*, fol. 13r, lines 20–22.

Saying 11. Sulamī, *Laṭāʾif al-miᶜrāj*, fol. 13v, lines 1–3. Compare Qushayrī, ["*Kitāb al-miᶜrāj*,"] Ms. 1891, fol. 58v–59r; Qushayrī, *Kitāb al-miᶜrāj*, ed. ᶜAbd al-Qādir, 112–13.

Saying 12. Sulamī, *Laṭāʾif al-miᶜrāj*, fol. 13v, lines 4–7. Compare a portion to Sulamī, "*Ḥaqāʾiq al-tafsīr*," Ms. 261 Fatih, fol. 267r; Ms. 9433 Or., fol. 317v.

Saying 13. Sulamī, *Laṭāʾif al-miᶜrāj*, fol. 13v, lines 8–13. Compare a portion to Sulamī, "*Ḥaqāʾiq al-tafsīr*," Ms. 261 Fatih, fol. 267v; Ms. 9433 Or., fol. 318v.

Saying 14. Sulamī, *Laṭāʾif al-miᶜrāj*, fol. 13v, lines 13–15.

Saying 15. Sulamī, *Laṭāʾif al-miᶜrāj*, fol. 13v, lines 16–20.

Saying 16. Sulamī, *Laṭāʾif al-miʿrāj*, fol. 13v line 21–fol. 14r line 6. Compare Qushayrī, ["*Kitāb al-miʿrāj*,"] Ms. 1891, fols. 59r–59v; Qushayrī, *Kitāb al-miʿrāj*, ed. ʿAbd al-Qādir, 113–14.

Saying 17. Sulamī, *Laṭāʾif al-miʿrāj*, fol. 14r, lines 6–11. Compare Qushayrī, ["*Kitāb al-miʿrāj*,"] Ms. 1891, fol. 59v; Qushayrī, *Kitāb al-miʿrāj*, ed. ʿAbd al-Qādir, 114. Compare the first portion to Sulamī, "*Ḥaqāʾiq al-tafsīr*," Ms. 261 Fatih, fol. 267r; Ms. 9433 Or., fols. 317v–318r.

Saying 18. Sulamī, *Laṭāʾif al-miʿrāj*, fol. 14r, lines 12–17. Compare the first paragraph to Qushayrī, ["*Kitāb al-miʿrāj*,"] Ms. 1891, fol. 60r; Qushayrī, *Kitāb al-miʿrāj*, ed. ʿAbd al-Qādir, 114. The second paragraph is missing in Q. Compare both paragraphs to the unattributed saying in Sulamī, "*Ḥaqāʾiq al-tafsīr*," Ms. 261 Fatih, fol. 267r; Ms. 9433 Or., fol. 318r. Unlike in the *Laṭāʾif al-miʿrāj* version, where the saying is explicitly linked to Jaʿfar al-Ṣādiq, the *Ḥaqāʾiq al-tafsīr* manuscripts begin with the words "He said" (Ms. 261 Fatih) or "He also said" (Ms. 9433 Or.), suggesting that the saying be attributed to the speaker in the previous saying, namely Wāsiṭī. This attribution is assumed by Böwering in his translation of the *Ḥaqāʾiq al-tafsīr* version, which he gives in his article "From the Word of God to the Vision of God," 215.

Saying 19. Sulamī, *Laṭāʾif al-miʿrāj*, fol. 14r line 18–fol. 14v line 2. Compare Qushayrī, ["*Kitāb al-miʿrāj*,"] Ms. 1891, fol. 60r; Qushayrī, *Kitāb al-miʿrāj*, ed. ʿAbd al-Qādir, 114–15.

Saying 20. Sulamī, *Laṭāʾif al-miʿrāj*, fol. 14v, lines 3–6.

Saying 21. Sulamī, *Laṭāʾif al-miʿrāj*, fol. 14v, lines 7–12.

Saying 22. Sulamī, *Laṭāʾif al-miʿrāj*, fol. 14v, lines 12–14. Compare Qushayrī, ["*Kitāb al-miʿrāj*,"] Ms. 1891, fol. 60v; Qushayrī, *Kitāb al-miʿrāj*, ed. ʿAbd al-Qādir, 115.

Saying 23. Sulamī, *Laṭāʾif al-miʿrāj*, fol. 14v, lines 14–19. Compare Qushayrī, ["*Kitāb al-miʿrāj*,"] Ms. 1891, fol. 60v; Qushayrī, *Kitāb al-miʿrāj*, ed. ʿAbd al-Qādir, 115.

Saying 24. Sulamī, *Laṭāʾif al-miʿrāj*, fol. 14v line 19–fol. 15v line 6. Compare the first portion to Sulamī, "*Ḥaqāʾiq al-tafsīr*," Ms. 261 Fatih, fols. 267r–267v; Ms. 9433 Or., fol. 318r; Nwyia, "Le Tafsīr mystique attribué à Jaʿfar Ṣādiq," *Mélanges de l'Université Saint Joseph* 43 (1968), 223. Compare the last portion to a separate saying on verse 53:10 in ibid. also attributed to Jaʿfar Ṣādiq, Ms. 261 Fatih, fol. 267v; Ms. 9433 Or., fol. 318v. The two fragments are combined into one in *Laṭāʾif al-miʿrāj*.

Saying 25. Sulamī, *Laṭāʾif al-miʿrāj*, fol. 15r, lines 7–13.

Saying 26. Sulamī, *Laṭāʾif al-miʿrāj*, fol. 15r, lines 14–19. Compare Qushayrī, ["*Kitāb al-miʿrāj*,"] Ms. 1891, fols. 60v–61r; Qushayrī, *Kitāb* *al-mi*ᶜ*rāj*, ed. ᶜAbd al-Qādir, 115–16. The version in Q leaves out the last sentence present in S, and Q also omits several key phrases near the beginning.

Saying 27. Sulamī, *Laṭāʾif al-mi*ᶜ*rāj*, fol. 15r line 19–fol. 15v line 2.

Saying 28. Sulamī, *Laṭāʾif al-mi*ᶜ*rāj*, fol. 15v, lines 3–4. Compare Qushayrī, ["*Kitāb al-mi*ᶜ*rāj*,"] Ms. 1891, fols. 58r–58v; Qushayrī, *Kitāb al-mi*ᶜ*rāj*, ed. ᶜAbd al-Qādir, 112. The version in Q leaves out the last sentence present in S.

Saying 29. Sulamī, *Laṭāʾif al-mi*ᶜ*rāj*, fol. 15v, lines 5–13.

Saying 30. Sulamī, *Laṭāʾif al-mi*ᶜ*rāj*, fol. 15v, lines 13–19.

Saying 31. Sulamī, *Laṭāʾif al-mi*ᶜ*rāj*, fol. 15v line 19– fol. 16r line 3.

Saying 32. Sulamī, *Laṭāʾif al-mi*ᶜ*rāj*, fol. 16r, lines 3–8.

Saying 33. Sulamī, *Laṭāʾif al-mi*ᶜ*rāj*, fol. 16r, lines 8–11. Compare Qushayrī, ["*Kitāb al-mi*ᶜ*rāj*,"] Ms. 1891, fol. 55r; Qushayrī, *Kitāb al-mi*ᶜ*rāj*, ed. ᶜAbd al-Qādir, 108, which substitutes the verb *ḍa*ᶜ*afat* for *ṣaghurat* in S. The final clause in S, *li'l-maqṣūd alladhī qaṣadahu*, does not appear in Q.

Saying 34. Sulamī, *Laṭāʾif al-mi*ᶜ*rāj*, fol. 16r, lines 12–15.

Saying 35. Sulamī, *Laṭāʾif al-mi*ᶜ*rāj*, fol. 16r, lines 15–19.

Saying 36. Sulamī, *Laṭāʾif al-mi*ᶜ*rāj*, fol. 16r, lines 19–20. Compare Qushayrī, ["*Kitāb al-mi*ᶜ*rāj*,"] Ms. 1891, fol. 58r; Qushayrī, *Kitāb al-mi*ᶜ*rāj*, ed. ᶜAbd al-Qādir, 112:

قال بعضهم اراد الله ان يشرف السموات بنور محمد (صل) كما اشرقت الارض بنوره فعرج به الى السماء.

Saying 37. Sulamī, *Laṭāʾif al-mi*ᶜ*rāj*, fol. 16r line 20–fol. 16v line 4.

Saying 38. Sulamī, *Laṭāʾif al-mi*ᶜ*rāj*, fol. 16v, lines 4–11. Compare Qushayrī, ["*Kitāb al-mi*ᶜ*rāj*,"] Ms. 1891, fol. 58r; Qushayrī, *Kitāb al-mi*ᶜ*rāj*, ed. ᶜAbd al-Qādir, 112, where an anonymous saying on the same subject appears:

قال بعضهم اكمل الله بحضور محمد (صل) ليلة المعراج خصائص المسجد الاقصى فإن الله قد اكرم تلك الجنة بكون الانبياء (ع س) بها فاكمل بالمصطفى ما اكرمها بالانبياء (ع س)

Saying 39. Sulamī, *Laṭāʾif al-mi*ᶜ*rāj*, fol. 16v, lines 11–14.

Saying 40. Sulamī, *Laṭāʾif al-mi*ᶜ*rāj*, fol. 16v, lines 14–18. Compare Abū al-Khaṭṭāb Ibn Dihya Kalbī, *al-Ibtihāj fī aḥādīth al-mi*ᶜ*rāj*, ed.

Rifᶜat Fawzī ᶜAbd al-Muṭṭalib (Cairo: Maktabat al-Khanjā, 1996), 145–46, where the same saying is erroneously ascribed to one "Junayd b. Manṣūr."

Saying 41. Sulamī, *Laṭāʾif al-miᶜrāj*, fol. 16v, lines 18–20. Compare Qushayrī, ["*Kitāb al-miᶜrāj*,"] Ms. 1891, fol. 56r; Qushayrī, *Kitāb al-miᶜrāj*, ed. ᶜAbd al-Qādir, 109. Note that this saying is incomplete as it stands. It poses a question, but never gives a verb "he said" to indicate the beginning of an answer. One solution to the problem is to insert the verb where it appears to belong. Doing so might render the following translation:

> Someone was asked, "On the night of the ascension, why was the pure one ﷺ made expansively cheerful through the witnessing and speech upon the carpet of nearness?" [He said,] "Bewilderment was eliminated from him at the times of witnessing, and contractive distress [was eliminated] during the conversation. He thus was made expansively cheerful in the intercession and requesting.

However, a different solution arises when one compares S and Q. Here is the Q version in its entirety (for the meaning of the asterixes, see below):

وسئل بعضهم: لِم انبسط النبي (صل) في عرصات القيمة عند خمود الانبياء؟ فقال: ذلك لأن كلّ طرف لم يكتحل بمشاهدة الحقّ يتحير في أوان التجلي، وكان لسان لم ينبسط بمكالمة الحقّ في القرب والدنوّ يعجز السؤال عند ظهور الهيبة. ولمّ خصّ النبيّ (صل) ليلة المعراج بالمشاهدة ** والكلام على بساط القرب، أزيل عنه [حيرة] أوان المشاهدة ** وانقباض [حين] المكالمة. فانبسط في الشفاعة والسؤال.

> Someone was asked, "Why was the Prophet made expansively cheerful in the courtyards of resurrection during the silence of the prophets?" He said, "That is because each eye that was not made up [i.e. colored with kohl] by the witnessing of the Real is bewildered at the time of the revelation [i.e. theophany]. The tongue that was not made expansively cheerful in the discourse of the Real at the nearness and approach is incapable of requesting upon the appearance of dread. When the Prophet was speci-

> fied on the night of the Ascension for witnessing ** and speaking on the carpet on nearness, [bewilderment] was eliminated from him at the times of the witnessing ** and constrictive distress eliminated [during] the conversation. He thus was made expansively cheerful in intercession and requesting."

Note that penultimate sentence of the saying in the published version of Q (Qushayrī, *Kitāb al-mi^c^rāj*, ed. ^c^Abd al-Qādir, 109) is rendered nearly incomprehensible by the fact that the editor skipped an entire phrase of text from the manuscript (f. 56a), the words contained between the double asterixes above. The printed text jumps from one instance of the word "witnessing" (*mushāhada*) to another instance of the same word later in the sentence. While such mistakes do happen, this error is even more remarkable given the fact that the omitted phrase contains the sentence's key verb.

The fragmentary sentence of S saying 41 can now be reconstructed by comparison with the Q manuscript. Notice that beginning with the words "*laylat al-mi^c^rāj*," the S and Q texts are nearly identical. One could postulate, then, that the copyist of S skipped one or more lines of text, and that Sulamī's text originally looked more similar to the way that the Q manuscript looks. One can thus propose a restored version of saying 41, one which I have offered in my English translation.

Saying 42. Sulamī, *Laṭā'if al-mi^c^rāj*, fol. 17r, lines 1–3. Compare Qushayrī, ["*Kitāb al-mi^c^rāj*,"] Ms. 1891, fol. 58r; Qushayrī, *Kitāb al-mi^c^rāj*, ed. ^c^Abd al-Qādir, 111–12.

Saying 43. Sulamī, *Laṭā'if al-mi^c^rāj*, fol. 17r, lines 4–5.

Saying 44. Sulamī, *Laṭā'if al-mi^c^rāj*, fol. 17r, lines 5–12.

Saying 45. Sulamī, *Laṭā'if al-mi^c^rāj*, fol. 17r, lines 12–14. Compare Qushayrī, ["*Kitāb al-mi^c^rāj*,"] Ms. 1891, fol. 56v; Qushayrī, *Kitāb al-mi^c^rāj*, ed. ^c^Abd al-Qādir, 110.

Saying 46. Sulamī, *Laṭā'if al-mi^c^rāj*, fol. 17r, lines 14–18. Compare Qushayrī, ["*Kitāb al-mi^c^rāj*,"] Ms. 1891, fol. 56v; Qushayrī, *Kitāb al-mi^c^rāj*, ed. ^c^Abd al-Qādir, 109–110; Nu^c^mānī, *al-Sirāj al-wahhāj*, 38. Qushayrī's version does not mention the source Isma^c^īl b. Nujayd (Sulamī's maternal grandfather), but Ibn Nujayd's name does appear in the version preserved by Nu^c^mānī.

Saying 47. Sulamī, *Laṭā'if al-mi^c^rāj*, fol. 17r, lines 18–20. Compare Qushayrī, ["*Kitāb al-mi^c^rāj*,"] Ms. 1891, fol. 56r–56v; Qushayrī, *Kitāb al-mi^c^rāj*, ed. ^c^Abd al-Qādir, 109.

Saying 48. Sulamī, *Laṭā'if al-mi^c^rāj*, fol. 17v, lines 1–5.

Saying 49. Sulamī, *Laṭā'if al-mi^c^rāj*, fol. 17v, lines 5–9. Compare Qushayrī, ["*Kitāb al-mi^c^rāj*,"] Ms. 1891, fol. 55v; Qushayrī, *Kitāb al-*

mi^crāj, ed. ᶜAbd al-Qādir, 108, where the two word phrase "*idh dhāka*" in S becomes the one word "*idrāk*" in Q.

Saying 50. Sulamī, *Laṭāʾif al-miᶜrāj*, fol. 17v, lines 9–11. Compare Qushayrī, ["*Kitāb al-miᶜrāj*,"] Ms. 1891, fol. 55v–56r; Qushayrī, *Kitāb al-miᶜrāj*, ed. ᶜAbd al-Qādir, 109.

Saying 51. Sulamī, *Laṭāʾif al-miᶜrāj*, fol. 17v, lines 11–13.

Saying 52. Sulamī, *Laṭāʾif al-miᶜrāj*, fol. 17v, lines 13–15.

Saying 53. Sulamī, *Laṭāʾif al-miᶜrāj*, fol. 17v, lines 15–20.

Saying 54. Sulamī, *Laṭāʾif al-miᶜrāj*, fol. 17v line 20–fol. 18r line 4. Compare Qushayrī, ["*Kitāb al-miᶜrāj*,"] Ms. 1891, fol. 55v; Qushayrī, *Kitāb al-miᶜrāj*, ed. ᶜAbd al-Qādir, 109.

Saying 55. Sulamī, *Laṭāʾif al-miᶜrāj*, fol. 18r, lines 4–8. Compare Qushayrī, ["*Kitāb al-miᶜrāj*,"] Ms. 1891, fols. 55r–55v; Qushayrī, *Kitāb al-miᶜrāj*, ed. ᶜAbd al-Qādir, 108.

Saying 56. Sulamī, *Laṭāʾif al-miᶜrāj*, fol. 18r, lines 8–10.

BIBLIOGRAPHY OF WORKS CITED

Abdul-Raof, Hussein. *Qurʾān Translation: Discourse, Texture and Exegesis*. Richmond, Surrey: Curzon Press, 2001.

Amir-Moezzi, Mohammad Ali. *The Divine Guide in Early Shiʿism*.

———. "L'Imām dans le ciel." In *Le Voyage initiatique en Terre d'Islam*. Edited by *idem*, 99-116. Leuven and Paris: Peeters, 1996.

Ayoub, Mahmoud. *The Qurʾān and its Interpreters*. Vol. 1. Albany, NY: State University of New York Press, 1984.

Bar-Asher, Meir. *Scripture and Exegesis in Early Imāmī Shiism*. Leiden: E. J. Brill, 1999.

Bencheikh, Jamel Eddine. *Le Voyage nocturne de Mahomet: L'Aventure de la Parole*. Paris: Gallimard, 1988.

Bevan, A. A. "Mohammad's Ascension to Heaven." In *Studien zur semitischen Philologie und Religionsgeschichte: Julius Wellhausen zum Geburtstag*. Edited by Karl Marti, 49-61. Giessen: Alfred Töpelman, 1914.

Birkeland, Harris. *The Legend of the Opening of Muhammad's Breast*. Oslo: I Kommisjos Hos Jacob Dybwad, 1955.

Böwering, Gerhard. "From the word of God to the vision of God: Muḥammad's heavenly journey in classical Ṣūfī Qurʾān commentary." In *Le Voyage Initiatique en Terre d'Islam*. Edited by Mohammad Ali Amir-Moezzi, 205-21. Louvain-Paris: Peeters, 1996.

———. "The Qurʾān Commentary of al-Sulamī." In *Islamic Studies Presented to Charles J. Adams*. Edited by Wael Hallaq and Donald Little. Leiden: E. J. Brill, 1991.

———. "al-Sulamī, Abu ʿAbd al-Raḥmān." *Encyclopaedia of Islam*, New Edition.

Brockelmann, Carl. *Geschichte der arabischen Litteratur*. Leiden: E. J. Brill, 1943-.

Bukhārī, Abū ʿAbd Allāh Muḥammad b. ʿIsmāʿīl. *Ṣaḥīḥ al-Bukhārī*. Edited by Muhammad Nizār Tamīm and Haytham Nizār Tamīm. Beirut: Sharikat Dār al-Arqām b. Abī Arqām, n.d.

Chittick, William. *The Sufi Path of Love: The Spiritual Teachings of Rumi*. Albany, NY: State University of New York Press, 1983.

———. *Sufism: A Short Introduction*. Oxford: Oneworld, 2000.

Colby, Frederick. "Constructing an Islamic Ascension Narrative: The Interplay of Official and Popular Culture in Pseudo-Ibn 'Abbas." Duke University Ph. D. Dissertation, 2002.

———. "The subtleties of the Ascension: al-Sulamī on the Miᶜrāj of the Prophet Muḥammad." *Studia Islamica* 94 (2002): 167-83.

Collins, John J. and Michael Fishbane. *Death, Ecstasy, and Other Worldly Journeys*. Albany, NY: State University of New York Press, 1995.

Cornell, Rkia. *Early Sufi Women*. Louisville KY: Fons Vitae, 1999.

Cornell, Vincent. *Realm of the Saint*. Austin: University of Texas Press, 1998.

Couliano, I. P. *Out of this World: Otherworldly Journeys from Gilgamesh to Albert Einstein*. Boston and London: Shambhala, 1991.

Dhahabī, Shams al-Dīn Muḥammad. *Siyar aᶜlām al-nubalāʾ*. Edited by Shuᶜayb Arnaʾūt. Beirut: al-Resalah, 1996-.

Elias, Jamal. "The Sufi Robe (*Khirqa*) as a Vehicle of Spiritual Authority." In *Robes and Honor: The Medieval World of Investiture*, edited by Stewart Gordon, 275-89. New York: Palgrave, 2001.

Ernst, Carl. *The Shambhala Guide to Sufism*. Boston and London: Shambhala, 1997.

———. *Teachings of Sufism*. Boston: Shambhala, 1999.

———. *Words of Ecstasy in Sufism*. Albany, NY: State University of New York Press, 1985.

Ess, Josef van. "Le Miᶜrāğ et la Vision de Dieu." In *Le Voyage Initiatique en Terre d'Islam*, edited by Mohammad Ali Amir-Moezzi, 27-56. Louvain-Paris, 1996.

———. "Vision and Ascension: Surat Najm and its Relationship with Muḥammad's Miᶜrāj." *Journal of Quʾānic Studies* 1 (1999): 47–62.

———. "The Youthful God: Anthropomorphism in Early Islam." Ninth Annual University Lecture in Religion, Arizona State University, 1988. Photocopy.

Gimaret, Daniel. "Au coeur du Mi[c]rāǧ, un hadith interpolé." In *Le Voyage Initiatique en Terre d'Islam*. Edited by Mohammad Ali Amir-Moezzi, 67-82. Louvain-Paris: Peeters, 1996.

Gramlich, Richard. *Alte Vorbilder des Sufitums*. Vol. 2: *Scheiche des Ostens*. Weisbaden: Harrassowitz, 1996.

Gruber, Christiane Jacqueline. "L'Ascension (Mi[c]rāj) du Prophète Mohammad dans la peinture et la littérature islamiques." *Luqmān* 39 no. 1 (Fall and Winter 2003-4): 55-79.

———. "The Prophet Muḥammad's Ascension (Mi[c]rāj) in Islamic Art and Literature, ca. 1300-1600." University of Pennsylvania Ph. D., 2005.

Guillaume, Alfred. "Where was al-Masyid al-Aqṣā?" *Andalus* 18 (1953): 323-36.

Heath, Peter. *Allegory and Philosophy in Avicenna (Ibn Sīnā)*. Philadelphia: The University of Pennsylvania Press, 1992.

Honerkamp, Kenneth. "Stations of the Righteous" and "The Stumbling of those Aspiring" (introduction and translation). In *Three Early Sufi Texts* by Nicholas Heer and Kenneth Honerkamp. Louisville, KY: Fons Vitae, 2003.

Hujwīrī, [c]Alī b. [c]Uthmān. *Kashf al-Maḥjūb of al-Hujwīrī*. Translated by Reynold Nicholson. New edition. London: E. J. W. Gibb Memorial, 1976.

Ibn [c]Arabī, Muḥyī al-Dīn. *Kitāb al-isrā᾽ ilā 'l-maqām al-asrā*. Edited by Su[c]ād Ḥakīm. Beirut: Dandara li'l-Ṭibā[c]a wa 'l-Nashr, 1988.

Ibn Diḥya, Abū al-Khaṭṭāb [c]Umar Kalbī. *al-Ibtihāj fī aḥādīth al-mi[c]rāj*. Edited by Rif[c]āt Fawzī [c]Abd al-Muṭṭalib. Cairo: Maktabat al-Khānjā, 1996.

Ibn Hishām, [c]Abd al-Malik. *Kitāb sīrat Rasūl Allāh: Das Leben Muhammed's nack Muhammed Ibn Isḥāk bearbeitet von Abd el-Malik Ibn Hichām*. Edited by Ferdinand Wüstenfeld. Göttingen, 1856.

———. *The Life of Muhammad*. Translated by Alfred Guillaume. Oxford: Oxford University Press, 1955.

Ibn Jawzī, Abū al-Faraj [c]Abd al-Raḥmān. *Ṣifat al-safwa*. Edited by [c]Abd al-Salām Muhammad Hārūn. Beirut: Dār al-Fikr, 1991.

Ibn Sa[c]d, Muhammad. *al-Ṭabaqāt al-kubrā*. Beirut: Dār al-Ṣādir, 1957-68.

Isbahānī, Abū Nu^caym. *Hilyat al-awliyā*ʾ. Beirut: Dār al-Fikr, [1980].
Kalabādhī, Abū Bakr Muhammad b. Isḥāq. *al-Ta*ᶜ*arruf li-madhhab ahl al-taṣawwuf*. Edited by Aḥmad Shams al-Dīn. Beirut: Dār al-Kutub al-ᶜIlmiyya, 1993.
Kappler, Claude. *Apocalypses et Voyages dans l'Au-Dela. Paris*: Editions of CERF, 1987.
Kister, M. J. "You Should Only Set Out for Three Mosques." *Le Muséon* 82 (1960): 173-96.
Kugle, Scott. *The Book of Illumination* (introduction and translation). Louisville, KY: Fons Vitae, 2005.
Olson, Brooke Elise. "Heavenly Journeys, Earthly Concerns: The Legacy of the Miᶜrāj in the Formation of Islam." University of Chicago Ph. D. Dissertation, 2002.
Maḥmūd, Muṣṭafā. "[Risale fī Mevlid al-Nabi ve Mi'rac]." MS. H Hüsnü Pasha 257, Sūleymaniye Kütüphanesı, Istanbul.
Massignon, Louis. *Le Passion d'Husayn Ibn Mansur Hallaj*. New Edition. Paris: Gallimard, 1975. Translated and abridged as *The Passion of Hallaj*. Translated by Herbert Mason. Princeton: Princeton University Press, 1994.
Morris, James. "The Spiritual Ascension: Ibn ᶜArabī and the Miᶜrāj, Part One." *Journal of the American Oriental Society* (107): 629-52.
———. "The Spiritual Ascension: Ibn ᶜArabī and the Miᶜrāj, Part Two." *Journal of the American Oriental Society* (108): 63-77.
Muslim b. Ḥajjāj Qurashī Naysabūrī. *Ṣaḥīḥ Muslim bi-sharḥ al-Nawawī*. Beirut: Dār al-Kitāb al-ᶜArabī, 1987.
Nicholson, Reynold. "An Early Arabic Version of the Miᶜrāj of Abū Yazīd al-Bisṭāmī." *Islamica* 2, no. 3 (1926): 402-15.
Niffarī, Muhammad b. ᶜAbd al-Jabbār. *Kitāb al-Mawāqif*. Edited by A. J. Arberrry. London: Luzac, 1935.
Nuᶜmānī, Abū Isḥāq Muhammad b. Ibrahīm. *al-Sirāj al-wahhāj*. Edited by ᶜAbd al-Qādir Aḥmad ᶜAṭā. Cairo: Maktabat al-Qurʾān, [1985].
Nwyia, Paul. *Exégèsis coranique et language mystique*. Beirut: Dār al-Machreq, 1970.
———. *Nuṣūṣ ṣūfiyya ghayr manshūra* [Trois oeuvres inédites de mystiques musulmans]. Beirut: Dār al-Machreq, 1973.

———. "Le Tafsīr Mystique Attribué a Gaᶜfar Ṣādiq: Édition critique." *Mélanges de l'Université Saint-Joseph* 43 (1968): 181-230.

Pourjavady, Nasrollah. *Ruᵓyai'ī māh dar asmān*. Tehran: Markaz-i Nashr-i Danishgahi, 1996.

Qummī, ᶜAlī b. Ibrahīm. *Kitāb tafsīr ᶜAlī b. Ibrahīm Qummī*. Tabriz: Lithograph, 1895.

Qushayrī, Abū al-Qasim ᶜAbd al-Karīm. [*Kitāb al-miᶜrāj*]. MS. 1891, Kahuda Bakhsh Oriental Public Library, Bankipore. Photostat, Institut Français des Études Arabes de Damas.

_______. *Kitāb al-miᶜrāj*. Edited by ᶜAlī Ḥusayn ᶜAbd al-Qādir. Cairo: Dār al-Kutub al-Ḥadītha, 1964.

———. *al-Risāla al-qushayriyya*. Edited by ᶜAbd al-Ḥalīm Maḥmūd and Maḥmūd b. al-Sharīf. Cairo: Dār al-Shaᶜb, 1989.

Rubin, Uri. *The Eye of the Beholder: The Life of Muhammad as Viewed by the Early Muslims*. Princeton: Darwin Press, 1995.

———. "Pre-existence and light: Aspects of the concept of *Nūr Muhammad*." *Israel Oriental Studies* 5 (1975): 62-119.

Samarrai, Qassim. *The Theme of Ascension in Mystical Writings*. Baghdad: National Printing and Publishing Company, 1968.

Sarrāj, Abū Naṣr. *al-Lumᶜā*. Edited by ᶜAbd al-Ḥalīm Maḥmūd and Ṭaha ᶜAbd al-Bāqī Surūr. Cairo: Dār al-Kutub al-Ḥadītha, 1960.

Scherberger, Max. *Das Miᶜragname: Die Himmel-und Höllenfahrt des Propheten Muhammad in der osttürkischen Überlieferung*. Würzburg: Ergon, 2003.

Schiffman, Lawrence. "The Recall of Rabbi Neḥuniah Ben ha-Qanah from Ecstasy in the *Hekhalot Rabbati*." *Association for Jewish Studies Review* (1976): 269-81.

Scholem, Gershom. *Jewish Gnosticism, Merkabah Mysticism, and Talmudic Tradition*. New York: Jewish Theological Seminary, 1965.

Schrieke, B. "Die Himmelsreise Muhammeds." *Der Islam* 6 (1916): 1-30.

Sells, Michael. *Early Islamic Mysticism: Sufi, Qur'an, Mi^crāj, Poetic and Theological Writings*. New York: Paulist Press, 1996.

———. *Mystical Languages of Unsaying*. Chicago: University of Chicago Press, 1994.

Séguy, Marie-Rose. *The Miraculous Journey of Mahomet: Mirāj Nameh*. Translated by Richard Pevear. New York: George Braziller, 1977.

Sezgin, Fuat. *Geschichte des arabischen Schrifttums*. Leiden: E. J. Brill, 1967-.

Silvers, Laury. "Tawhid in early Sufism: The Life and Work of Abu Bakr al-Wasitī." State University of New York at Stony Brook Ph. D. Dissertation, 2002.

———. "The Teaching Relationship in Early Sufism: A Reassessment of Fritz Meier's Definition of the *shaykh al-tarbiya* and the *shaykh al-ta^clīm*." *The Muslim World* 93 (January 2003): 69-97.

Sulamī, Abu ^cAbd al-Raḥmān. *Dhikr al-niswa al-muta^cabbidāt al-ṣūfiyyāt*. Edited by Maḥmūd Muḥammad Ṭanāḥī. Cairo: Maktabat al-Khānjī, 1993.

———. *Ḥaqā^ʾiq al-tafsīr*. MS. 9433 Or., British Library.

———. *Ḥaqā^ʾiq al-tafsīr*. MS. 261 Fatih, Sülaymaniye Kütüphanisı, Istanbul.

———. *Kitāb Ṭabaqāt al-Ṣūfiyya*. Edited by Johannes Pederson. Leiden: E. J. Brill, 1960.

———. [*Laṭā^ʾif al-mi^crāj*]. MS 2118 Muḥammad b. Sa^cūd. Riyadh.

———. *Majmū^cah-'i asār-i Abū 'Abd al-Raḥmān Sulamī*, ed. Nasr Allāh Pūrjavādī. Tehran: Markaz-i Nashr-i Dānishgāhī, 1990-.

———. *Ṭabaqāt al-ṣūfiyya*. Edited by Nūr al-Dīn Sharība. Cairo: Maktabat al-Khānjā, 1986.

———. *Tis^ca kutub fī uṣūl al-taṣawwuf wa 'l-zuhd*. Edited by Sulaymān Ibrahīm Ātesh. N.p.: al-Nāshir, 1993.

Suyūṭī, Jalāl al-Dīn. *al-Lālī al-maṣnū^ca fī aḥādīth al-mawḍū^ca*. Edited by Abū ^cAbd al-Raḥmān Ṣalāḥ b. Muhammad b. ^cUwayḍa. Beirut: Dār al-Kutub al^cIlmiyya, 1996.

Ṭabarī, Muhammad. *Tafsīr al-Ṭabarī*. Beirut: Dār al-Kutub al-^cIlmiyya, 1992.

Thackston, Wheeler. "The Paris *Mi*[c]*rājnāma*." *Journal of Turkish Studies* 18 (1994): 263-99.

Tirmidhī, Abu [c]Īsā. *Jāmi*[c] *al-ṣaḥīḥ*. In *al-*[c]*Āriḍat al-aḥwazī bi-sharḥ ṣaḥīḥ al-Tirmidhī* by Ibn [c]Arabī al-Mālikī. Edited by Hishām Samīr Bukhārī. Beirut: Dār Iḥyā' al-Turāth al-[c]Arabī, 1995.

Vuckovic, Brooke Olson. *Heavenly Journeys, Earthly Concerns: The Legacy of the Mi*[c]*rāj in the Formation of Islam*. New York and London: Routledge, 2005.

Wensinck, A. J. *Concordance et Indices de la Tradition Musulmanse*. 2nd Edition. Leiden: E. J. Brill, 1992.

INDEX

INDEX OF QUR'ANIC VERSES